THE SECRET TORTURE MEMOS

BUSH ADMINISTRATION MEMOS
ON TORTURE AS RELEASED BY
THE UNITED STATES DEPARTMENT
OF JUSTICE, APRIL 16, 2009

ROCKVILLE, MARYLAND

The Secret Torture Memos: Bush Administration Memos on Torture as Released by the United Sates Department of Justice in its current format, copyright © Arc Manor 2009. The contents themselves have been released to the public domain by the US Department of Justice, The Central Intelligence Agency and/or other agencies/departments of the US Federal Government.

Arc Manor, Arc Manor Classic Reprints, Manor Classics, TARK Classic Fiction and the Arc Manor logo are trademarks or registered trademarks of Arc Manor Publishers, Rockville, Maryland. All other trademarks are properties of their respective owners.

This book is presented as is, without any warranties (implied or otherwise) as to the accuracy of the production, text or translation. The publisher does not take responsibility for any typesetting, formatting, translation or other errors which may have occurred during the production of this book.

ISBN: 978-1-60450-439-2

These documents are presented exactly as released by the Department of Justice. All redactions and corrections are as presented in the original released documents. Some pages, as provided by the Department of Justice in the electronic file provided, are presented at an angle. These have been left as provided as attempts to correct them made the text less legible.

Information contained in this book has been released to the public by the US Depatrmet of Justice and other agencies/departments of the U.S. Federal Governemnt. Arc Manor, LLC is not associated with the the Central Intelligence Agency or any other agency of the US Federal Government. Arc Manor has compiled the information contained in this book through many means which may include (but are not limited to) US Government documents and web-sites and other information released through the Freedom of Information Act (FOIA) and otherwise made public by relevant federal departments/agencies.

Published by Arc Manor
P. O. Box 10339
Rockville, MD 20849-0339
www.ArcManor.com

Printed in the United States of America/United Kingdom

CONTENTS

DEPARTMENT OF JUSTICE PRESS RELEASE REGARDING
DISCLOSURE OF FOUR MEMOS ON TORTURE   5

MEMO ONE   7
DATED AUGUST 1, 2002, FROM JAY BYBEE, ASSISTANT ATTORNEY GENERAL,
OLC, TO JOHN A. RIZZO, GENERAL COUNSEL CIA.   7

MEMO TWO   27
DATED MAY 10, 2005, FROM STEVEN
BRADBURY, ACTING ASSISTANT ATTORNEY GENERAL, OLC, TO JOHN A.
RIZZO, GENERAL COUNSEL CIA   27

MEMO THREE   75
DATED MAY 10, 2005, FROM STEVEN
BRADBURY, ACTING ASSISTANT ATTORNEY GENERAL, OLC, TO JOHN A.
RIZZO, GENERAL COUNSEL CIA   75

MEMO FOUR   97
DATED MAY 30, 2005, FROM STEVEN
BRADBURY, ACTING ASSISTANT ATTORNEY GENERAL, OLC, TO JOHN A.
RIZZO, GENERAL COUNSEL CIA   97

DEPARTMENT OF JUSTICE PRESS RELEASE REGARDING DISCLOSURE OF FOUR MEMOS ON TORTURE

FOR IMMEDIATE RELEASE
Thursday, April 16, 2009
WWW.USDOJ.GOV

AG
(202) 514-2007
TDD (202) 514-1888

Department of Justice Releases Four Office of Legal Counsel Opinions

In connection with ongoing litigation, the Department of Justice today released four previously undisclosed Office of Legal Counsel ("OLC") opinions – one that OLC issued to the Central Intelligence Agency in August 2002 and three that OLC issued to the CIA in May 2005.

"The President has halted the use of the interrogation techniques described in these opinions, and this administration has made clear from day one that it will not condone torture," said Attorney General Eric Holder. "We are disclosing these memos consistent with our commitment to the rule of law."

Holder also stressed that intelligence community officials who acted reasonably and relied in good faith on authoritative legal advice from the Justice Department that their conduct was lawful, and conformed their conduct to that advice, would not face federal prosecutions for that conduct.

The Attorney General has informed the Central Intelligence Agency that the government would provide legal representation to any employee, at no cost to the employee, in any state or federal judicial or administrative proceeding brought against the employee based on such conduct and would take measures to respond to any proceeding initiated against the employee in any international or foreign tribunal, including appointing counsel to act on the employee's behalf and asserting any available immunities and other defenses in the proceeding itself.

To the extent permissible under federal law, the government will also indemnify any employee for any monetary judgment or penalty ultimately imposed against him for such conduct and will provide representation in congressional investigations.

"It would be unfair to prosecute dedicated men and women working to protect America for conduct that was sanctioned in advance by the Justice Department," Holder said.

After reviewing these opinions, OLC has decided to withdraw them: They no longer represent the views of the Office of Legal Counsel.

###

09-356

MEMO ONE

DATED AUGUST 1, 2002, FROM JAY BYBEE, ASSISTANT ATTORNEY GENERAL, OLC, TO JOHN A. RIZZO, GENERAL COUNSEL CIA

U.S. Department of Justice

Office of Legal Counsel

Office of the Assistant Attorney General

Washington, D.C. 20530

August 1, 2002

Memorandum for John Rizzo
Acting General Counsel of the Central Intelligence Agency

Interrogation of al Qaeda Operative

You have asked for this Office's views on whether certain proposed conduct would violate the prohibition against torture found at Section 2340A of title 18 of the United States Code. You have asked for this advice in the course of conducting interrogations of Abu Zubaydah. As we understand it, Zubaydah is one of the highest ranking members of the al Qaeda terrorist organization, with which the United States is currently engaged in an international armed conflict following the attacks on the World Trade Center and the Pentagon on September 11, 2001. This letter memorializes our previous oral advice, given on July 24, 2002 and July 26, 2002, that the proposed conduct would not violate this prohibition.

I.

Our advice is based upon the following facts, which you have provided to us. We also understand that you do not have any facts in your possession contrary to the facts outlined here, and this opinion is limited to these facts. If these facts were to change, this advice would not necessarily apply. Zubaydah is currently being held by the United States. The interrogation team is certain that he has additional information that he refuses to divulge. Specifically, he is withholding information regarding terrorist networks in the United States or in Saudi Arabia and information regarding plans to conduct attacks within the United States or against our interests overseas. Zubaydah has become accustomed to a certain level of treatment and displays no signs of willingness to disclose further information. Moreover, your intelligence indicates that there is currently a level of "chatter" equal to that which preceded the September 11 attacks. In light of the information you believe Zubaydah has and the high level of threat you believe now exists, you wish to move the interrogations into what you have described as an "increased pressure phase."

As part of this increased pressure phase, Zubaydah will have contact only with a new interrogation specialist, whom he has not met previously, and the Survival, Evasion, Resistance, Escape ("SERE") training psychologist who has been involved with the interrogations since they began. This phase will likely last no more than several days but could last up to thirty days. In this phase, you would like to employ ten techniques that you believe will dislocate his

expectations regarding the treatment he believes he will receive and encourage him to disclose the crucial information mentioned above. These ten techniques are: (1) attention grasp, (2) walling, (3) facial hold, (4) facial slap (insult slap), (5) cramped confinement, (6) wall standing, (7) stress positions, (8) sleep deprivation, (9) insects placed in a confinement box, and (10) the waterboard. You have informed us that the use of these techniques would be on an as-needed basis and that not all of these techniques will necessarily be used. The interrogation team would use these techniques in some combination to convince Zubaydah that the only way he can influence his surrounding environment is through cooperation. You have, however, informed us that you expect these techniques to be used in some sort of escalating fashion, culminating with the waterboard, though not necessarily ending with this technique. Moreover, you have also orally informed us that although some of these techniques may be used with more than once, that repetition will not be substantial because the techniques generally lose their effectiveness after several repetitions. You have also informed us that Zabaydah sustained a wound during his capture, which is being treated.

Based on the facts you have given us, we understand each of these techniques to be as follows. The attention grasp consists of grasping the individual with both hands, one hand on each side of the collar opening, in a controlled and quick motion. In the same motion as the grasp, the individual is drawn toward the interrogator.

For walling, a flexible false wall will be constructed. The individual is placed with his heels touching the wall. The interrogator pulls the individual forward and then quickly and firmly pushes the individual into the wall. It is the individual's shoulder blades that hit the wall. During this motion, the head and neck are supported with a rolled hood or towel that provides a c-collar effect to help prevent whiplash. To further reduce the probability of injury, the individual is allowed to rebound from the flexible wall. You have orally informed us that the false wall is in part constructed to create a loud sound when the individual hits it, which will further shock or surprise in the individual. In part, the idea is to create a sound that will make the impact seem far worse than it is and that will be far worse than any injury that might result from the action.

The facial hold is used to hold the head immobile. One open palm is placed on either side of the individual's face. The fingertips are kept well away from the individual's eyes.

With the facial slap or insult slap, the interrogator slaps the individual's face with fingers slightly spread. The hand makes contact with the area directly between the tip of the individual's chin and the bottom of the corresponding earlobe. The interrogator invades the individual's personal space. The goal of the facial slap is not to inflict physical pain that is severe or lasting. Instead, the purpose of the facial slap is to induce shock, surprise, and/or humiliation.

Cramped confinement involves the placement of the individual in a confined space, the dimensions of which restrict the individual's movement. The confined space is usually dark.

~~TOP SECRET~~

The duration of confinement varies based upon the size of the container. For the larger confined space, the individual can stand up or sit down; the smaller space is large enough for the subject to sit down. Confinement in the larger space can last up to eighteen hours; for the smaller space, confinement lasts for no more than two hours.

Wall standing is used to induce muscle fatigue. The individual stands about four to five feet from a wall, with his feet spread approximately to shoulder width. His arms are stretched out in front of him, with his fingers resting on the wall. His fingers support all of his body weight. The individual is not permitted to move or reposition his hands or feet.

A variety of stress positions may be used. You have informed us that these positions are not designed to produce the pain associated with contortions or twisting of the body. Rather, somewhat like walling, they are designed to produce the physical discomfort associated with muscle fatigue. Two particular stress positions are likely to be used on Zubaydah: (1) sitting on the floor with legs extended straight out in front of him with his arms raised above his head; and (2) kneeling on the floor while leaning back at a 45 degree angle. You have also orally informed us that through observing Zubaydah in captivity, you have noted that he appears to be quite flexible despite his wound.

Sleep deprivation may be used. You have indicated that your purpose in using this technique is to reduce the individual's ability to think on his feet and, through the discomfort associated with lack of sleep, to motivate him to cooperate. The effect of such sleep deprivation will generally remit after one or two nights of uninterrupted sleep. You have informed us that your research has revealed that, in rare instances, some individuals who are already predisposed to psychological problems may experience abnormal reactions to sleep deprivation. Even in those cases, however, reactions abate after the individual is permitted to sleep. Moreover, personnel with medical training are available to and will intervene in the unlikely event of an abnormal reaction. You have orally informed us that you would not deprive Zubaydah of sleep for more than eleven days at a time and that you have previously kept him awake for 72 hours, from which no mental or physical harm resulted.

You would like to place Zubaydah in a cramped confinement box with an insect. You have informed us that he appears to have a fear of insects. In particular, you would like to tell Zubaydah that you intend to place a stinging insect into the box with him. You would, however, place a harmless insect in the box. You have orally informed us that you would in fact place a harmless insect such as a caterpillar in the box with him.

Finally, you would like to use a technique called the "waterboard." In this procedure, the individual is bound securely to an inclined bench, which is approximately four feet by seven feet. The individual's feet are generally elevated. A cloth is placed over the forehead and eyes. Water

~~TOP SECRET~~

is then applied to the cloth in a controlled manner. As this is done, the cloth is lowered until it covers both the nose and mouth. Once the cloth is saturated and completely covers the mouth and nose, air flow is slightly restricted for 20 to 40 seconds due to the presence of the cloth. This causes an increase in carbon dioxide level in the individual's blood. This increase in the carbon dioxide level stimulates increased effort to breathe. This effort plus the cloth produces the perception of "suffocation and incipient panic," i.e., the perception of drowning. The individual does not breathe any water into his lungs. During those 20 to 40 seconds, water is continuously applied from a height of twelve to twenty-four inches. After this period, the cloth is lifted, and the individual is allowed to breathe unimpeded for three or four full breaths. The sensation of drowning is immediately relieved by the removal of the cloth. The procedure may then be repeated. The water is usually applied from a canteen cup or small watering can with a spout. You have orally informed us that this procedure triggers an automatic physiological sensation of drowning that the individual cannot control even though he may be aware that he is in fact not drowning. You have also orally informed us that it is likely that this procedure would not last more than 20 minutes in any one application.

We also understand that a medical expert with SERE experience will be present throughout this phase and that the procedures will be stopped if deemed medically necessary to prevent severe mental or physical harm to Zubaydah. As mentioned above, Zubaydah suffered an injury during his capture. You have informed us that steps will be taken to ensure that this injury is not in any way exacerbated by the use of these methods and that adequate medical attention will be given to ensure that it will heal properly.

II.

In this part, we review the context within which these procedures will be applied. You have informed us that you have taken various steps to ascertain what effect, if any, these techniques would have on Zubaydah's mental health. These same techniques, with the exception of the insect in the cramped confined space, have been used and continue to be used on some members of our military personnel during their SERE training. Because of the use of these procedures in training our own military personnel to resist interrogations, you have consulted with various individuals who have extensive experience in the use of these techniques. You have done so in order to ensure that no prolonged mental harm would result from the use of these proposed procedures.

Through your consultation with various individuals responsible for such training, you have learned that these techniques have been used as elements of a course of conduct without any reported incident of prolonged mental harm. ███████████████ of the SERE school, ███████████████████████████████████ has reported that, during the seven-year period that he spent in those positions, there were two requests from Congress for information concerning alleged injuries resulting from the training. One of these inquiries was prompted by the temporary physical injury a trainee sustained as result of being placed in a

TOP SECRET

confinement box. The other inquiry involved claims that the SERE training caused two individuals to engage in criminal behavior, namely, felony shoplifting and downloading child pornography onto a military computer. According to this official, these claims were found to be baseless. Moreover, he has indicated that during the three and a half years he spent as ▓▓▓ of the SERE program, he trained 10,000 students. Of those students, only two dropped out of the training following the use of these techniques. Although on rare occasions some students temporarily postponed the remainder of their training and received psychological counseling, those students were able to finish the program without any indication of subsequent mental health effects.

You have informed us that you have consulted with ▓▓▓ who has ten years of experience with SERE training ▓▓▓ He stated that, during those ten years, insofar as he is aware, none of the individuals who completed the program suffered any adverse mental health effects. He informed you that there was one person who did not complete the training. That person experienced an adverse mental health reaction that lasted only two hours. After those two hours, the individual's symptoms spontaneously dissipated without requiring treatment or counseling and no other symptoms were ever reported by this individual. According to the information you have provided to us, this assessment of the use of these procedures includes the use of the waterboard.

Additionally, you received a memorandum from the ▓▓▓ which you supplied to us. ▓▓▓ has experience with the use of all of these procedures in a course of conduct, with the exception of the insect in the confinement box and the waterboard. This memorandum confirms that the use of these procedures has not resulted in any reported instances of prolonged mental harm, and very few instances of immediate and temporary adverse psychological responses to the training. ▓▓▓ reported that a small minority of students have had temporary adverse psychological reactions during training. Of the 26,829 students trained from 1992 through 2001 in the Air Force SERE training, 4.3 percent of those students had contact with psychology services. Of those 4.3 percent, only 3.2 percent were pulled from the program for psychological reasons. Thus, out of the students trained overall, only 0.14 percent were pulled from the program for psychological reasons. Furthermore, although ▓▓▓ indicated that surveys of students having completed this training are not done, he expressed confidence that the training did not cause any long-term psychological impact. He based his conclusion on the debriefing of students that is done after the training. More importantly, he based this assessment on the fact that although training is required to be extremely stressful in order to be effective, very few complaints have been made regarding the training. During his tenure, in which 10,000 students were trained, no congressional complaints have been made. While there was one Inspector General complaint, it was not due to psychological concerns. Moreover, he was aware of only one letter inquiring about the long-term impact of these techniques from an individual trained

TOP SECRET

over twenty years ago. He found that it was impossible to attribute this individual's symptoms to his training. ▮▮▮▮ concluded that if there are any long-term psychological effects of the United States Air Force training using the procedures outlined above they "are certainly minimal."

With respect to the waterboard, you have also orally informed us that the Navy continues to use it in training. You have informed us that your on-site psychologists, who have extensive experience with the use of the waterboard in Navy training, have not encountered any significant long-term mental health consequences from its use. Your on-site psychologists have also indicated that JPRA has likewise not reported any significant long-term mental health consequences from the use of the waterboard. You have informed us that other services ceased use of the waterboard because it was so successful as an interrogation technique, but not because of any concerns over any harm, physical or mental, caused by it. It was also reported to be almost 100 percent effective in producing cooperation among the trainees. ▮▮▮▮ also indicated that he had observed the use of the waterboard in Navy training some ten to twelve times. Each time it resulted in cooperation but it did not result in any physical harm to the student.

You have also reviewed the relevant literature and found no empirical data on the effect of these techniques, with the exception of sleep deprivation. With respect to sleep deprivation, you have informed us that is not uncommon for someone to be deprived of sleep for 72 hours and still perform excellently on visual-spatial motor tasks and short-term memory tests. Although some individuals may experience hallucinations, according to the literature you surveyed, those who experience such psychotic symptoms have almost always had such episodes prior to the sleep deprivation. You have indicated the studies of lengthy sleep deprivation showed no psychosis, loosening of thoughts, flattening of emotions, delusions, or paranoid ideas. In one case, even after eleven days of deprivation, no psychosis or permanent brain damaged occurred. In fact the individual reported feeling almost back to normal after one night's sleep. Further, based on the experiences with its use in military training (where it is induced for up to 48 hours), you found that rarely, if ever, will the individual suffer harm after the sleep deprivation is discontinued. Instead, the effects remit after a few good nights of sleep.

You have taken the additional step of consulting with U.S. interrogations experts, and other individuals with oversight over the SERE training process. None of these individuals was aware of any prolonged psychological effect caused by the use of any of the above techniques either separately or as a course of conduct. Moreover, you consulted with outside psychologists who reported that they were unaware of any cases where long-term problems have occurred as a result of these techniques.

Moreover, in consulting with a number of mental health experts, you have learned that the effect of any of these procedures will be dependant on the individual's personal history, cultural history and psychological tendencies. To that end, you have informed us that you have

6

completed a psychological assessment of Zubaydah. This assessment is based on interviews with Zubaydah, observations of him, and information collected from other sources such as intelligence and press reports. Our understanding of Zubaydah's psychological profile, which we set forth below, is based on that assessment.

According to this assessment, Zubaydah, though only 31, rose quickly from very low level mujahedin to third or fourth man in al Qaeda. He has served as Usama Bin Laden's senior lieutenant. In that capacity, he has managed a network of training camps. He has been instrumental in the training of operatives for al Qaeda, the Egyptian Islamic Jihad, and other terrorist elements inside Pakistan and Afghanistan. He acted as the Deputy Camp Commander for al Qaeda training camp in Afghanistan, personally approving entry and graduation of all trainees during 1999-2000. From 1996 until 1999, he approved all individuals going in and out of Afghanistan to the training camps. Further, no one went in and out of Peshawar, Pakistan without his knowledge and approval. He also acted as al Qaeda's coordinator of external contacts and foreign communications. Additionally, he has acted as al Qaeda's counter-intelligence officer and has been trusted to find spies within the organization.

Zubaydah has been involved in every major terrorist operation carried out by al Qaeda. He was a planner for the Millennium plot to attack U.S. and Israeli targets during the Millennium celebrations in Jordan. Two of the central figures in this plot who were arrested have identified Zubaydah as the supporter of their cell and the plot. He also served as a planner for the Paris Embassy plot in 2001. Moreover, he was one of the planners of the September 11 attacks. Prior to his capture, he was engaged in planning future terrorist attacks against U.S. interests.

Your psychological assessment indicates that it is believed Zubaydah wrote al Qaeda's manual on resistance techniques. You also believe that his experiences in al Qaeda make him well-acquainted with and well-versed in such techniques. As part of his role in al Qaeda, Zubaydah visited individuals in prison and helped them upon their release. Through this contact and activities with other al Qaeda mujahedin, you believe that he knows many stories of capture, interrogation, and resistance to such interrogation. Additionally, he has spoken with Ayman al-Zawahiri, and you believe it is likely that the two discussed Zawahiri's experiences as a prisoner of the Russians and the Egyptians.

Zubaydah stated during interviews that he thinks of any activity outside of jihad as "silly." He has indicated that his heart and mind are devoted to serving Allah and Islam through jihad and he has stated that he has no doubts or regrets about committing himself to jihad. Zubaydah believes that the global victory of Islam is inevitable. You have informed us that he continues to express his unabated desire to kill Americans and Jews.

Your psychological assessment describes his personality as follows. He is "a highly self-directed individual who prizes his independence." He has "narcissistic features," which are evidenced in the attention he pays to his personal appearance and his "obvious 'efforts' to demonstrate that he is really a rather 'humble and regular guy.'" He is "somewhat compulsive" in how he organizes his environment and business. He is confident, self-assured, and possesses an air of authority. While he admits to at times wrestling with how to determine who is an "innocent," he has acknowledged celebrating the destruction of the World Trade Center. He is intelligent and intellectually curious. He displays "excellent self-discipline." The assessment describes him as a perfectionist, persistent, private, and highly capable in his social interactions. He is very guarded about opening up to others and your assessment repeatedly emphasizes that he tends not to trust others easily. He is also "quick to recognize and assess the moods and motivations of others." Furthermore, he is proud of his ability to lie and deceive others successfully. Through his deception he has, among other things, prevented the location of al Qaeda safehouses and even acquired a United Nations refugee identification card.

According to your reports, Zubaydah does not have any pre-existing mental conditions or problems that would make him likely to suffer prolonged mental harm from your proposed interrogation methods. Through reading his diaries and interviewing him, you have found no history of "mood disturbance or other psychiatric pathology[,]" "thought disorder[,] . . . enduring mood or mental health problems." He is in fact "remarkably resilient and confident that he can overcome adversity." When he encounters stress or low mood, this appears to last only for a short time. He deals with stress by assessing its source, evaluating the coping resources available to him, and then taking action. Your assessment notes that he is "generally self-sufficient and relies on his understanding and application of religious and psychological principles, intelligence and discipline to avoid and overcome problems." Moreover, you have found that he has a "reliable and durable support system" in his faith, "the blessings of religious leaders, and camaraderie of like-minded mujahedin brothers." During detention, Zubaydah has managed his mood, remaining at most points "circumspect, calm, controlled, and deliberate." He has maintained this demeanor during aggressive interrogations and reductions in sleep. You describe that in an initial confrontational incident, Zubaydah showed signs of sympathetic nervous system arousal, which you think was possibly fear. Although this incident led him to disclose intelligence information, he was able to quickly regain his composure, his air of confidence, and his "strong resolve" not to reveal any information.

Overall, you summarize his primary strengths as the following: ability to focus, goal-directed discipline, intelligence, emotional resilience, street savvy, ability to organize and manage people, keen observation skills, fluid adaptability (can anticipate and adapt under duress and with minimal resources), capacity to assess and exploit the needs of others, and ability to adjust goals to emerging opportunities.

You anticipate that he will draw upon his vast knowledge of interrogation techniques to cope with the interrogation. Your assessment indicates that Zubaydah may be willing to die to protect the most important information that he holds. Nonetheless, you are of the view that his belief that Islam will ultimately dominate the world and that this victory is inevitable may provide the chance that Zubaydah will give information and rationalize it solely as a temporary setback. Additionally, you believe he may be willing to disclose some information, particularly information he deems to not be critical, but which may ultimately be useful to us when pieced together with other intelligence information you have gained.

III.

Section 2340A makes it a criminal offense for any person "outside of the United States [to] commit[] or attempt[] to commit torture." Section 2340(1) defines torture as:

> an act committed by a person acting under the color of law specifically intended to inflict severe physical or mental pain or suffering (other than pain or suffering incidental to lawful sanctions) upon another person within his custody of physical control.

18 U.S.C. § 2340(1). As we outlined in our opinion on standards of conduct under Section 2340A, a violation of 2340A requires a showing that: (1) the torture occurred outside the United States; (2) the defendant acted under the color of law; (3) the victim was within the defendant's custody or control; (4) the defendant specifically intended to inflict severe pain or suffering; and (5) that the acted inflicted severe pain or suffering. *See* Memorandum for John Rizzo, Acting General Counsel for the Central Intelligence Agency, from Jay S. Bybee, Assistant Attorney General, Office of Legal Counsel, Re: *Standards of Conduct for Interrogation under 18 U.S.C. §§ 2340–2340A* at 3 (August 1, 2002) ("Section 2340A Memorandum"). You have asked us to assume that Zubaydah is being held outside the United States, Zubaydah is within U.S. custody, and the interrogators are acting under the color of law. At issue is whether the last two elements would be met by the use of the proposed procedures, namely, whether those using these procedures would have the requisite mental state and whether these procedures would inflict severe pain or suffering within the meaning of the statute.

<u>Severe Pain or Suffering.</u> In order for pain or suffering to rise to the level of torture, the statute requires that it be severe. As we have previously explained, this reaches only extreme acts. *See id.* at 13. Nonetheless, drawing upon cases under the Torture Victim Protection Act (TVPA), which has a definition of torture that is similar to Section 2340's definition, we found that a single event of sufficiently intense pain may fall within this prohibition. *See id.* at 26. As a result, we have analyzed each of these techniques separately. In further drawing upon those cases, we also have found that courts tend to take a totality-of-the-circumstances approach and consider an entire course of conduct to determine whether torture has occurred. *See id.* at 27. Therefore, in addition to considering each technique separately, we consider them together as a course of conduct.

Section 2340 defines torture as the infliction of severe physical or mental pain or suffering. We will consider physical pain and mental pain separately. *See* 18 U.S.C. § 2340(1). With respect to *physical* pain, we previously concluded that "severe pain" within the meaning of

TOP SECRET

Section 2340 is pain that is difficult for the individual to endure and is of an intensity akin to the pain accompanying serious physical injury. *See* Section 2340A Memorandum at 6. Drawing upon the TVPA precedent, we have noted that examples of acts inflicting severe pain that typify torture are, among other things, severe beatings with weapons such as clubs, and the burning of prisoners. *See id.* at 24. We conclude below that none of the proposed techniques inflicts such pain.

The facial hold and the attention grasp involve no physical pain. In the absence of such pain it is obvious that they cannot be said to inflict severe physical pain or suffering. The stress positions and wall standing both may result in muscle fatigue. Each involves the sustained holding of a position. In wall standing, it will be holding a position in which all of the individual's body weight is placed on his finger tips. The stress positions will likely include sitting on the floor with legs extended straight out in front and arms raised above the head, and kneeling on the floor and leaning back at a 45 degree angle. Any pain associated with muscle fatigue is not of the intensity sufficient to amount to "severe physical pain or suffering" under the statute, nor, despite its discomfort, can it be said to be difficult to endure. Moreover, you have orally informed us that no stress position will be used that could interfere with the healing of Zubaydah's wound. Therefore, we conclude that these techniques involve discomfort that falls far below the threshold of severe physical pain.

Similarly, although the confinement boxes (both small and large) are physically uncomfortable because their size restricts movement, they are not so small as to require the individual to contort his body to sit (small box) or stand (large box). You have also orally informed us that despite his wound, Zubaydah remains quite flexible, which would substantially reduce any pain associated with being placed in the box. We have no information from the medical experts you have consulted that the limited duration for which the individual is kept in the boxes causes any substantial physical pain. As a result, we do not think the use of these boxes can be said to cause pain that is of the intensity associated with serious physical injury.

The use of one of these boxes with the introduction of an insect does not alter this assessment. As we understand it, no actually harmful insect will be placed in the box. Thus, though the introduction of an insect may produce trepidation in Zubaydah (which we discuss below), it certainly does not cause physical pain.

As for sleep deprivation, it is clear that depriving someone of sleep does not involve severe physical pain within the meaning of the statute. While sleep deprivation may involve some physical discomfort, such as the fatigue or the discomfort experienced in the difficulty of keeping one's eyes open, these effects remit after the individual is permitted to sleep. Based on the facts you have provided us, we are not aware of any evidence that sleep deprivation results in severe physical pain or suffering. As a result, its use does not violate Section 2340A.

Even those techniques that involve physical contact between the interrogator and the

TOP SECRET

individual do not result in severe pain. The facial slap and walling contain precautions to ensure that no pain even approaching this level results. The slap is delivered with fingers slightly spread, which you have explained to us is designed to be less painful than a closed-hand slap. The slap is also delivered to the fleshy part of the face, further reducing any risk of physical damage or serious pain. The facial slap does not produce pain that is difficult to endure. Likewise, walling involves quickly pulling the person forward and then thrusting him against a flexible false wall. You have informed us that the sound of hitting the wall will actually be far worse than any possible injury to the individual. The use of the rolled towel around the neck also reduces any risk of injury. While it may hurt to be pushed against the wall, any pain experienced is not of the intensity associated with serious physical injury.

As we understand it, when the waterboard is used, the subject's body responds as if the subject were drowning—even though the subject may be well aware that he is in fact not drowning. You have informed us that this procedure does not inflict actual physical harm. Thus, although the subject may experience the fear or panic associated with the feeling of drowning, the waterboard does not inflict physical pain. As we explained in the Section 2340A Memorandum, "pain and suffering" as used in Section 2340 is best understood as a single concept, not distinct concepts of "pain" as distinguished from "suffering." *See* Section 2340A Memorandum at 6 n.3. The waterboard, which inflicts no pain or actual harm whatsoever, does not, in our view inflict "severe pain or suffering." Even if one were to parse the statute more finely to attempt to treat "suffering" as a distinct concept, the waterboard could not be said to inflict severe suffering. The waterboard is simply a controlled acute episode, lacking the connotation of a protracted period of time generally given to suffering.

Finally, as we discussed above, you have informed us that in determining which procedures to use and how you will use them, you have selected techniques that will not harm Zubaydah's wound. You have also indicated that numerous steps will be taken to ensure that none of these procedures in any way interferes with the proper healing of Zubaydah's wound. You have also indicated that, should it appear at any time that Zubaydah is experiencing severe pain or suffering, the medical personnel on hand will stop the use of any technique.

Even when all of these methods are considered combined in an overall course of conduct, they still would not inflict severe physical pain or suffering. As discussed above, a number of these acts result in no physical pain, others produce only physical discomfort. You have indicated that these acts will not be used with substantial repetition, so that there is no possibility that severe physical pain could arise from such repetition. Accordingly, we conclude that these acts neither separately nor as part of a course of conduct would inflict severe physical pain or suffering within the meaning of the statute.

We next consider whether the use of these techniques would inflict severe *mental* pain or suffering within the meaning of Section 2340. Section 2340 defines severe mental pain or suffering as "the prolonged mental harm caused by or resulting from" one of several predicate

11

acts. 18 U.S.C. § 2340(2). Those predicate acts are: (1) the intentional infliction or threatened infliction of severe physical pain or suffering; (2) the administration or application, or threatened administration or application of mind-altering substances or other procedures calculated to disrupt profoundly the senses or the personality; (3) the threat of imminent death; or (4) the threat that any of the preceding acts will be done to another person. *See* 18 U.S.C. § 2340(2)(A)–(D). As we have explained, this list of predicate acts is exclusive. *See* Section 2340A Memorandum at 8. No other acts can support a charge under Section 2340A based on the infliction of severe mental pain or suffering. *See id.* Thus, if the methods that you have described do not either in and of themselves constitute one of these acts or as a course of conduct fulfill the predicate act requirement, the prohibition has not been violated. *See id.* Before addressing these techniques, we note that it is plain that none of these procedures involves a threat to any third party, the use of any kind of drugs, or for the reasons described above, the infliction of severe physical pain. Thus, the question is whether any of these acts, separately or as a course of conduct, constitutes a threat of severe physical pain or suffering, a procedure designed to disrupt profoundly the senses, or a threat of imminent death. As we previously explained, whether an action constitutes a threat must be assessed from the standpoint of a reasonable person in the subject's position. *See id.* at 9.

No argument can be made that the attention grasp or the facial hold constitute threats of imminent death or are procedures designed to disrupt profoundly the senses or personality. In general the grasp and the facial hold will startle the subject, produce fear, or even insult him. As you have informed us, the use of these techniques is not accompanied by a specific verbal threat of severe physical pain or suffering. To the extent that these techniques could be considered a threat of severe physical pain or suffering, such a threat would have to be inferred from the acts themselves. Because these actions themselves involve no pain, neither could be interpreted by a reasonable person in Zubaydah's position to constitute a threat of severe pain or suffering. Accordingly, these two techniques are not predicate acts within the meaning of Section 2340.

The facial slap likewise falls outside the set of predicate acts. It plainly is not a threat of imminent death, under Section 2340(2)(C), or a procedure designed to disrupt profoundly the senses or personality, under Section 2340(2)(B). Though it may hurt, as discussed above, the effect is one of smarting or stinging and surprise or humiliation, but not severe pain. Nor does it alone constitute a threat of severe pain or suffering, under Section 2340(2)(A). Like the facial hold and the attention grasp, the use of this slap is not accompanied by a specific verbal threat of further escalating violence. Additionally, you have informed us that in one use this technique will typically involve at most two slaps. Certainly, the use of this slap may dislodge any expectation that Zubaydah had that he would not be touched in a physically aggressive manner. Nonetheless, this alteration in his expectations could hardly be construed by a reasonable person in his situation to be tantamount to a threat of severe physical pain or suffering. At most, this technique suggests that the circumstances of his confinement and interrogation have changed. Therefore, the facial slap is not within the statute's exclusive list of predicate acts.

Walling plainly is not a procedure calculated to disrupt profoundly the senses or personality. While walling involves what might be characterized as rough handling, it does not involve the threat of imminent death or, as discussed above, the infliction of severe physical pain. Moreover, once again we understand that use of this technique will not be accompanied by any specific verbal threat that violence will ensue absent cooperation. Thus, like the facial slap, walling can only constitute a threat of severe physical pain if a reasonable person would infer such a threat from the use of the technique itself. Walling does not in and of itself inflict severe pain or suffering. Like the facial slap, walling may alter the subject's expectation as to the treatment he believes he will receive. Nonetheless, the character of the action falls so far short of inflicting severe pain or suffering within the meaning of the statute that even if he inferred that greater aggressiveness was to follow, the type of actions that could be reasonably be anticipated would still fall below anything sufficient to inflict severe physical pain or suffering under the statute. Thus, we conclude that this technique falls outside the proscribed predicate acts.

Like walling, stress positions and wall-standing are not procedures calculated to disrupt profoundly the senses, nor are they threats of imminent death. These procedures, as discussed above, involve the use of muscle fatigue to encourage cooperation and do not themselves constitute the infliction of severe physical pain or suffering. Moreover, there is no aspect of violence to either technique that remotely suggests future severe pain or suffering from which such a threat of future harm could be inferred. They simply involve forcing the subject to remain in uncomfortable positions. While these acts may indicate to the subject that he may be placed in these positions again if he does not disclose information, the use of these techniques would not suggest to a reasonable person in the subject's position that he is being threatened with severe pain or suffering. Accordingly, we conclude that these two procedures do not constitute any of the predicate acts set forth in Section 2340(2).

As with the other techniques discussed so far, cramped confinement is not a threat of imminent death. It may be argued that, focusing in part on the fact that the boxes will be without light, placement in these boxes would constitute a procedure designed to disrupt profoundly the senses. As we explained in our recent opinion, however, to "disrupt profoundly the senses" a technique must produce an extreme effect in the subject. *See* Section 2340A Memorandum at 10–12. We have previously concluded that this requires that the procedure cause substantial interference with the individual's cognitive abilities or fundamentally alter his personality. *See id.* at 11. Moreover, the statute requires that such procedures must be calculated to produce this effect. *See id.* at 10; 18 U.S.C. § 2340(2)(B).

With respect to the small confinement box, you have informed us that he would spend at most two hours in this box. You have informed us that your purpose in using these boxes is not to interfere with his senses or his personality, but to cause him physical discomfort that will encourage him to disclose critical information. Moreover, your imposition of time limitations on the use of either of the boxes also indicates that the use of these boxes is not designed or calculated to disrupt profoundly the senses or personality. For the larger box, in which he can both stand and sit, he may be placed in this box for up to eighteen hours at a time, while you have informed us that he will never spend more than an hour at time in the smaller box. These time limits further ensure that no profound disruption of the senses or personality, were it even possible, would result. As such, the use of the confinement boxes does not constitute a procedure calculated to disrupt profoundly the senses or personality.

Nor does the use of the boxes threaten Zubaydah with severe physical pain or suffering. While additional time spent in the boxes may be threatened, their use is not accompanied by any express threats of severe physical pain or suffering. Like the stress positions and walling, placement in the boxes is physically uncomfortable but any such discomfort does not rise to the level of severe physical pain or suffering. Accordingly, a reasonable person in the subject's position would not infer from the use of this technique that severe physical pain is the next step in his interrogator's treatment of him. Therefore, we conclude that the use of the confinement boxes does not fall within the statute's required predicate acts.

In addition to using the confinement boxes alone, you also would like to introduce an insect into one of the boxes with Zubaydah. As we understand it, you plan to inform Zubaydah that you are going to place a stinging insect into the box, but you will actually place a harmless insect in the box, such as a caterpillar. If you do so, to ensure that you are outside the predicate act requirement, you must inform him that the insects will not have a sting that would produce death or severe pain. If, however, you were to place the insect in the box without informing him that you are doing so, then, in order to not commit a predicate act, you should not affirmatively lead him to believe that any insect is present which has a sting that could produce severe pain or suffering or even cause his death. ███████████████ so long as you take either of the approaches we have described, the insect's placement in the box would not constitute a threat of severe physical pain or suffering to a reasonable person in his position. An individual placed in a box, even an individual with a fear of insects, would not reasonably feel threatened with severe physical pain or suffering if a caterpillar was placed in the box. Further, you have informed us that you are not aware that Zubaydah has any allergies to insects, and you have not informed us of any other factors that would cause a reasonable person in that same situation to believe that an unknown insect would cause him severe physical pain or death. Thus, we conclude that the placement of the insect in the confinement box with Zubaydah would not constitute a predicate act.

Sleep deprivation also clearly does not involve a threat of imminent death. Although it produces physical discomfort, it cannot be said to constitute a threat of severe physical pain or suffering from the perspective of a reasonable person in Zubaydah's position. Nor could sleep deprivation constitute a procedure calculated to disrupt profoundly the senses, so long as sleep deprivation (as you have informed us is your intent) is used for limited periods, before hallucinations or other profound disruptions of the senses would occur. To be sure, sleep deprivation may reduce the subject's ability to think on his feet. Indeed, you indicate that this is the intended result. His mere reduced ability to evade your questions and resist answering does not, however, rise to the level of disruption required by the statute. As we explained above, a disruption within the meaning of the statute is an extreme one, substantially interfering with an individual's cognitive abilities, for example, inducing hallucinations, or driving him to engage in uncharacteristic self-destructive behavior. *See infra* 13; Section 2340A Memorandum at 11. Therefore, the limited use of sleep deprivation does not constitute one of the required predicate acts.

We find that the use of the waterboard constitutes a threat of imminent death. As you have explained the waterboard procedure to us, it creates in the subject the uncontrollable physiological sensation that the subject is drowning. Although the procedure will be monitored by personnel with medical training and extensive SERE school experience with this procedure who will ensure the subject's mental and physical safety, the subject is not aware of any of these precautions. From the vantage point of any reasonable person undergoing this procedure in such circumstances, he would feel as if he is drowning at very moment of the procedure due to the uncontrollable physiological sensation he is experiencing. Thus, this procedure cannot be viewed as too uncertain to satisfy the imminence requirement. Accordingly, it constitutes a threat of imminent death and fulfills the predicate act requirement under the statute.

Although the waterboard constitutes a threat of imminent death, prolonged mental harm must nonetheless result to violate the statutory prohibition on infliction of severe mental pain or suffering. *See* Section 2340A Memorandum at 7. We have previously concluded that prolonged mental harm is mental harm of some lasting duration, e.g., mental harm lasting months or years. *See id.* Prolonged mental harm is not simply the stress experienced in, for example, an interrogation by state police. *See id.* Based on your research into the use of these methods at the SERE school and consultation with others with expertise in the field of psychology and interrogation, you do not anticipate that any prolonged mental harm would result from the use of the waterboard. Indeed, you have advised us that the relief is almost immediate when the cloth is removed from the nose and mouth. In the absence of prolonged mental harm, no severe mental pain or suffering would have been inflicted, and the use of these procedures would not constitute torture within the meaning of the statute.

When these acts are considered as a course of conduct, we are unsure whether these acts may constitute a threat of severe physical pain or suffering. You have indicated to us that you have not determined either the order or the precise timing for implementing these procedures. It is conceivable that these procedures could be used in a course of escalating conduct, moving incrementally and rapidly from least physically intrusive, e.g., facial hold, to the most physical contact, e.g., walling or the waterboard. As we understand it, based on his treatment so far, Zubaydah has come to expect that no physical harm will be done to him. By using these techniques in increasing intensity and in rapid succession, the goal would be to dislodge this expectation. Based on the facts you have provided to us, we cannot say definitively that the entire course of conduct would cause a reasonable person to believe that he is being threatened

with severe pain or suffering within the meaning of section 2340. On the other hand, however, under certain circumstances—for example, rapid escalation in the use of these techniques culminating in the waterboard (which we acknowledge constitutes a threat of imminent death) accompanied by verbal or other suggestions that physical violence will follow—might cause a reasonable person to believe that they are faced with such a threat. Without more information, we are uncertain whether the course of conduct would constitute a predicate act under Section 2340(2).

Even if the course of conduct were thought to pose a threat of physical pain or suffering, it would nevertheless—on the facts before us—not constitute a violation of Section 2340A. Not only must the course of conduct be a predicate act, but also those who use the procedure must actually cause prolonged mental harm. Based on the information that you have provided to us, indicating that no evidence exists that this course of conduct produces any prolonged mental harm, we conclude that a course of conduct using these procedures and culminating in the waterboard would not violate Section 2340A.

Specific Intent. To violate the statute, an individual must have the specific intent to inflict severe pain or suffering. Because specific intent is an element of the offense, the absence of specific intent negates the charge of torture. As we previously opined, to have the required specific intent, an individual must expressly intend to cause such severe pain or suffering. *See* Section 2340A Memorandum at 3 *citing Carter v. United States*, 530 U.S. 255, 267 (2000). We have further found that if a defendant acts with the good faith belief that his actions will not cause such suffering, he has not acted with specific intent. *See id.* at 4 *citing South Atl. Lmtd. Ptrshp. of Tenn. v. Reise*, 218 F.3d 518, 531 (4th Cir. 2002). A defendant acts in good faith when he has an honest belief that his actions will not result in severe pain or suffering. *See id. citing Cheek v. United States*, 498 U.S. 192, 202 (1991). Although an honest belief need not be reasonable, such a belief is easier to establish where there is a reasonable basis for it. *See id.* at 5. Good faith may be established by, among other things, the reliance on the advice of experts. *See id.* at 8.

Based on the information you have provided us, we believe that those carrying out these procedures would not have the specific intent to inflict severe physical pain or suffering. The objective of these techniques is not to cause severe physical pain. First, the constant presence of personnel with medical training who have the authority to stop the interrogation should it appear it is medically necessary indicates that it is not your intent to cause severe physical pain. The personnel on site have extensive experience with these specific techniques as they are used in SERE school training. Second, you have informed us that you are taking steps to ensure that Zubaydah's injury is not worsened or his recovery impeded by the use of these techniques.

Third, as you have described them to us, the proposed techniques involving physical contact between the interrogator and Zubaydah actually contain precautions to prevent any serious physical harm to Zubaydah. In "walling," a rolled hood or towel will be used to prevent

whiplash and he will be permitted to rebound from the flexible wall to reduce the likelihood of injury. Similarly, in the "facial hold," the fingertips will be kept well away from the his eyes to ensure that there is no injury to them. The purpose of that facial hold is not injure him but to hold the head immobile. Additionally, while the stress positions and wall standing will undoubtedly result in physical discomfort by tiring the muscles, it is obvious that these positions are not intended to produce the kind of extreme pain required by the statute.

Furthermore, no specific intent to cause severe mental pain or suffering appears to be present. As we explained in our recent opinion, an individual must have the specific intent to cause prolonged mental harm in order to have the specific intent to inflict severe mental pain or suffering. See Section 2340A Memorandum at 8. Prolonged mental harm is substantial mental harm of a sustained duration, e.g., harm lasting months or even years after the acts were inflicted upon the prisoner. As we indicated above, a good faith belief can negate this element. Accordingly, if an individual conducting the interrogation has a good faith belief that the procedures he will apply, separately or together, would not result in prolonged mental harm, that individual lacks the requisite specific intent. This conclusion concerning specific intent is further bolstered by the due diligence that has been conducted concerning the effects of these interrogation procedures.

The mental health experts that you have consulted have indicated that the psychological impact of a course of conduct must be assessed with reference to the subject's psychological history and current mental health status. The healthier the individual, the less likely that the use of any one procedure or set of procedures as a course of conduct will result in prolonged mental harm. A comprehensive psychological profile of Zubaydah has been created. In creating this profile, your personnel drew on direct interviews, Zubaydah's diaries, observation of Zubaydah since his capture, and information from other sources such as other intelligence and press reports.

As we indicated above, you have informed us that your proposed interrogation methods have been used and continue to be used in SERE training. It is our understanding that these techniques are not used one by one in isolation, but as a full course of conduct to resemble a real interrogation. Thus, the information derived from SERE training bears both upon the impact of the use of the individual techniques and upon their use as a course of conduct. You have found that the use of these methods together or separately, including the use of the waterboard, has not resulted in any negative long-term mental health consequences. The continued use of these methods without mental health consequences to the trainees indicates that it is highly improbable that such consequences would result here. Because you have conducted the due diligence to determine that these procedures, either alone or in combination, do not produce prolonged mental harm, we believe that you do not meet the specific intent requirement necessary to violate Section 2340A.

You have also informed us that you have reviewed the relevant literature on the subject, and consulted with outside psychologists. Your review of the literature uncovered no empirical data on the use of these procedures, with the exception of sleep deprivation for which no long-term health consequences resulted. The outside psychologists with whom you consulted indicated were unaware of any cases where long-term problems have occurred as a result of these techniques.

As described above, it appears you have conducted an extensive inquiry to ascertain what impact, if any, these procedures individually and as a course of conduct would have on Zubaydah. You have consulted with interrogation experts, including those with substantial SERE school experience, consulted with outside psychologists, completed a psychological assessment and reviewed the relevant literature on this topic. Based on this inquiry, you believe that the use of the procedures, including the waterboard, and as a course of conduct would not result in prolonged mental harm. Reliance on this information about Zubaydah and about the effect of the use of these techniques more generally demonstrates the presence of a good faith belief that no prolonged mental harm will result from using these methods in the interrogation of Zubaydah. Moreover, we think that this represents not only an honest belief but also a reasonable belief based on the information that you have supplied to us. Thus, we believe that the specific intent to inflict prolonged mental is not present, and consequently, there is no specific intent to inflict severe mental pain or suffering. Accordingly, we conclude that on the facts in this case the use of these methods separately or a course of conduct would not violate Section 2340A.

Based on the foregoing, and based on the facts that you have provided, we conclude that the interrogation procedures that you propose would not violate Section 2340A. We wish to emphasize that this is our best reading of the law; however, you should be aware that there are no cases construing this statute; just as there have been no prosecutions brought under it.

Please let us know if we can be of further assistance.

Jay S. Bybee
Assistant Attorney General

MEMO TWO

DATED MAY 10, 2005, FROM STEVEN BRADBURY, ACTING ASSISTANT ATTORNEY GENERAL, OLC, TO JOHN A. RIZZO, GENERAL COUNSEL CIA

~~TOP SECRET~~ / ~~NOFORN~~   0000013

U.S. Department of Justice

Office of Legal Counsel

Office of the Principal Deputy Assistant Attorney General   Washington, D.C. 20530

May 10, 2005

MEMORANDUM FOR JOHN A. RIZZO
SENIOR DEPUTY GENERAL COUNSEL, CENTRAL INTELLIGENCE AGENCY

Re: Application of 18 U.S.C. §§ 2340-2340A to ~~Certain Techniques~~ That May Be Used in the Interrogation of a High Value al Qaeda Detainee

You have asked us to address whether certain specified interrogation techniques designed to be used on a high value al Qaeda detainee in the War on Terror comply with the federal prohibition on torture, codified at 18 U.S.C. §§ 2340-2340A. Our analysis of this question is controlled by this Office's recently published opinion interpreting the anti-torture statute. *See* Memorandum for James B. Comey, Deputy Attorney General, from Daniel Levin, Acting Assistant Attorney General, Office of Legal Counsel, *Re: Legal Standards Applicable Under 18 U.S.C. §§ 2340-2340A* (Dec. 30, 2004) ("*2004 Legal Standards Opinion*"), *available at* www.usdoj.gov. (We provided a copy of that opinion to you at the time it was issued.) Much of the analysis from our *2004 Legal Standards Opinion* is reproduced below; all of it is incorporated by reference herein. Because you have asked us to address the application of sections 2340-2340A to specific interrogation techniques, the present memorandum necessarily includes additional discussion of the applicable legal standards and their application to particular facts. We stress, however, that the legal standards we apply in this memorandum are fully consistent with the interpretation of the statute set forth in our *2004 Legal Standards Opinion* and ~~constitute~~ our authoritative view of the legal standards applicable under sections 2340-2340A. Our task is to explicate those standards in order to assist you in complying with the law.

A paramount recognition emphasized in our *2004 Legal Standards Opinion* merits re-emphasis at the outset and guides our analysis: Torture is abhorrent both to American law and values and to international norms. The universal repudiation of torture is reflected not only in our criminal law, *see, e.g.,* 18 U.S.C. §§ 2340-2340A, but also in international agreements,[1] in

---

[1] *See, e.g.,* United Nations Convention Against Torture and Other Cruel, Inhuman or Degrading Treatment or Punishment, Dec. 10, 1984, S. Treaty Doc. No. 100-20, 1465 U.N.T.S. 85 (entered into force for U.S. Nov. 20,

centuries of Anglo-American law, see, e.g., John H. Langbein, *Torture and the Law of Proof: Europe and England in the Ancien Regime* (1977) ("*Torture and the Law of Proof*"), and in the longstanding policy of the United States, repeatedly and recently reaffirmed by the President.[2] Consistent with these norms, the President has directed unequivocally that the United States is not to engage in torture.[3]

The task of interpreting and applying sections 2340-2340A is complicated by the lack of precision in the statutory terms and the lack of relevant case law. In defining the federal crime of torture, Congress required that a defendant "*specifically intend*[] to inflict *severe* physical or mental pain or suffering," and Congress narrowly defined "severe mental pain or suffering" to mean "the *prolonged* mental harm caused by" enumerated predicate acts, including "the threat of *imminent* death" and "procedures *calculated* to disrupt *profoundly* the senses or personality." 18 U.S.C. § 2340 (emphases added). These statutory requirements are consistent with U.S. obligations under the United Nations Convention Against Torture, the treaty that obligates the United States to ensure that torture is a crime under U.S. law and that is implemented by sections 2340-2340A. The requirements in sections 2340-2340A closely track the understandings and reservations required by the Senate when it gave its advice and consent to ratification of the Convention Against Torture. They reflect a clear intent by Congress to limit the scope of the prohibition on torture under U.S. law. However, many of the key terms used in the statute (for example, "severe," "prolonged," "suffering") are imprecise and necessarily bring a degree of uncertainty to addressing the reach of sections 2340-2340A. Moreover, relevant judicial decisions in this area provide only limited guidance.[4] This imprecision and lack of judicial guidance, coupled with the President's clear directive that the United States does not condone or engage in torture, counsel great care in applying the statute to specific conduct. We have attempted to exercise such care throughout this memorandum.

With these considerations in mind, we turn to the particular question before us: whether certain specified interrogation techniques may be used by the Central Intelligence Agency ("CIA.") on a high value al Qaeda detainee consistent with the federal statutory prohibition on

---

1994) ("Convention Against Torture" or "CAT"); International Covenant on Civil and Political Rights, Dec. 16, 1966, art. 7, 999 U.N.T.S. 171.

[2] *See, e.g.*, Statement on United Nations International Day in Support of Victims of Torture, 40 Weekly Comp. Pres. Doc. 1167 (July 5, 2004) ("Freedom from torture is an inalienable human right . . . ."); Statement on United Nations International Day in Support of Victims of Torture, 39 Weekly Comp. Pres. Doc. 824 (June 30, 2003) ("Torture anywhere is an affront to human dignity everywhere."); *see also Letter of Transmittal from President Ronald Reagan to the Senate* (May 20, 1988), *in Message from the President of the United States Transmitting the Convention Against Torture and Other Cruel, Inhuman or Degrading Treatment or Punishment*, S. Treaty Doc. No. 100-20, at ii (1988) ("Ratification of the Convention by the United States will clearly express United States opposition to torture, an abhorrent practice still prevalent in the world today.").

[3] *See, e.g.*, 40 Weekly Comp. Pres. Doc. at 1167-68 ("America stands against and will not tolerate torture. . . . Torture is wrong no matter where it occurs, and the United States will continue to lead the fight to eliminate it everywhere.").

[4] What judicial guidance there is comes from decisions that apply a related but separate statute (the Torture Victims Protection Act ("TVPA"), 28 U.S.C. § 1350 note (2000)). These judicial opinions generally contain little if any analysis of specific conduct or of the relevant statutory standards.

torture, 18 U.S.C. §§ 2340-2340A.[5] For the reasons discussed below, and based on the representations we have received from you (or officials of your Agency) about the particular techniques in question, the circumstances in which they are authorized for use, and the physical and psychological assessments made of the detainee to be interrogated, we conclude that the separate authorized use of each of the specific techniques at issue, subject to the limitations and safeguards described herein, would not violate sections 2340-2340A.[6] Our conclusion is straightforward with respect to all but two of the techniques discussed herein. As discussed below, use of sleep deprivation as an enhanced technique and use of the waterboard involve more substantial questions, with the waterboard presenting the most substantial question.

We base our conclusions on the statutory language enacted by Congress in sections 2340-2340A. We do not rely on any consideration of the President's authority as Commander in Chief under the Constitution, any application of the principle of constitutional avoidance (or any conclusion about constitutional issues), or any arguments based on possible defenses of "necessity" or self-defense.[7]

---

[5] We have previously advised you that the use by the CIA of the techniques of interrogation discussed herein is consistent with the Constitution and applicable statutes and treaties. In the present memorandum, you have asked us to address only the requirements of 18 U.S.C. §§ 2340-2340A. Nothing in this memorandum or in our prior advice to the CIA should be read to suggest that the use of these techniques would conform to the requirements of the Uniform Code of Military Justice that governs members of the Armed Forces or to United States obligations under the Geneva Conventions in circumstances where those Conventions would apply. We do not address the possible application of article 16 of the CAT, nor do we address any question relating to conditions of confinement or detention, as distinct from the interrogation of detainees. We stress that our advice on the application of sections 2340-2340A does not represent the policy views of the Department of Justice concerning interrogation practices. Finally, we note that section 6057(a) of H.R. 1268 (109th Cong. 1st Sess.), if it becomes law, would forbid expending or obligating funds made available by that bill "to subject any person in the custody or under the physical control of the United States to torture," but because the bill would define "torture" to have "the meaning given that term in section 2340(1) of title 18, United States Code," § 6057(b)(1), the provision (to the extent it might apply here at all) would merely reaffirm the preexisting prohibitions on torture in sections 2340-2340A.

[6] The present memorandum addresses only the separate use of each individual technique, not the combined use of techniques as part of an integrated regimen of interrogation. You have informed us that most of the CIA's authorized techniques are designed to be used with particular detainees in an interrelated or combined manner as part of an overall interrogation program, and you have provided us with a description of a typical scenario for the CIA's combined use of techniques. See Background Paper on CIA's Combined Use of Interrogation Techniques (Dec. 30, 2004) ("Background Paper"). A full assessment of whether the use of interrogation techniques is consistent with sections 2340-2340A should take into account the potential combined effects of using multiple techniques on a given detainee, either simultaneously or sequentially within a short time. We will address in a separate memorandum whether the combined use of certain techniques, as reflected in the Background Paper, is consistent with the legal requirements of sections 2340-2340A.

[7] In preparing the present memorandum, we have reviewed and carefully considered the report prepared by the CIA Inspector General, Counterterrorism Detention and Interrogation Activities (September 2001-October 2003), No. 2003-7123-IG (May 7, 2004) ("IG Report")  Various aspects of the IG Report are addressed below.

TOP SECRET/ ███████ /NOFORN

I.

A.

In asking us to consider certain specific techniques to be used in the interrogation of a particular al Qaeda operative, you have provided background information common to the use of all of the techniques. You have advised that these techniques would be used only on an individual who is determined to be a "High Value Detainee," defined as:

> a detainee who, until time of capture, we have reason to believe: (1) is a senior member of al-Qai'da or an al-Qai'da associated terrorist group (Jemaah Islamiyyah, Eqyptian Islamic Jihad, al-Zarqawi Group, etc.); (2) has knowledge of imminent terrorist threats against the USA, its military forces, its citizens and organizations, or its allies; or that has/had direct involvement in planning and preparing terrorist actions against the USA or its allies, or assisting the al-Qai'da leadership in planning and preparing such terrorist actions; and (3) if released, constitutes a clear and continuing threat to the USA or its allies.

Fax for Daniel Levin, Acting Assistant Attorney General, Office of Legal Counsel, from ███████ Assistant General Counsel, CIA, at 3 (Jan. 4, 2005) ("*January 4 ███ Fax*"). For convenience, below we will generally refer to such individuals simply as detainees.

You have also explained that, prior to interrogation, each detainee is evaluated by medical and psychological professionals from the CIA's Office of Medical Services ("OMS") to ensure that he is not likely to suffer any severe physical or mental pain or suffering as a result of interrogation.

> [T]echnique-specific advanced approval is required for all "enhanced" measures and is conditional on on-site medical and psychological personnel confirming from direct detainee examination that the enhanced technique(s) is not expected to produce "severe physical or mental pain or suffering." As a practical matter, the detainee's physical condition must be such that these interventions will not have lasting effect, and his psychological state strong enough that no severe psychological harm will result.

OMS Guidelines on Medical and Psychological Support to Detainee Rendition, Interrogation and Detention at 9 (Dec. 2004) ("*OMS Guidelines*") (footnote omitted). New detainees are also subject to a general intake examination, which includes "a thorough initial medical assessment . . . with a complete, documented history and physical addressing in depth any chronic or previous medical problems. This assessment should especially attend to cardio-vascular, pulmonary, neurological and musculoskeletal findings. . . . Vital signs and weight should be recorded, and blood work drawn. . . ." *Id.* at 6. In addition, "subsequent medical rechecks during the interrogation period should be performed on a regular basis." *Id.* As an additional precaution, and to ensure the objectivity of their medical and psychological assessments, OMS personnel do not participate in administering interrogation techniques; their function is to monitor interrogations and the health of the detainee.

TOP SECRET/ ███████ /NOFORN

TOP SECRET/ NOFORN

The detainee is then interviewed by trained and certified interrogators to determine whether he is actively attempting to withhold or distort information. If so, the on-scene interrogation team develops an interrogation plan, which may include only those techniques for which there is no medical or psychological contraindication. You have informed us that the initial OMS assessments have ruled out the use of some—or all—of the interrogation techniques as to certain detainees. If the plan calls for the use of any of the interrogation techniques discussed herein, it is submitted to CIA Headquarters, which must review the plan and approve the use of any of these interrogation techniques before they may be applied. *See* George J. Tenet, Director of Central Intelligence, *Guidelines on Interrogations Conducted Pursuant to the* ▮▮▮▮▮ (Jan. 28, 2003) ("*Interrogation Guidelines*"). Prior written approval "from the Director, DCI Counterterrorist Center, with the concurrence of the Chief, CTC Legal Group," is required for the use of any enhanced interrogation techniques. *Id.* We understand that, as to the detainee here, this written approval has been given for each of the techniques we discuss, except the waterboard.

We understand that, when approved, interrogation techniques are generally used in an escalating fashion, with milder techniques used first. Use of the techniques is not continuous. Rather, one or more techniques may be applied—during or between interrogation sessions—based on the judgment of the interrogators and other team members and subject always to the monitoring of the on-scene medical and psychological personnel. Use of the techniques may be continued if the detainee is still believed to have and to be withholding actionable intelligence. The use of these techniques may not be continued for more than 30 days without additional approval from CIA Headquarters. *See generally Interrogation Guidelines* at 1-2 (describing approval procedures required for use of enhanced interrogation techniques). Moreover, even within that 30-day period, any further use of these interrogation techniques is discontinued if the detainee is judged to be consistently providing accurate intelligence or if he is no longer believed to have actionable intelligence. This memorandum addresses the use of these techniques during no more than one 30-day period. We do not address whether the use of these techniques beyond the initial 30-day period would violate the statute.

Medical and psychological personnel are on-scene throughout (and, as detailed below, physically present or otherwise observing during the application of many techniques, including all techniques involving physical contact with detainees), and "[d]aily physical and psychological evaluations are continued throughout the period of [enhanced interrogation technique] use." *IG Report* at 30 n.35; *see also* George J. Tenet, Director of Central Intelligence, *Guidelines on Confinement Conditions for CIA Detainees*, at 1 (Jan. 28, 2003) ("*Confinement Guidelines*") ("Medical and, as appropriate, psychological personnel shall be physically present at, or reasonably available to, each Detention Facility. Medical personnel shall check the physical condition of each detainee at intervals appropriate to the circumstances and shall keep appropriate records."); *IG Report* at 28-29.[8] In addition, "[i]n each interrogation session in which an Enhanced Technique is employed, a contemporaneous record shall be created setting forth the nature and duration of each such technique employed." *Interrogation Guidelines* at 3.

---

[8] In addition to monitoring the application and effects of enhanced interrogation techniques, OMS personnel are instructed more generally to ensure that "[a]dequate medical care shall be provided to detainees, even those undergoing enhanced interrogation." *OMS Guidelines* at 10.

TOP SECRET/ ~~██████~~ NOFORN

At any time, any on-scene personnel (including the medical or psychological personnel, the chief of base, substantive experts, security officers, and other interrogators) can intervene to stop the use of any technique if it appears that the technique is being used improperly, and on-scene medical personnel can intervene if the detainee has developed a condition making the use of the technique unsafe. More generally, medical personnel watch for signs of physical distress or mental harm so significant as possibly to amount to the "severe physical or mental pain or suffering" that is prohibited by sections 2340-2340A. As the *OMS Guidelines* explain, "[m]edical officers must remain cognizant at all times of their obligation to prevent 'severe physical or mental pain or suffering.'" *OMS Guidelines* at 10. Additional restrictions on certain techniques are described below.

These techniques have all been imported from military Survival, Evasion, Resistance, Escape ("SERE") training, where they have been used for years on U.S. military personnel, although with some significant differences described below. *See IG Report* at 13-14. Although we refer to the SERE experience below, we note at the outset an important limitation on reliance on that experience. Individuals undergoing SERE training are obviously in a very different situation from detainees undergoing interrogation; SERE trainees know it is part of a training program, not a real-life interrogation regime, they presumably know it will last only a short time, and they presumably have assurances that they will not be significantly harmed by the training.

B.

You have described the specific techniques at issue as follows:[9]

---

[9] The descriptions of these techniques are set out in a number of documents including: the *OMS Guidelines; Interrogations Guidelines; Confinement Guidelines; Background Paper;* Letter from ████ ████ Associate General Counsel, CIA, to Dan Levin, Acting Assistant Attorney General, Office of Legal Counsel ("OLC") (July 30, 2004) ("*July 30 ████ ████*"); Letter from John A. Rizzo, Acting General Counsel, CIA, to Daniel Levin, Acting Assistant Attorney General, OLC (Aug. 2, 2004) ("*August 2 Rizzo Letter*"); Letter from ████ ████ Associate General Counsel, CIA, to Dan Levin, Acting Assistant Attorney General, OLC (Aug. 19, 2004) ("*August 19 ████ Letter*"); Letter from ████ ████ Associate General Counsel, CIA, to Dan Levin, Acting Assistant Attorney General, OLC (Aug. 25, 2004) ("*August 25 ████ Letter*"); Letter from ████ ████ Associate General Counsel, CIA, to Dan Levin, Acting Assistant Attorney General, OLC (Oct. ██ 2004) ("*October ██ ████ Letter*"); Letter from ████ ████ Associate General Counsel, CIA, to Dan Levin, Acting Assistant Attorney General, OLC (Oct. 22, 2004) ("*October 22 ████ Letter*"). Several of the techniques are described and discussed in an earlier memorandum to you. *See* Memorandum for John Rizzo, Acting General Counsel, Central Intelligence Agency, from Jay S. Bybee, Assistant Attorney General, Office of Legal Counsel, *Re: Interrogation of al Qaeda Operative* (Aug. 1, 2002) ("*Interrogation Memorandum*") (TS). We have separately reanalyzed all techniques in the present memorandum, and we will note below where aspects of particular techniques differ from those addressed in the *Interrogation Memorandum*. In order to avoid any confusion in this extremely sensitive and important area, the discussions of the statute in the *2004 Legal Standards Opinion* and this memorandum supersede that in the *Interrogation Memorandum*; however, this memorandum confirms the conclusion of *Interrogation Memorandum* that the use of these techniques on a particular high value al Qaeda detainee, subject to the limitations imposed herein, would not violate sections 2340-2340A. In some cases additional facts set forth below have been provided to us in communications with CIA personnel. The CIA has reviewed this memorandum and confirmed the accuracy of the descriptions and limitations. Our analysis assumes adherence to these descriptions and limitations.

TOP SECRET/ ~~██████~~ NOFORN

1. *Dietary manipulation.* This technique involves the substitution of commercial liquid meal replacements for normal food, presenting detainees with a bland, unappetizing, but nutritionally complete diet. You have informed us that the CIA believes dietary manipulation makes other techniques, such as sleep deprivation, more effective. *See August 25* ███ *Letter* at 4. Detainees on dietary manipulation are permitted as much water as they want. In general, minimum daily fluid and nutritional requirements are estimated using the following formula:

- Fluid requirement: 35 ml/kg/day. This may be increased depending on ambient temperature, body temperature, and level of activity. Medical officers must monitor fluid intake, and although detainees are allowed as much water as they want, monitoring of urine output may be necessary in the unlikely event that the officers suspect that the detainee is becoming dehydrated.

- Calorie requirement: The CIA generally follows as a guideline a calorie requirement of 900 kcal/day + 10 kcal/kg/day. This quantity is multiplied by 1.2 for a sedentary activity level or 1.4 for a moderate activity level. Regardless of this formula, the recommended minimum calorie intake is 1500 kcal/day, and in no event is the detainee allowed to receive less than 1000 kcal/day.[10] Calories are provided using commercial liquid diets (such as Ensure Plus), which also supply other essential nutrients and make for nutritionally complete meals.[11]

Medical officers are required to ensure adequate fluid and nutritional intake, and frequent medical monitoring takes place while any detainee is undergoing dietary manipulation. All detainees are weighed weekly, and in the unlikely event that a detainee were to lose more than 10 percent of his body weight, the restricted diet would be discontinued.

2. *Nudity.* This technique is used to cause psychological discomfort, particularly if a detainee, for cultural or other reasons, is especially modest. When the technique is employed, clothing can be provided as an instant reward for cooperation. During and between interrogation sessions, a detainee may be kept nude, provided that ambient temperatures and the health of the detainee permit. For this technique to be employed, ambient temperature must be at least 68°F.[12] No sexual abuse or threats of sexual abuse are permitted. Although each detention cell has full-time closed-circuit video monitoring, the detainee is not intentionally exposed to other detainees or unduly exposed to the detention facility staff. We understand that interrogators "are trained to

---

[10] This is the calorie requirement for males; the CIA presently has no female detainees.

[11] While detainees subject to dietary manipulation are obviously situated differently from individuals who voluntarily engage in commercial weight-loss programs, we note that widely available commercial weight-loss programs in the United States employ diets of 1000 kcal/day for sustained periods of weeks or longer without requiring medical supervision. While we do not equate commercial weight loss programs and this interrogation technique, the fact that these calorie levels are used in the weight-loss programs, in our view, is instructive in evaluating the medical safety of the interrogation technique.

[12] You have informed us that it is very unlikely that nudity would be employed at ambient temperatures below 75°F. *See October 12* ███ *Letter* at 1. For purposes of our analysis, however, we will assume that ambient temperatures may be as low as 68°F.

TOP SECRET// ███████ //NOFORN

avoid sexual innuendo or any acts of implicit or explicit sexual degradation." *October 12* ███████ *Letter* at 2. Nevertheless, interrogators can exploit the detainee's fear of being seen naked. In addition, female officers involved in the interrogation process may see the detainees naked; and for purposes of our analysis, we will assume that detainees subjected to nudity as an interrogation technique are aware that they may be seen naked by females.

3. *Attention grasp.* This technique consists of grasping the individual with both hands, one hand on each side of the collar opening, in a controlled and quick motion. In the same motion as the grasp, the individual is drawn toward the interrogator.

4. *Walling.* This technique involves the use of a flexible, false wall. The individual is placed with his heels touching the flexible wall. The interrogator pulls the individual forward and then quickly and firmly pushes the individual into the wall. It is the individual's shoulder blades that hit the wall. During this motion, the head and neck are supported with a rolled hood or towel that provides a C-collar effect to help prevent whiplash. To reduce further the risk of injury, the individual is allowed to rebound from the flexible wall. You have informed us that the false wall is also constructed to create a loud noise when the individual hits it in order to increase the shock or surprise of the technique. We understand that walling may be used when the detainee is uncooperative or unresponsive to questions from interrogators. Depending on the extent of the detainee's lack of cooperation, he may be walled one time during an interrogation session (one impact with the wall) or many times (perhaps 20 or 30 times) consecutively. We understand that this technique is not designed to, and does not, cause severe pain, even when used repeatedly as you have described. Rather, it is designed to wear down the detainee and to shock or surprise the detainee and alter his expectations about the treatment he believes he will receive. In particular, we specifically understand that the repetitive use of the walling technique is intended to contribute to the shock and drama of the experience, to dispel a detainee's expectations that interrogators will not use increasing levels of force, and to wear down his resistance. It is not intended to—and based on experience you have informed us that it does not—inflict any injury or cause severe pain. Medical and psychological personnel are physically present or otherwise observing whenever this technique is applied (as they are with any interrogation technique involving physical contact with the detainee).

5. *Facial hold.* This technique is used to hold the head immobile during interrogation. One open palm is placed on either side of the individual's face. The fingertips are kept well away from the individual's eyes.

6. *Facial slap or insult slap.* With this technique, the interrogator slaps the individual's face with fingers slightly spread. The hand makes contact with the area directly between the tip of the individual's chin and the bottom of the corresponding earlobe. The interrogator thus "invades" the individual's "personal space." We understand that the goal of the facial slap is not to inflict physical pain that is severe or lasting. Instead, the purpose of the facial slap is to induce shock, surprise, or humiliation. Medical and psychological personnel are physically present or otherwise observing whenever this technique is applied.

7. *Abdominal slap.* In this technique, the interrogator strikes the abdomen of the detainee with the back of his open hand. The interrogator must have no rings or other jewelry on

TOP SECRET// ███████ //NOFORN

his hand. The interrogator is positioned directly in front of the detainee, generally no more than 18 inches from the detainee. With his fingers held tightly together and fully extended, and with his palm toward the interrogator's own body, using his elbow as a fixed pivot point, the interrogator slaps the detainee in the detainee's abdomen. The interrogator may not use a fist, and the slap must be delivered above the navel and below the sternum. This technique is used to condition a detainee to pay attention to the interrogator's questions and to dislodge expectations that the detainee will not be touched. It is not intended to—and based on experience you have informed us that it does not—inflict any injury or cause any significant pain. Medical and psychological personnel are physically present or otherwise observing whenever this technique is applied.

8. *Cramped confinement.* This technique involves placing the individual in a confined space, the dimensions of which restrict the individual's movement. The confined space is usually dark. The duration of confinement varies based upon the size of the container. For the larger confined space, the individual can stand up or sit down; the smaller space is large enough for the subject to sit down. Confinement in the larger space may last no more than 8 hours at a time for no more than 18 hours a day; for the smaller space, confinement may last no more than two hours. Limits on the duration of cramped confinement are based on considerations of the detainee's size and weight, how he responds to the technique, and continuing consultation between the interrogators and OMS officers.[13]

9. *Wall standing.* This technique is used only to induce temporary muscle fatigue. The individual stands about four to five feet from a wall, with his feet spread approximately to shoulder width. His arms are stretched out in front of him, with his fingers resting on the wall and supporting his body weight. The individual is not permitted to move or reposition his hands or feet.

10. *Stress positions.* There are three stress positions that may be used. You have informed us that these positions are not designed to produce the pain associated with contortions or twisting of the body. Rather, like wall standing, they are designed to produce the physical discomfort associated with temporary muscle fatigue. The three stress positions are (1) sitting on the floor with legs extended straight out in front and arms raised above the head, (2) kneeling on the floor while leaning back at a 45 degree angle, and (3) leaning against a wall generally about three feet away from the detainee's feet, with only the detainee's head touching the wall, while his wrists are handcuffed in front of him or behind his back, and while an interrogator stands next to him to prevent injury if he loses his balance. As with wall standing, we understand that these positions are used only to induce temporary muscle fatigue.

11. *Water dousing.* Cold water is poured on the detainee either from a container or from a hose without a nozzle. This technique is intended to weaken the detainee's resistance and persuade him to cooperate with interrogators. The water poured on the detainee must be potable,

---

[13] In *Interrogation Memorandum*, we also addressed the use of harmless insects placed in a confinement box and concluded that it did not violate the statute. We understand that—for reasons unrelated to any concern that it might violate the statute—the CIA never used that technique and has removed it from the list of authorized interrogation techniques; accordingly, we do not address it again here.

TOP SECRET//NOFORN

and the interrogators must ensure that water does not enter the detainee's nose, mouth, or eyes. A medical officer must observe and monitor the detainee throughout application of this technique, including for signs of hypothermia. Ambient temperatures must remain above 64°F. If the detainee is lying on the floor, his head is to remain vertical, and a poncho, mat, or other material must be placed between him and the floor to minimize the loss of body heat. At the conclusion of the water dousing session, the detainee must be moved to a heated room if necessary to permit his body temperature to return to normal in a safe manner. To ensure an adequate margin of safety, the maximum period of time that a detainee may be permitted to remain wet has been set at two-thirds the time at which, based on extensive medical literature and experience, hypothermia could be expected to develop in healthy individuals who are submerged in water of the same temperature. For example, in employing this technique:

- For water temperature of 41°F, total duration of exposure may not exceed 20 minutes without drying and rewarming.

- For water temperature of 50°F, total duration of exposure may not exceed 40 minutes without drying and rewarming.

- For water temperature of 59°F, total duration of exposure may not exceed 60 minutes without drying and rewarming.

The minimum permissible temperature of the water used in water dousing is 41°F, though you have informed us that in practice the water temperature is generally not below 50°F, since tap water rather than refrigerated water is generally used. We understand that a version of water dousing routinely used in SERE training is much more extreme in that it involves complete immersion of the individual in cold water (where water temperatures may be below 40°F) and is usually performed outdoors where ambient air temperatures may be as low as 10°F. Thus, the SERE training version involves a far greater impact on body temperature; SERE training also involves a situation where the water may enter the trainee's nose and mouth.[14]

You have also described a variation of water dousing involving much smaller quantities of water; this variation is known as "flicking." Flicking of water is achieved by the interrogator wetting his fingers and then flicking them at the detainee, propelling droplets at the detainee. Flicking of water is done "in an effort to create a distracting effect, to awaken, to startle, to irritate, to instill humiliation, or to cause temporary insult." *October 22 Letter* at 2. The water used in the "flicking" variation of water dousing also must be potable and within the water and ambient air temperature ranges for water dousing described above. Although water may be flicked into the detainee's face with this variation, the flicking of water at all times is done in such a manner as to avoid the inhalation or ingestion of water by the detainee. *See id.*

---

[14] *See October 12 Letter* at 2-3. Comparison of the time limits for water dousing with those used in SERE training is somewhat difficult as we understand that the SERE training time limits are based on the ambient air temperature rather than water temperature.

TOP SECRET/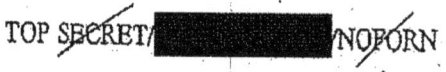/NOFORN

12. *Sleep deprivation (more than 48 hours).* This technique subjects a detainee to an extended period without sleep. You have informed us that the primary purpose of this technique is to weaken the subject and wear down his resistance.

The primary method of sleep deprivation involves the use of shackling to keep the detainee awake. In this method, the detainee is standing and is handcuffed, and the handcuffs are attached by a length of chain to the ceiling. The detainee's hands are shackled in front of his body, so that the detainee has approximately a two- to three-foot diameter of movement. The detainee's feet are shackled to a bolt in the floor. Due care is taken to ensure that the shackles are neither too loose nor too tight for physical safety. We understand from discussions with OMS that the shackling does not result in any significant physical pain for the subject. The detainee's hands are generally between the level of his heart and his chin. In some cases, the detainee's hands may be raised above the level of his head, but only for a period of up to two hours. All of the detainee's weight is borne by his legs and feet during standing sleep deprivation. You have informed us that the detainee is not allowed to hang from or support his body weight with the shackles. Rather, we understand that the shackles are only used as a passive means to keep the detainee standing and thus to prevent him from falling asleep; should the detainee begin to fall asleep, he will lose his balance and awaken, either because of the sensation of losing his balance or because of the restraining tension of the shackles. The use of this passive means for keeping the detainee awake avoids the need for using means that would require interaction with the detainee and might pose a danger of physical harm.

We understand from you that no detainee subjected to this technique by the CIA has suffered any harm or injury, either by falling down and forcing the handcuffs to bear his weight or in any other way. You have assured us that detainees are continuously monitored by closed-circuit television, so that if a detainee were unable to stand, he would immediately be removed from the standing position and would not be permitted to dangle by his wrists. We understand that standing sleep deprivation may cause edema, or swelling, in the lower extremities because it forces detainees to stand for an extended period of time. OMS has advised us that this condition is not painful, and that the condition disappears quickly once the detainee is permitted to lie down. Medical personnel carefully monitor any detainee being subjected to standing sleep deprivation for indications of edema or other physical or psychological conditions. The *OMS Guidelines* include extensive discussion on medical monitoring of detainees being subjected to shackling and sleep deprivation, and they include specific instructions for medical personnel to require alternative, non-standing positions or to take other actions, including ordering the cessation of sleep deprivation, in order to relieve or avoid serious edema or other significant medical conditions. *See OMS Guidelines* at 14-16.

In lieu of standing sleep deprivation, a detainee may instead be seated on and shackled to a small stool. The stool supports the detainee's weight, but is too small to permit the subject to balance himself sufficiently to be able to go to sleep. On rare occasions, a detainee may also be restrained in a horizontal position when necessary to enable recovery from edema without interrupting the course of sleep deprivation.[15] We understand that these alternative restraints,

---

[15] Specifically, you have informed us that on three occasions early in the program, the interrogation team and the attendant medical officers identified the potential for unacceptable edema in the lower limbs of detainees

although uncomfortable, are not significantly painful, according to the experience and professional judgment of OMS and other personnel.

We understand that a detainee undergoing sleep deprivation is generally fed by hand by CIA personnel so that he need not be unshackled; however, "[i]f progress is made during interrogation, the interrogators may unshackle the detainee and let him feed himself as a positive incentive." October 12 ▮▮▮ Letter at 4. If the detainee is clothed, he wears an adult diaper under his pants. Detainees subject to sleep deprivation who are also subject to nudity as a separate interrogation technique will at times be nude and wearing a diaper. If the detainee is wearing a diaper, it is checked regularly and changed as necessary. The use of the diaper is for sanitary and health purposes of the detainee; it is not used for the purpose of humiliating the detainee, and it is not considered to be an interrogation technique. The detainee's skin condition is monitored, and diapers are changed as needed so that the detainee does not remain in a soiled diaper. You have informed us that to date no detainee has experienced any skin problems resulting from use of diapers.

The maximum allowable duration for sleep deprivation authorized by the CIA is 180 hours, after which the detainee must be permitted to sleep without interruption for at least eight hours. You have informed us that to date, more than a dozen detainees have been subjected to sleep deprivation of more than 48 hours, and three detainees have been subjected to sleep deprivation of more than 96 hours; the longest period of time for which any detainee has been deprived of sleep by the CIA is 180 hours. Under the CIA's guidelines, sleep deprivation could be resumed after a period of eight hours of uninterrupted sleep, but only if OMS personnel specifically determined that there are no medical or psychological contraindications based on the detainee's condition at that time. As discussed below, however, in this memorandum we will evaluate only one application of up to 180 hours of sleep deprivation.[15]

---

undergoing standing sleep deprivation, and in order to permit the limbs to recover without impairing interrogation requirements, the subjects underwent horizontal sleep deprivation. Fax for Steven G. Bradbury, Principal Deputy Assistant Attorney General, OLC, from ▮▮▮ Assistant General Counsel, CIA, at 2 (Apr. 22, 2005) ("April 22 ▮▮▮ Fax"). In horizontal sleep deprivation, the detainee is placed prone on the floor on top of a thick towel or blanket (a precaution designed to prevent reduction of body temperature through direct contact with the cell floor). The detainee's hands are manacled together and the arms placed in an outstretched position—either extended beyond the head or extended to either side of the body—and anchored to a far point on the floor in such a manner that the arms cannot be bent or used for balance or comfort. At the same time, the ankles are shackled together and the legs are extended in a straight line with the body and also anchored to a far point on the floor in such a manner that the legs cannot be bent or used for balance or comfort. Id. You have specifically informed us that the manacles and shackles are anchored without additional stress on any of the arm or leg joints that might force the limbs beyond natural extension or create tension on any joint. Id. The position is sufficiently uncomfortable to detainees to deprive them of unbroken sleep, while allowing their lower limbs to recover from the effects of standing sleep deprivation. We understand that all standard precautions and procedures for shackling are observed for both hands and feet while in this position. Id. You have informed us that horizontal sleep deprivation has been used until the detainee's affected limbs have demonstrated sufficient recovery to return to sitting or standing sleep deprivation mode, as warranted by the requirements of the interrogation team, and subject to a determination by the medical officer that there is no contraindication to resuming other sleep deprivation modes. Id.

[16] We express no view on whether any further use of sleep deprivation following a 180-hour application of the technique and 8 hours of sleep would violate sections 2340-2340A.

TOP SECRET/ ███████ /NOFORN

You have informed us that detainees are closely monitored by the interrogation team at all times (either directly or by closed-circuit video camera) while being subjected to sleep deprivation, and that these personnel will intervene and the technique will be discontinued if there are medical or psychological contraindications. Furthermore, as with all interrogation techniques used by the CIA, sleep deprivation will not be used on any detainee if the prior medical and psychological assessment reveals any contraindications.

13. The "waterboard." In this technique, the detainee is lying on a gurney that is inclined at an angle of 10 to 15 degrees to the horizontal, with the detainee on his back and his head toward the lower end of the gurney. A cloth is placed over the detainee's face, and cold water is poured on the cloth from a height of approximately 6 to 18 inches. The wet cloth creates a barrier through which it is difficult—or in some cases not possible—to breathe. A single "application" of water may not last for more than 40 seconds, with the duration of an "application" measured from the moment when water—of whatever quantity—is first poured onto the cloth until the moment the cloth is removed from the subject's face. *See August 19* ███ *Letter* at 1. When the time limit is reached, the pouring of water is immediately discontinued and the cloth is removed. We understand that if the detainee makes an effort to defeat the technique (e.g., by twisting his head to the side and breathing out of the corner of his mouth), the interrogator may cup his hands around the detainee's nose and mouth to dam the runoff, in which case it would not be possible for the detainee to breathe during the application of the water. In addition, you have informed us that the technique may be applied in a manner to defeat efforts by the detainee to hold his breath by, for example, beginning an application of water as the detainee is exhaling. Either in the normal application, or where countermeasures are used, we understand that water may enter—and may accumulate in—the detainee's mouth and nasal cavity, preventing him from breathing.[17] In addition, you have indicated that the detainee as a countermeasure may swallow water, possibly in significant quantities. For that reason, based on advice of medical personnel, the CIA requires that saline solution be used instead of plain water to reduce the possibility of hyponatremia (i.e., reduced concentration of sodium in the blood) if the detainee drinks the water.

We understand that the effect of the waterboard is to induce a sensation of drowning. This sensation is based on a deeply rooted physiological response. Thus, the detainee experiences this sensation even if he is aware that he is not actually drowning. We are informed that, based on extensive experience, the process is not physically painful, but that it usually does cause fear and panic. The waterboard has been used many thousands of times in SERE training provided to American military personnel, though in that context it is usually limited to one or two applications of no more than 40 seconds each.[18]

---

[17] In most applications of this technique, including as it is used in SERE training, it appears that the individual undergoing the technique is not in fact completely prevented from breathing, but his airflow is restricted by the wet cloth, creating a sensation of drowning. *See IG Report* at 15 ("Airflow is restricted . . . and the technique produces the sensation of drowning and suffocation."). For purposes of our analysis, however, we will assume that the individual is unable to breathe during the entire period of any application of water during the waterboard technique.

[18] The Inspector General was critical of the reliance on the SERE experience with the waterboard in light of these and other differences in the application of the technique. We discuss the Inspector General's criticisms

TOP SECRET/ ███████ /NOFORN

TOP SECRET/███████████/NOFORN

You have explained that the waterboard technique is used only if: (1) the CIA has credible intelligence that a terrorist attack is imminent; (2) there are "substantial and credible indicators the subject has actionable intelligence that can prevent, disrupt or delay this attack"; and (3) other interrogation methods have failed or are unlikely to yield actionable intelligence in time to prevent the attack. *See* Attachment to *August 2 Rizzo Letter.* You have also informed us that the waterboard may be approved for use with a given detainee only during, at most, one single 30-day period, and that during that period, the waterboard technique may be used on no more than five days. We further understand that in any 24-hour period, interrogators may use no more than two "sessions" of the waterboard on a subject—with a "session" defined to mean the time that the detainee is strapped to the waterboard—and that no session may last more than two hours. Moreover, during any session, the number of individual applications of water lasting 10 seconds or longer may not exceed six. As noted above, the maximum length of any application of water is 40 seconds (you have informed us that this maximum has rarely been reached). Finally, the total cumulative time of all applications of whatever length in a 24-hour period may not exceed 12 minutes. *See August 19* ███████ *Letter* at 1-2. We understand that these limitations have been established with extensive input from OMS, based on experience to date with this technique and OMS's professional judgment that use of the waterboard on a healthy individual subject to these limitations would be "medically acceptable." *See OMS Guidelines* at 18-19.

During the use of the waterboard, a physician and a psychologist are present at all times. The detainee is monitored to ensure that he does not develop respiratory distress. If the detainee is not breathing freely after the cloth is removed from his face, he is immediately moved to a vertical position in order to clear the water from his mouth, nose, and nasopharynx. The gurney used for administering this technique is specially designed so that this can be accomplished very quickly if necessary. Your medical personnel have explained that the use of the waterboard does pose a small risk of certain potentially significant medical problems and that certain measures are taken to avoid or address such problems. First, a detainee might vomit and then aspirate the emesis. To reduce this risk, any detainee on whom this technique will be used is first placed on a liquid diet. Second, the detainee might aspirate some of the water, and the resulting water in the lungs might lead to pneumonia. To mitigate this risk, a potable saline solution is used in the procedure. Third, it is conceivable (though, we understand from OMS, highly unlikely) that a detainee could suffer spasms of the larynx that would prevent him from breathing even when the application of water is stopped and the detainee is returned to an upright position. In the event of such spasms, a qualified physician would immediately intervene to address the problem, and, if necessary, the intervening physician would perform a tracheotomy. Although the risk of such spasms is considered remote (it apparently has never occurred in thousands of instances of SERE training), we are informed that the necessary emergency medical equipment is always present—although not visible to the detainee—during any application of the waterboard. *See generally id* at 17-20.[19]

---

further below. Moreover, as noted above, the very different situations of detainees undergoing interrogation and military personnel undergoing training counsels against undue reliance on the experience in SERE training. That experience is nevertheless of some value in evaluating the technique.

[19] OMS identified other potential risks:

TOP SECRET/███████████/NOFORN

We understand that in many years of use on thousands of participants in SERE training, the waterboard technique (although used in a substantially more limited way) has not resulted in any cases of serious physical pain or prolonged mental harm. In addition, we understand that the waterboard has been used by the CIA on three high level al Qaeda detainees, two of whom were subjected to the technique numerous times, and, according to OMS, none of these three individuals has shown any evidence of physical pain or suffering or mental harm in the more than 25 months since the technique was used on them. As noted, we understand that OMS has been involved in imposing strict limits on the use of the waterboard, limits that, when combined with careful monitoring, in their professional judgment should prevent physical pain or suffering or mental harm to a detainee. In addition, we understand that any detainee is closely monitored by medical and psychological personnel whenever the waterboard is applied, and that there are additional reporting requirements beyond the normal reporting requirements in place when other interrogation techniques are used. *See OMS Guidelines* at 20.

* * *

As noted, all of the interrogation techniques described above are subject to numerous restrictions, many based on input from OMS. Our advice in this memorandum is based on our understanding that there will be careful adherence to all of these guidelines, restrictions, and safeguards, and that there will be ongoing monitoring and reporting by the team, including OMS medical and psychological personnel, as well as prompt intervention by a team member, as necessary, to prevent physical distress or mental harm so significant as possibly to amount to the "severe physical or mental pain or suffering" that is prohibited by sections 2340-2340A. Our advice is also based on our understanding that all interrogators who will use these techniques are adequately trained to understand that the authorized use of the techniques is not designed or intended to cause severe physical or mental pain or suffering, and also to understand and respect the medical judgment of OMS and the important role that OMS personnel play in the program.

C.

You asked for our advice concerning these interrogation techniques in connection with their use on a specific high value al Qaeda detainee named  You informed us that the

---

In our limited experience, extensive sustained use of the waterboard can introduce new risks. Most seriously, for reasons of physical fatigue or psychological resignation, the subject may simply give up, allowing excessive filling of the airways and loss of consciousness. An unresponsive subject should be righted immediately, and the interrogator should deliver a sub-xyphoid thrust to expel the water. If this fails to restore normal breathing, aggressive medical intervention is required. Any subject who has reached this degree of compromise is not considered an appropriate candidate for the waterboard, and the physician on the scene can not concur in the further use of the waterboard without specific [Chief, OMS] consultation and approval.

OMS Guidelines at 18. OMS has also stated that "[b]y days 3-5 of an aggressive program, cumulative effects become a potential concern. Without any hard data to quantify either this risk or the advantages of this technique, we believe that beyond this point continued intense waterboard applications may not be medically appropriate." *Id.* at 19. As noted above, based on OMS input, the CIA has adopted and imposed a number of strict limitations on the frequency and duration of use of the waterboard.

TOP SECRET/ ▮▮▮▮ /NOFORN

▮▮▮▮ had information about al Qaeda's plans to launch an attack within the United States. According to ▮▮▮▮ had extensive connections to various al Qaeda leaders, members of the Taliban, and the al-Zarqawi network, and had arranged meetings between an associate and ▮▮▮▮ to discuss such an attack. *August 25 Letter* at 2-3. You advised us that medical and psychological assessments ▮▮▮▮ were completed by a CIA physician and psychologist, and that based on this examination, the physician concluded "▮▮▮▮ medically stable and has no medical contraindications to interrogation, including the use of interrogation techniques" addressed in this memorandum.[20] *Medical and Psychological Assessment of* ▮▮▮▮ attached to *August 2 Rizzo Letter* at 1.[21] The psychological assessment found ▮▮▮▮ was alert and oriented and his concentration and attention were appropriate." *Id.* at 2. The psychologist further found ▮▮▮▮ "thought processes were clear and logical; there was no evidence of a thought disorder, delusions, or hallucinations[, and t]here were not significant signs of depression, anxiety or other mental disturbance." *Id.* The psychologist evaluated ▮▮▮▮ "psychologically stable, reserved and defensive," and "opined that there was no evidence that the use of the approved interrogation methods would cause any severe or prolonged psychological disturbance ▮▮▮▮ *Id.* at 2. Our conclusions depend on these assessments. Before using the techniques on other detainees, the CIA would need to ensure, in each case, that all medical and psychological assessments indicate that the detainee is fit to undergo the use of the interrogation techniques.

II.

A.

Section 2340A provides that "[w]hoever outside the United States commits or attempts to commit torture shall be fined under this title or imprisoned not more than 20 years, or both, and if death results to any person from conduct prohibited by this subsection, shall be punished by death or imprisoned for any term of years or for life."[22] Section 2340(1) defines "torture" as "an

---

[20] You have advised us that the waterboard has not been used ▮▮▮▮ We understand that there may have been medical reasons against using that technique in his case. Of course, our advice assumes that the waterboard could be used only in the absence of medical contraindications.

[21] The medical examination reported ▮▮▮▮ was obese, and that he reported a "5-6 year history of non-exertional chest pressures, which are intermittent, at times accompanied by nausea and depression and shortness of breath." *Medical and Psychological Assessment of* ▮▮▮▮ at 1, attached to *August 2 Rizzo Letter*. ▮▮▮▮ he has never consulted a physician for this problem," and was "unable or unwilling to be more specific about the frequency or intensity of the aforementioned symptoms." *Id.* He also reported suffering "long-term medical and mental problems" from a motor vehicle accident "many years ago," and stated that he took medication as a result of that accident until ten years ago. *Id.* He stated that he was not currently taking any medication. He also reported seeing a physician for kidney problems that caused him to urinate frequently and complained of a toothache. *Id.* The medical examination ▮▮▮▮ showed a rash on his chest and shoulders and that "his nose and chest were clear, [and] his heart sounds were normal with no murmurs or gallops." *Id.* The physician opined ▮▮▮▮ "likely has some reflux esophagitis and mild check folliculitis, but doubt[ed] that he has any coronary pathology." *Id.*

[22] Section 2340A provides in full:

(a) Offense.—Whoever outside the United States commits or attempts to commit torture shall be fined under this title or imprisoned not more than 20 years, or both, and if death results to any

TOP SECRET/  NOFORN

act committed by a person acting under color of law specifically intended to inflict severe physical or mental pain or suffering (other than pain or suffering incidental to lawful sanctions) upon another person within his custody or physical control."[23]

Congress enacted sections 2340-2340A to carry out the obligations of the United States under the CAT. *See* H.R. Conf. Rep. No. 103-482, at 229 (1994). The CAT, among other things, requires the United States, as a state party, to ensure that acts of torture, along with attempts and complicity to commit such acts, are crimes under U.S. law. *See* CAT arts. 2, 4-5. Sections 2340-2340A satisfy that requirement with respect to acts committed outside the United States.[24] Conduct constituting "torture" within the United States already was—and remains—prohibited by various other federal and state criminal statutes.

[footnotes continued]

person from conduct prohibited by this subsection, shall be punished by death or imprisoned for any term of years or for life.

(b) Jurisdiction.—There is jurisdiction over the activity prohibited in subsection (a) if—

(1) the alleged offender is a national of the United States; or

(2) the alleged offender is present in the United States, irrespective of the nationality of the victim or alleged offender.

(c) Conspiracy.—A person who conspires to commit an offense under this section shall be subject to the same penalties (other than the penalty of death) as the penalties prescribed for the offense, the commission of which was the object of the conspiracy.

18 U.S.C. § 2340A.

[23] Section 2340 provides in full:

As used in this chapter—

(1) "torture" means an act committed by a person acting under color of law specifically intended to inflict severe physical or mental pain or suffering (other than pain or suffering incidental to lawful sanctions) upon another person within his custody or physical control;

(2) "severe mental pain or suffering" means the prolonged mental harm caused by or resulting from—

(A) the intentional infliction or threatened infliction of severe physical pain or suffering;

(B) the administration or application, or threatened administration or application, of mind-altering substances or other procedures calculated to disrupt profoundly the senses or the personality;

(C) the threat of imminent death; or

(D) the threat that another person will imminently be subjected to death, severe physical pain or suffering, or the administration or application of mind-altering substances or other procedures calculated to disrupt profoundly the senses or personality; and

(3) "United States" means the several States of the United States, the District of Columbia, and the commonwealths, territories, and possessions of the United States.

18 U.S.C. § 2340 (as amended by Pub. L. No. 108-375, 118 Stat. 1811 (2004)).

[24] Congress limited the territorial reach of the federal torture statute by providing that the prohibition applies only to conduct occurring "outside the United States," 18 U.S.C. § 2340A(a), which is currently defined in the statute to mean outside "the several States of the United States, the District of Columbia, and the commonwealths, territories, and possessions of the United States." *Id.* § 2340(3) (as amended by Pub. L. No. 108-375, 118 Stat. 1811

The CAT defines "torture" so as to require the intentional infliction of "severe pain or suffering, whether physical or mental." Article 1(1) of the CAT provides:

> For the purposes of this Convention, the term "torture" means any act by which severe pain or suffering, whether physical or mental, is intentionally inflicted on a person for such purposes as obtaining from him or a third person information or a confession, punishing him for an act he or a third person has committed or is suspected of having committed, or intimidating or coercing him or a third person, or for any reason based on discrimination of any kind, when such pain or suffering is inflicted by or at the instigation of or with the consent or acquiescence of a public official or other person acting in an official capacity. It does not include pain or suffering arising only from, inherent in or incidental to lawful sanctions.

The Senate included the following understanding in its resolution of advice and consent to ratification of the CAT:

> The United States understands that, in order to constitute torture, an act must be specifically intended to inflict severe physical or mental pain or suffering and that mental pain or suffering refers to prolonged mental harm caused by or resulting from (1) the intentional infliction or threatened infliction of severe physical pain or suffering; (2) the administration or application, or threatened administration or application, of mind altering substances or other procedures calculated to disrupt profoundly the senses or the personality; (3) the threat of imminent death; or (4) the threat that another person will imminently be subjected to death, severe physical pain or suffering, or the administration or application of mind altering substances or other procedures calculated to disrupt profoundly the senses or personality.

S. Exec. Rep. No. 101-30, at 36 (1990). This understanding was deposited with the U.S. instrument of ratification, see 1830 U.N.T.S. 320 (Oct. 21, 1994), and thus defines the scope of United States obligations under the treaty. See *Relevance of Senate Ratification History to Treaty Interpretation*, 11 Op. O.L.C. 28, 32-33 (1987). The criminal prohibition against torture that Congress codified In 18 U.S.C. §§ 2340-2340A generally tracks the CAT's definition of torture, subject to the U.S. understanding.

B.

Under the language adopted by Congress in sections 2340-2340A, to constitute "torture," conduct must be "specifically intended to inflict severe physical or mental pain or suffering." In the discussion that follows, we will separately consider each of the principal components of this key phrase: (1) the meaning of "severe"; (2) the meaning of "severe physical pain or suffering";

(2004). You have advised us that the CIA's use of the techniques addressed in this memorandum would occur "outside the United States" as defined in sections 2340-2340A.

(3) the meaning of "severe mental pain or suffering"; and (4) the meaning of "specifically intended."

(1) The meaning of "severe."

Because the statute does not define "severe," "we construe [the] term in accordance with its ordinary or natural meaning." *FDIC v. Meyer*, 510 U.S. 471, 476 (1994). The common understanding of the term "torture" and the context in which the statute was enacted also inform our analysis. Dictionaries define "severe" (often conjoined with "pain") to mean "extremely violent or intense: *severe pain.*" *American Heritage Dictionary of the English Language* 1653 (3d ed. 1992); *see also* XV *Oxford English Dictionary* 101 (2d ed. 1989) ("Of pain, suffering, loss, or the like: Grievous, extreme" and "Of circumstances . . . : Hard to sustain or endure."). The common understanding of "torture" further supports the statutory concept that the pain or suffering must be severe. *See Black's Law Dictionary* 1528 (8th ed. 2004) (defining "torture" as "[t]he infliction of *intense pain* to the body or mind to punish, to extract a confession or information, or to obtain sadistic pleasure") (emphasis added); *Webster's Third New International Dictionary of the English Language Unabridged* 2414 (2002) (defining "torture" as "the infliction of *intense pain* (as from burning, crushing, wounding) to punish or coerce someone") (emphasis added); *Oxford American Dictionary and Language Guide* 1064 (1999) (defining "torture" as "the infliction of *severe bodily pain*, esp. as a punishment or a means of persuasion") (emphasis added). Thus, the use of the word "severe" in the statutory prohibition on torture clearly denotes a sensation or condition that is extreme in intensity and difficult to endure.

This interpretation is also consistent with the historical understanding of torture, which has generally involved the use of procedures and devices designed to inflict intense or extreme pain. The devices and procedures historically used were generally intended to cause extreme pain while not killing the person being questioned (or at least not doing so quickly) so that questioning could continue. Descriptions in Lord Hope's lecture, "Torture," University of Essex/Clifford Chance Lecture at 7-8 (Jan. 28, 2004) (describing the "boot," which involved crushing of the victim's legs and feet; repeated pricking with long needles; and thumbscrews), and in Professor Langbein's book, *Torture and the Law of Proof*, cited *supra* p. 2, make this clear. As Professor Langbein summarized:

> The commonest torture devices—strappado, rack, thumbscrews, legscrews—worked upon the extremities of the body, either by distending or compressing them. We may suppose that these modes of torture were preferred because they were somewhat less likely to maim or kill than coercion directed to the trunk of the body, and because they would be quickly adjusted to take account of the victim's responses during the examination.

Torture and the Law of Proof at 15 (footnote omitted).[25]

The statute, moreover, was intended to implement United States obligations under the CAT, which, as quoted above, defines "torture" as acts that intentionally inflict "severe pain or suffering." CAT art. 1(1). As the Senate Foreign Relations Committee explained in its report recommending that the Senate consent to ratification of the CAT:

> The [CAT] seeks to define "torture" in a relatively limited fashion, corresponding to the common understanding of torture as an extreme practice which is universally condemned. . . .
>
> . . . .
>
> . . . The term "torture," in United States and international usage, is usually reserved for extreme, deliberate and unusually cruel practices, for example, sustained systematic beating, application of electric currents to sensitive parts of the body, and tying up or hanging in positions that cause extreme pain.

S. Exec. Rep. No. 101-30 at 13-14; *See also* David P. Stewart, *The Torture Convention and the Reception of International Criminal Law Within the United States*, 15 Nova L. Rev. 449, 455 (1991) ("By stressing the extreme nature of torture, . . . [the] definition [of torture in the CAT] describes a relatively limited set of circumstances likely to be illegal under most, if not all, domestic legal systems.").

Drawing distinctions among gradations of pain is obviously not an easy task, especially given the lack of any precise, objective scientific criteria for measuring pain.[26] We are given some aid in this task by judicial interpretations of the Torture Victims Protection Act ("TVPA"), 28 U.S.C. § 1350 note (2000). The TVPA, also enacted to implement the CAT, provides a civil remedy to victims of torture. The TVPA defines "torture" to include:

> any act, directed against an individual in the offender's custody or physical control, by which *severe pain or suffering* (other than pain or suffering arising

---

[25] We emphatically are not saying that only such historical techniques—or similar ones—can constitute "torture" under sections 2340-2340A. But the historical understanding of torture is relevant in interpreting Congress's intent in prohibiting the crime of "torture." *Cf. Morissette v. United States*, 342 U.S. 246, 263 (1952).

[26] Despite extensive efforts to develop objective criteria for measuring pain, there is no clear, objective, consistent measurement. As one publication explains:

> Pain is a complex, subjective, perceptual phenomenon with a number of dimensions—intensity, quality, time course, impact, and personal meaning—that are uniquely experienced by each individual and, thus, can only be assessed indirectly. *Pain is a subjective experience and there is no way to objectively quantify it.* Consequently, assessment of a patient's pain depends on the patient's overt communications, both verbal and behavioral. Given pain's complexity, one must assess not only its somatic (sensory) component but also patients' moods, attitudes, coping efforts, resources, responses of family members, and the impact of pain on their lives.

Dennis C. Turk, *Assess the Person, Not Just the Pain*, Pain: Clinical Updates, Sept. 1993 (emphasis added). This lack of clarity further complicates the effort to define "severe" pain or suffering.

TOP SECRET/ / NOFORN

only from or inherent in, or incidental to, lawful sanctions), *whether physical or mental*, is intentionally inflicted on that individual for such purposes as obtaining from that individual or a third person information or a confession, punishing that individual for an act that individual or a third person has committed or is suspected of having committed, intimidating or coercing that individual or a third person, or for any reason based on discrimination of any kind . . . .

28 U.S.C. § 1350 note, § 3(b)(1) (emphases added). The emphasized language is similar to section 2340's phrase "severe physical or mental pain or suffering."[27] As the Court of Appeals for the District of Columbia Circuit has explained:

> The severity requirement is crucial to ensuring that the conduct proscribed by the [CAT] and the TVPA is sufficiently extreme and outrageous to warrant the universal condemnation that the term "torture" both connotes and invokes. The drafters of the [CAT], as well as the Reagan Administration that signed it, the Bush Administration that submitted it to Congress, and the Senate that ultimately ratified it, therefore all sought to ensure that "only acts of a certain gravity shall be considered to constitute torture."
>
> The critical issue is the degree of pain and suffering that the alleged torturer intended to, and actually did, inflict upon the victim. The more intense, lasting, or heinous the agony, the more likely it is to be torture.

Price v. Socialist People's Libyan Arab Jamahiriya, 294 F.3d 82, 92-93 (D.C. Cir. 2002) (citations omitted). The D.C. Circuit in *Price* concluded that a complaint that alleged beatings at the hands of police but that did not provide details concerning "the severity of plaintiffs' alleged beatings, including their frequency, duration, the parts of the body at which they were aimed, and the weapons used to carry them out," did not suffice "to ensure that [it] satisf[ied] the TVPA's rigorous definition of torture." *Id.* at 93.

In *Simpson v. Socialist People's Libyan Arab Jamahiriya*, 326 F.3d 230 (D.C. Cir. 2003), the D.C. Circuit again considered the types of acts that constitute torture under the TVPA definition. The plaintiff alleged, among other things, that Libyan authorities had held her incommunicado and threatened to kill her if she tried to leave. *See id.* at 232, 234. The court acknowledged that "these alleged acts certainly reflect a bent toward cruelty on the part of their perpetrators," but, reversing the district court, went on to hold that "they are not in themselves so unusually cruel or sufficiently extreme and outrageous as to constitute torture within the meaning of the [TVPA]." *Id.* at 234. Cases in which courts have found torture illustrate the extreme nature of conduct that falls within the statutory definition. *See, e.g., Hilao v. Estate of Marcos*, 103 F.3d 789, 790-91, 795 (9th Cir. 1996) (concluding that a course of conduct that included, among other things, severe beatings of plaintiff, repeated threats of death and electric shock, sleep deprivation, extended shackling to a cot (at times with a towel over his nose and mouth and water poured down his nostrils), seven months of confinement in a "suffocatingly hot" and

---

[27] Section 3(b)(2) of the TVPA defines "mental pain or suffering" using substantially identical language to section 2340(2)'s definition of "severe mental pain or suffering."

TOP SECRET/ / NOFORN

49

cramped cell, and eight years of solitary or near-solitary confinement, constituted torture); *Mehinovic v. Vuckovic*, 198 F. Supp. 2d 1322, 1332-40, 1345-46 (N.D. Ga. 2002) (concluding that a course of conduct that included, among other things, severe beatings to the genitals, head, and other parts of the body with metal pipes, brass knuckles, batons, a baseball bat, and various other items; removal of teeth with pliers; kicking in the face and ribs; breaking of bones and ribs and dislocation of fingers; cutting a figure into the victim's forehead; hanging the victim and beating him; extreme limitations of food and water; and subjection to games of "Russian roulette," constituted torture); *Daliberti v. Republic of Iraq*, 146 F. Supp. 2d 19, 22-23 (D.D.C. 2001) (entering default judgment against Iraq where plaintiffs alleged, among other things, threats of "physical torture, such as cutting off . . . fingers, pulling out . . . fingernails," and electric shocks to the testicles); *Cicippio v. Islamic Republic of Iran*, 18 F. Supp. 2d 62, 64-66 (D.D.C. 1998) (concluding that a course of conduct that included frequent beatings, pistol whipping, threats of imminent death, electric shocks, and attempts to force confessions by playing Russian roulette and pulling the trigger at each denial, constituted torture).

(2) The meaning of "severe physical pain or suffering."

The statute provides a specific definition of "severe mental pain or suffering," *see* 18 U.S.C. § 2340(2), but does not define the term "severe physical pain or suffering." The meaning of "severe physical pain" is relatively straightforward; it denotes physical pain that is extreme in intensity and difficult to endure. In our *2004 Legal Standards Opinion*, we concluded that under some circumstances, conduct intended to inflict "severe physical suffering" may constitute torture even if it is not intended to inflict "severe physical pain." *Id.* at 10. That conclusion follows from the plain language of sections 2340-2340A. The inclusion of the words "or suffering" in the phrase "severe physical pain or suffering" suggests that the statutory category of physical torture is not limited to "severe physical pain." *See, e.g., Duncan v. Walker*, 533 U.S. 167, 174 (2001) (explaining presumption against surplusage).

"Severe physical suffering," however, is difficult to define with precision. As we have previously noted, the text of the statute and the CAT, and their history, provide little concrete guidance as to what Congress intended by the concept of "severe physical suffering." *See 2004 Legal Standards Opinion* at 11. We interpret the phrase in a statutory context where Congress expressly distinguished "severe physical pain or suffering" from "severe mental pain or suffering." Consequently, we believe it a reasonable inference that "physical suffering" was intended by Congress to mean something distinct from "mental pain or suffering."[28] We presume that where Congress uses different words in a statute, those words are intended to have different meanings. *See, e.g., Barnes v. United States*, 199 F.3d 386, 389 (7th Cir. 1999) ("Different language in separate clauses in a statute indicates Congress intended distinct meanings."). Moreover, given that Congress precisely defined "mental pain or suffering" in sections 2340-2340A, it is unlikely to have intended to undermine that careful definition by

---

[28] Common dictionary definitions of "physical" support reading "physical suffering" to mean something different from mental pain or suffering. *See, e.g., American Heritage Dictionary of the English Language* at 1366 ("Of or relating to the body as distinguished from the mind or spirit"); *Oxford American Dictionary and Language Guide* at 748 ("of or concerning the body (*physical exercise*; *physical education*)").

including essentially mental distress within the separate category of "physical suffering."[29]

In our *2004 Legal Standards Opinion*, we concluded, based on the understanding that "suffering" denotes a "state" or "condition" that must be "endured" over time, that there is "an extended temporal element, or at least an element of persistence" to the concept of physical suffering in sections 2340-2340A. *Id.* at 12 & n.22. Consistent with this analysis in our *2004 Legal Standards Opinion*, and in light of standard dictionary definitions, we read the word "suffering," when used in reference to physical or bodily sensations, to mean a state or condition of physical distress, misery, affliction, or torment (usually associated with physical pain) that persists for a significant period of time. *See, e.g., Webster's Third New International Dictionary* at 2284 (defining "suffering" as "the state or experience of one who suffers: the endurance of or submission to affliction, pain, loss"; "a pain endured or a distress, loss, or injury incurred"); *Random House Dictionary of the English Language* 572, 1229, 1998 (2d ed. unabridged 1987) (giving "distress," "misery," and "torment" as synonyms of "suffering"). Physical distress or discomfort that is merely transitory and that does not persist over time does not constitute "physical suffering" within the meaning of the statute. Furthermore, in our *2004 Legal Standards Opinion*, we concluded that "severe physical suffering" for purposes of sections 2340-2340A requires "a condition of some extended duration or persistence as well as intensity" and "is reserved for physical distress that is 'severe' considering its intensity and duration or persistence, rather than merely mild or transitory." *Id.* at 12.

We therefore believe that "severe physical suffering" under the statute means a state or condition of physical distress, misery, affliction, or torment, usually involving physical pain, that is both extreme in intensity and significantly protracted in duration or persistent over time. Accordingly, judging whether a particular state or condition may amount to "severe physical suffering" requires a weighing of both its intensity and its duration. The more painful or intense is the physical distress involved—i.e., the closer it approaches the level of severe physical pain separately proscribed by the statute—the less significant would be the element of duration or persistence over time. On the other hand, depending on the circumstances, a level of physical

---

[29] This conclusion is reinforced by the expressions of concern at the time the Senate gave its advice and consent to the CAT about the potential for vagueness in including the concept of mental pain or suffering as a definitional element in any criminal prohibition on torture. *See, e.g., Convention Against Torture: Hearing Before the Senate Comm. On Foreign Relations*, 101st Cong. 8, 10 (1990) (prepared statement of Abraham Sofaer, Legal Adviser, Department of State: "The Convention's wording . . . is not in all respects as precise as we believe necessary. . . . [B]ecause [the Convention] requires establishment of criminal penalties under our domestic law, we must pay particular attention to the meaning and interpretation of its provisions, especially concerning the standards by which the Convention will be applied as a matter of U.S. law. . . . [W]e prepared a codified proposal which . . . clarifies the definition of mental pain and suffering."); *id.* at 15-16 (prepared statement of Mark Richard: "The basic problem with the Torture Convention—one that permeates all our concerns—is its imprecise definition of torture, especially as that term is applied to actions which result solely in mental anguish. This definitional vagueness makes it very doubtful that the United States can, consistent with Constitutional due process constraints, fulfill its obligation under the Convention to adequately engraft the definition of torture into the domestic criminal law of the United States."); *id.* at 17 (prepared statement of Mark Richard: "Accordingly, the Torture Convention's vague definition concerning the mental suffering aspect of torture cannot be resolved by reference to established principles of international law. In an effort to overcome this unacceptable element of vagueness in Article I of the Convention, we have proposed an understanding which defines severe mental pain constituting torture with sufficient specificity to . . . meet Constitutional due process requirements.").

distress or discomfort that is lacking in extreme intensity may not constitute "severe physical suffering" regardless of its duration—i.e., even if it lasts for a very long period of time. In defining conduct proscribed by sections 2340-2340A, Congress established a high bar. The ultimate question is whether the conduct "is sufficiently extreme and outrageous to warrant the universal condemnation that the term 'torture' both connotes and invokes." *See Price v. Socialist People's Libyan Arab Jamahiriya*, 294 F.3d at 92 (interpreting the TVPA); *cf. Mehinovic v. Vuckovic*, 198 F. Supp. 2d at 1332-40, 1345-46 (standard met under the TVPA by a course of conduct that included severe beatings to the genitals, head, and other parts of the body with metal pipes and various other items; removal of teeth with pliers; kicking in the face and ribs; breaking of bones and ribs and dislocation of fingers; cutting a figure into the victim's forehead; hanging the victim and beating him; extreme limitations of food and water; and subjection to games of "Russian roulette").

(3) The meaning of "severe mental pain or suffering."

Section 2340 defines "severe mental pain or suffering" to mean:

the prolonged mental harm caused by or resulting from—

(A) the intentional infliction or threatened infliction of severe physical pain or suffering;
(B) the administration or application, or threatened administration or application, of mind-altering substances or other procedures calculated to disrupt profoundly the senses or the personality;
(C) the threat of imminent death; or
(D) the threat that another person will imminently be subjected to death, severe physical pain or suffering, or the administration or application of mind-altering substances or other procedures calculated to disrupt profoundly the senses or personality[.]

18 U.S.C. § 2340(2). Torture is defined under the statute to include an act specifically intended to inflict severe mental pain or suffering. *See id.* § 2340(1).

An important preliminary question with respect to this definition is whether the statutory list of the four "predicate acts" in section 2340(2)(A)-(D) is exclusive. We have concluded that Congress intended the list of predicate acts to be exclusive—that is, to satisfy the definition of "severe mental pain or suffering" under the statute, the prolonged mental harm must be caused by acts falling within one of the four statutory categories of predicate acts. *2004 Legal Standards Opinion* at 13. We reached this conclusion based on the clear language of the statute, which provides a detailed definition that includes four categories of predicate acts joined by the disjunctive and does not contain a catchall provision or any other language suggesting that additional acts might qualify (for example, language such as "including" or "such acts as"). *Id.*[30]

---

[30] These four categories of predicate acts "are members of an 'associated group or series,' justifying the inference that items not mentioned were excluded by deliberate choice, not inadvertence." *Barnhart v. Peabody Coal Co.*, 537 U.S. 149, 168 (2003) (quoting *United States v. Vonn*, 535 U.S. 55, 65 (2002)). *See also, e.g.,*

Congress plainly considered very specific predicate acts, and this definition tracks the Senate's understanding concerning mental pain or suffering on which its advice and consent to ratification of the CAT was conditioned. The conclusion that the list of predicate acts is exclusive is consistent with both the text of the Senate's understanding, and with the fact that the understanding was required out of concern that the CAT's definition of torture would not otherwise meet the constitutional requirement for clarity in defining crimes. *See 2004 Legal Standards Opinion* at 13. Adopting an interpretation of the statute that expands the list of predicate acts for "severe mental pain or suffering" would constitute an impermissible rewriting of the statute and would introduce the very imprecision that prompted the Senate to require this understanding as a condition of its advice and consent to ratification of the CAT.

Another question is whether the requirement of "prolonged mental harm" caused by or resulting from one of the enumerated predicate acts is a separate requirement, or whether such "prolonged mental harm" is to be presumed any time one of the predicate acts occurs. Although it is possible to read the statute's reference to "*the* prolonged mental harm caused by or resulting from" the predicate acts as creating a statutory presumption that each of the predicate acts will always cause prolonged mental harm, we concluded in our *2004 Legal Standards Opinion* that that was not Congress's intent, since the statutory definition of "severe mental pain or suffering" was meant to track the understanding that the Senate required as a condition to its advice and consent to ratification of the CAT:

> in order to constitute torture, an act must be specifically intended to inflict severe physical or mental pain or suffering and that mental pain or suffering refers to prolonged mental harm caused by or resulting from (1) the intentional infliction or threatened infliction of severe physical pain or suffering; (2) the administration or application, or threatened administration or application, of mind altering substances or other procedures calculated to disrupt profoundly the senses or the personality; (3) the threat of imminent death; or (4) the threat that another person will imminently be subjected to death, severe physical pain or suffering, or the administration or application of mind altering substances or other procedures calculated to disrupt profoundly the senses or personality.

S. Exec. Rep. No. 101-30 at 36. As we previously stated, "[w]e do not believe that simply by adding the word 'the' before 'prolonged harm,' Congress intended a material change in the definition of mental pain or suffering as articulated in the Senate's understanding to the CAT." *2004 Legal Standards Opinion* at 13-14. "The definition of torture emanates directly from article 1 of the [CAT]. The definition for 'severe mental pain and suffering' incorporates the [above mentioned] understanding." S. Rep. No. 103-107, at 58-59 (1993) (emphasis added). This understanding, embodied in the statute, defines the obligation undertaken by the United States. Given this understanding, the legislative history, and the fact that section 2340(2) defines "severe mental pain or suffering" carefully in language very similar to the understanding, we believe that Congress did not intend to create a presumption that any time one of the predicate

---

Leatherman v. Tarrant County Narcotics Intelligence & Coordination Unit, 507 U.S. 163, 168 (1993); 2A Norman J. Singer, *Statutes and Statutory Construction* § 47.23 (6th ed. 2000). Nor do we see any "contrary indications" that would rebut this inference. *Vonn*, 535 U.S. at 65.

acts occurs, prolonged mental harm is automatically deemed to result. *See 2004 Legal Standards Opinion* at 13-14. At the same time, it is conceivable that the occurrence of one of the predicate acts alone could, depending on the circumstances of a particular case, give rise to an inference of intent to cause prolonged mental harm, as required by the statute.

Turning to the question of what constitutes "prolonged mental harm caused by or resulting from" a predicate act, we have concluded that Congress intended this phrase to require mental "harm" that has some lasting duration. *Id.* at 14. There is little guidance to draw upon in interpreting the phrase "prolonged mental harm," which does not appear in the relevant medical literature. Nevertheless, our interpretation is consistent with the ordinary meaning of the statutory terms. First, the use of the word "harm"—as opposed to simply repeating "pain or suffering"—suggests some mental damage or injury. Ordinary dictionary definitions of "harm," such as "physical or mental *damage: injury*," *Webster's Third New International Dictionary* at 1034 (emphasis added), or "[p]hysical or psychological *injury or damage*," *American Heritage Dictionary of the English Language* at 825 (emphasis added), support this interpretation. Second, to "prolong" means to "lengthen in time," "extend in duration," or "draw out," *Webster's Third New International Dictionary* at 1815, further suggesting that to be "prolonged," the mental damage must extend for some period of time. This damage need not be permanent, but it must be intended to continue for a "prolonged" period of time.[31] Moreover, under section 2340(2), the "prolonged mental harm" must be "caused by" or "resulting from" one of the enumerated predicate acts. As we pointed out in *2004 Legal Standards Opinion*, this conclusion is not meant to suggest that, if the predicate act or acts continue for an extended period, "prolonged mental harm" cannot occur until after they are completed. *Id.* at 14-15 n.26. Early occurrences of the predicate act could cause mental harm that could continue—and become prolonged—during the extended period the predicate acts continued to occur. *See, e.g., Sackie v. Ashcroft*, 270 F. Supp. 2d 596, 601-02 (E.D. Pa. 2003) (finding that predicate acts had continued over a three-to-four-year period and concluding that "prolonged mental harm" had occurred during that time).

Although there are few judicial opinions discussing the question of "prolonged mental harm," those cases that have addressed the issue are consistent with our view. For example, in the TVPA case of *Mehinovic v. Vuckovic*, the district court explained that:

---

[31] Although we do not suggest that the statute is limited to such cases, development of a mental disorder—such as post-traumatic stress disorder or perhaps chronic depression—could constitute "prolonged mental harm." *See* American Psychiatric Association, *Diagnostic and Statistical Manual of Mental Disorders* 369-76, 463-68 (4th ed. 2000) ("DSM-IV-TR"). *See also, e.g., Report of the Special Rapporteur on Torture and Other Cruel, Inhuman or Degrading Treatment or Punishment*, U.N. Doc. A/59/324, at 14 (2004) ("The most common diagnosis of psychiatric symptoms among torture survivors is said to be post-traumatic stress disorder."); *see also* Metin Basoglu et al., *Torture and Mental Health: A Research Overview, in* Ellen Gerrity et al. eds., *The Mental Health Consequences of Torture* 48-49 (2001) (referring to findings of higher rates of post-traumatic stress disorder in studies involving torture survivors); Murat Parker et al., *Psychological Effects of Torture: An Empirical Study of Tortured and Non-Tortured Non-Political Prisoners, in* Metin Basoglu ed., *Torture and Its Consequences: Current Treatment Approaches* 77 (1992) (referring to findings of post-traumatic stress disorder in torture survivors). OMS has advised that—although the ability to predict is imperfect—they would object to the initial or continued use of any technique if their psychological assessment of the detainee suggested that the use of the technique might result in PTSD, chronic depression, or other condition that could constitute prolonged mental harm.

> [The defendant] also caused or participated in the plaintiffs' mental torture. Mental torture consists of "prolonged mental harm caused by or resulting from: the intentional infliction or threatened infliction of severe physical pain or suffering; ... the threat of imminent death...." As set out above, plaintiffs noted in their testimony that they feared that they would be killed by [the defendant] during the beatings he inflicted or during games of "Russian roulette." *Each plaintiff continues to suffer long-term psychological harm as a result of the ordeals they suffered at the hands of defendant and others.*

198 F. Supp. 2d at 1346 (emphasis added; first ellipsis in original). In reaching its conclusion, the court noted that each of the plaintiffs were continuing to suffer serious mental harm even ten years after the events in question. *See id.* at 1334-40. In each case, these mental effects were continuing years after the infliction of the predicate acts. *See also Sackie v. Ashcroft*, 270 F. Supp. 2d at 597-98, 601-02 (victim was kidnapped and "forcibly recruited" as a child soldier at the age of 14, and, over a period of three to four years, was repeatedly forced to take narcotics and threatened with imminent death, all of which produced "prolonged mental harm" during that time). Conversely, in *Villeda Aldana v. Fresh Del Monte Produce, Inc.*, 305 F. Supp. 2d 1285 (S.D. Fla. 2003), the court rejected a claim under the TVPA brought by individuals who had been held at gunpoint overnight and repeatedly threatened with death. While recognizing that the plaintiffs had experienced an "ordeal," the court concluded that they had failed to show that their experience caused lasting damage, noting that "there is simply no allegation that Plaintiffs have suffered any prolonged mental harm or physical injury as a result of their alleged intimidation." *Id.* at 1294-95.

(4) The meaning of "specifically intended."

It is well recognized that the term "specific intent" has no clear, settled definition, and that the courts do not use it consistently. *See* 1 Wayne R. LaFave, *Substantive Criminal Law* § 5.2(e), at 355 & n.79 (2d ed. 2003). "Specific intent" is most commonly understood, however, "to designate a special mental element which is required above and beyond any mental state required with respect to the *actus reus* of the crime." *Id.* at 354; *see also Carter v. United States*, 530 U.S. 255, 268 (2000) (explaining that general intent, as opposed to specific intent, requires "that the defendant possessed knowledge [only] with respect to the *actus reus* of the crime"). Some cases suggest that only a conscious desire to produce the proscribed result constitutes specific intent; others suggest that even reasonable foreseeability may suffice. In *United States v. Bailey*, 444 U.S. 394 (1980), for example, the Court suggested that, at least "[i]n a general sense," *id.* at 405, "specific intent" requires that one consciously desire the result. *Id.* at 403-05. The Court compared the common law's *mens rea* concepts of specific intent and general intent to the Model Penal Code's *mens rea* concepts of acting purposefully and acting knowingly. *See id.* at 404-05. "[A] person who causes a particular result is said to act purposefully," wrote the Court, "if 'he consciously desires that result, whatever the likelihood of that result happening from his conduct.'" *Id.* at 404 (internal quotation marks omitted). A person "is said to act knowingly," in contrast, "if he is aware 'that that result is practically certain to follow from his conduct, whatever his desire may be as to that result.'" *Id.* (internal quotation marks omitted). The Court then stated: "In a general sense, 'purpose' corresponds loosely with the common-law concept of specific intent, while 'knowledge' corresponds loosely with the concept of general intent." *Id.* at 405. In contrast, cases such as *United States v. Neiswender*, 590 F.2d 1269 (4th Cir. 1979), suggest that to prove specific intent it is enough that the defendant simply have "knowledge or notice" that his act "would have likely resulted in" the proscribed outcome. *Id.* at 1273. "Notice," the court held, "is provided by the reasonable foreseeability of the natural and probable consequences of one's acts." *Id.*

As in *2004 Legal Standards Opinion*, we will not attempt to ascertain the precise meaning of "specific intent" in sections 2340-2340A. *See id.* at 16-17. It is clear, however, that the necessary specific intent would be present if an individual performed an act and "consciously desire[d]" that act to inflict severe physical or mental pain or suffering. 1 LaFave, *Substantive Criminal Law* § 5.2(a), at 341. Conversely, if an individual acted in good faith, and only after reasonable investigation establishing that his conduct would not be expected to inflict severe physical or mental pain or suffering, he would not have the specific intent necessary to violate sections 2340-2340A. Such an individual could be said neither consciously to desire the proscribed result, *see, e.g., Bailey*, 444 U.S. at 405, nor to have "knowledge or notice" that his act "would likely have resulted in" the proscribed outcome, *Neiswender*, 590 F.2d at 1273.

As we did in *2004 Legal Standards Opinion*, we stress two additional points regarding specific intent: First, specific intent is distinguished from motive. A good motive, such as to protect national security, does not excuse conduct that is specifically intended to inflict severe physical or mental pain or suffering, as proscribed by the statute. Second, specific intent to take a given action can be found even if the actor would take the action only upon certain conditions. *Cf., e.g., Holloway v. United States*, 526 U.S. 1, 11 (1999) ("[A] defendant may not negate a proscribed intent by requiring the victim to comply with a condition the defendant has no right to impose."). *See also id.* at 10-11 & nn. 9-12; Model Penal Code § 2.02(6). Thus, for example, the fact that a victim might have avoided being tortured by cooperating with the perpetrator would not render permissible the resort to conduct that would otherwise constitute torture under the statute. *2004 Legal Standards Opinion* at 17.[22]

III.

In the discussion that follows, we will address each of the specific interrogation techniques you have described. Subject to the understandings, limitations, and safeguards discussed herein, including ongoing medical and psychological monitoring and team intervention as necessary, we conclude that the authorized use of each of these techniques, considered individually, would not violate the prohibition that Congress has adopted in sections 2340-2340A. This conclusion is straightforward with respect to all but two of the techniques. Use of sleep deprivation as an enhanced technique and use of the waterboard, however, involve more substantial questions, with the waterboard presenting the most substantial question. Although we conclude that the use of these techniques—as we understand them and subject to the limitations you have described—would not violate the statute, the issues raised by these two techniques counsel great caution in their use, including both careful adherence to the limitations and

---

[22] The Criminal Division of the Department of Justice has reviewed this memorandum and is satisfied that our general interpretation of the legal standards under sections 2340-2340A is consistent with its concurrence in the *2004 Legal Standards Opinion*.

TOP SECRET  NOFORN

restrictions you have described and also close and continuing medical and psychological monitoring.

Before addressing the application of sections 2340-2340A to the specific techniques in question, we note certain overall features of the CIA's approach that are significant to our conclusions. Interrogators are trained and certified in a course that you have informed us currently lasts approximately four weeks. Interrogators (and other personnel deployed as part of this program) are required to review and acknowledge the applicable interrogation guidelines. *See Confinement Guidelines* at 2; *Interrogation Guidelines* at 2 ("The Director, DCI Counterterrorist Center shall ensure that all personnel directly engaged in the interrogation of persons detained pursuant to the authorities set forth in ▇▇▇▇ have been appropriately screened (from the medical, psychological and security standpoints), have reviewed these Guidelines, have received appropriate training in their implementation, and have completed the attached Acknowledgement."). We assume that all interrogators are adequately trained, that they understand the design and purpose of the interrogation techniques, and that they will apply the techniques in accordance with their authorized and intended use.

In addition, the involvement of medical and psychological personnel in the adaptation and application of the established SERE techniques is particularly noteworthy for purposes of our analysis.[33] Medical personnel have been involved in imposing limitations on—and requiring changes to—certain procedures, particularly the use of the waterboard.[34] We have had extensive

---

[33] As noted above, each of these techniques has been adapted (although in some cases with significant modifications) from SERE training. Through your consultation with various individuals responsible for such training, you have learned facts relating to experience with them, which you have reported to us. Again, fully recognizing the limitations of reliance on this experience, you have advised us that these techniques have been used as elements of a course of training without any reported incidents of prolonged mental harm or of any severe physical pain, injury, or suffering. With respect to the psychological impact ▇▇▇▇ of the SERE school advised that during his three and a half years in that position, he trained 10,000 students, only two of whom dropped out following use of the techniques. Although on rare occasions students temporarily postponed the remainder of the training and received psychological counseling, we understand that those students were able to finish the program without any indication of subsequent mental health effects. ▇▇▇▇ who has had over ten years experience with SERE training, told you that he was not aware of any individuals who completed the program suffering any adverse mental health effects (though he advised of one person who did not complete the training who had an adverse mental health reaction that lasted two hours and spontaneously dissipated without requiring treatment and with no further symptoms reported). In addition, the ▇▇▇▇ who has had experience with all of the techniques discussed herein, has advised that the use of these procedures has not resulted in any reported instances of prolonged mental harm and very few instances of immediate and temporary adverse psychological responses to the training. Of 26,829 students in Air Force SERE training from 1992 through 2001, only 0.14% were pulled from the program for psychological reasons (specifically, although 4.3% had some contact with psychology services, only 3% of those individuals with such contact in fact withdrew from the program). We understand that the ▇▇▇▇ expressed confidence—based on debriefing of students and other information—that the training did not cause any long-term psychological harm and that if there are any long-term psychological effects of the training at all, they "are certainly minimal."

[34] We note that this involvement of medical personnel in designing safeguards for, and in monitoring implementation of, the procedures is a significant difference from earlier uses of the techniques catalogued in the Inspector General's Report. *See IG Report* at 21 n.26 ("OMS was neither consulted nor involved in the initial analysis of the risk and benefits of [enhanced interrogation techniques], nor provided with the OTS report cited in the OLC opinion [the *Interrogation Memorandum*]."). Since that time, based on comments from OMS, additional constraints have been imposed on use of the techniques.

meetings with the medical personnel involved in monitoring the use of these techniques. It is clear that they have carefully worked to ensure that the techniques do not result in severe physical or mental pain or suffering to the detainees.[35] Medical and psychological personnel evaluate each detainee before the use of these techniques on the detainee is approved, and they continue to monitor each detainee throughout his interrogation and detention. Moreover, medical personnel are physically present throughout application of the waterboard (and present or otherwise observing the use of all techniques that involve physical contact, as discussed more fully above), and they carefully monitor detainees who are undergoing sleep deprivation or dietary manipulation. In addition, they regularly assess both the medical literature and the experience with detainees.[36] OMS has specifically declared that "[m]edical officers must remain cognizant at all times of their obligation to prevent 'severe physical or mental pain or suffering.'" *OMS Guidelines* at 10. In fact, we understand that medical and psychological personnel have discontinued the use of techniques as to a particular detainee when they believed he might suffer such pain or suffering, and in certain instances, OMS medical personnel have not cleared certain detainees for some—or any—techniques based on the initial medical and psychological assessments. They have also imposed additional restrictions on the use of techniques (such as the waterboard) in order to protect the safety of detainees, thus reducing further the risk of severe pain or suffering. You have informed us that they will continue to have this role and authority. We assume that all interrogators understand the important role and authority of OMS personnel and will cooperate with OMS in the exercise of these duties.

  Finally, in sharp contrast to those practices universally condemned as torture over the centuries, the techniques we consider here have been carefully evaluated to avoid causing severe pain or suffering to the detainees. As OMS has described these techniques as a group:

> In all instances the general goal of these techniques is a psychological impact, and not some physical effect, with a specific goal of "dislocat[ing] [the detainee's] expectations regarding the treatment he believes he will receive. . . ." The more physical techniques are delivered in a manner carefully limited to avoid serious pain. The slaps, for example, are designed "to induce shock, surprise, and/or humiliation" and "not to inflict physical pain that is severe or lasting."

Id. at 8-9.

---

 [35] We are mindful that, historically, medical personnel have sometimes been used to enhance, not prevent, torture—for example, by keeping a torture victim alive and conscious so as to extend his suffering. It is absolutely clear, as you have informed us and as our own dealings with OMS personnel have confirmed, that the involvement of OMS is intended to prevent harm to the detainees and not to extend or increase pain or suffering. As the *OMS Guidelines* explain, "OMS is responsible for assessing and monitoring the health of all Agency detainees subject to 'enhanced' interrogation techniques, and for determining that the authorized administration of these techniques would not be expected to cause serious or permanent harm." *OMS Guidelines* at 9 (footnote omitted).

 [36] To assist in monitoring experience with the detainees, we understand that there is regular reporting on medical and psychological experience with the use of these techniques on detainees and that there are special instructions on documenting experience with sleep deprivation and the waterboard. *See OMS Guidelines* at 6-7, 16, 20.

With this background, we turn to the application of sections 2340-2340A to each of the specific interrogation techniques.

1. *Dietary manipulation.* Based on experience, it is evident that this technique is not expected to cause any physical pain, let alone pain that is extreme in intensity. The detainee is carefully monitored to ensure that he does not suffer acute weight loss or any dehydration. Further, there is nothing in the experience of caloric intake at this level that could be expected to cause physical pain. Although we do not equate a person who voluntarily enters a weight-loss program with a detainee subjected to dietary manipulation as an interrogation technique, we believe that it is relevant that several commercial weight-loss programs available in the United States involve similar or even greater reductions in caloric intake. Nor could this technique reasonably be thought to induce "severe physical suffering." Although dietary manipulation may cause some degree of hunger, such an experience is far from extreme hunger (let alone starvation) and cannot be expected to amount to "severe physical suffering" under the statute. The caloric levels are set based on the detainee's weight, so as to ensure that the detainee does not experience extreme hunger. As noted, many people participate in weight-loss programs that involve similar or more stringent caloric limitations, and, while such participation cannot be equated with the use of dietary manipulation as an interrogation technique, we believe that the existence of such programs is relevant to whether dietary manipulation would cause "severe physical suffering" within the meaning of sections 2340-2340A. Because there is no prospect that the technique would cause severe physical pain or suffering, we conclude that the authorized use of this technique by an adequately trained interrogator could not reasonably be considered specifically intended to do so.

This technique presents no issue of "severe mental pain or suffering" within the meaning of sections 2340-2340A, because the use of this technique would involve no qualifying predicate act. The technique does not, for example, involve "the intentional infliction or threatened infliction of severe physical pain or suffering," 18 U.S.C. § 2340(2)(A), or the "application ... of ... procedures calculated to disrupt profoundly the senses or the personality," *id.* § 2340(2)(B). Moreover, there is no basis to believe that dietary manipulation could cause "prolonged mental harm." Therefore, we conclude that the authorized use of this technique by an adequately trained interrogator could not reasonably be considered specifically intended to cause such harm.[37]

2. *Nudity.* We understand that nudity is used as a technique to create psychological discomfort, not to inflict any physical pain or suffering. You have informed us that during the use of this technique, detainees are kept in locations with ambient temperatures that ensure there is no threat to their health. Specifically, this technique would not be employed at temperatures below 68°F (and is unlikely to be employed below 75°F). Even if this technique involves some physical discomfort, it cannot be said to cause "suffering" (as we have explained the term

---

[37] In *Ireland v. United Kingdom*, 25 Eur. Ct. H.R. (ser. A) (1978), the European Court of Human Rights concluded by a vote of 13-4 that a reduced diet, even in conjunction with a number of other techniques, did not amount to "torture," as defined in the European Convention on Human Rights. The reduced diet there consisted of one "round" of bread and a pint of water every six hours, *see id.*, separate opinion of Judge Zekia, Part A. The duration of the reduced diet in that case is not clear.

above), let alone "severe physical pain or suffering," and we therefore conclude that its authorized use by an adequately trained interrogator could not reasonably be considered specifically intended to do so. Although some detainees might be humiliated by this technique, especially given possible cultural sensitivities and the possibility of being seen by female officers, it cannot constitute "severe mental pain or suffering" under the statute because it does not involve any of the predicate acts specified by Congress.

3. *Attention grasp.* The attention grasp involves no physical pain or suffering for the detainee and does not involve any predicate act for purposes of severe mental pain or suffering under the statute. Accordingly, because this technique cannot be expected to cause severe physical or mental pain or suffering, we conclude that its authorized use by an adequately trained interrogator could not reasonably be considered specifically intended to do so.

4. *Walling.* Although the walling technique involves the use of considerable force to push the detainee against the wall and may involve a large number of repetitions in certain cases, we understand that the false wall that is used is flexible and that this technique is not designed to, and does not, cause severe physical pain to the detainee. We understand that there may be some pain or irritation associated with the collar, which is used to help avoid injury such as whiplash to the detainee, but that any physical pain associated with the use of the collar would not approach the level of intensity needed to constitute severe physical pain. Similarly, we do not believe that the physical distress caused by this technique or the duration of its use, even with multiple repetitions, could amount to severe physical suffering within the meaning of sections 2340-2340A. We understand that medical and psychological personnel are present or observing during the use of this technique (as with all techniques involving physical contact with a detainee), and that any member of the team or the medical staff may intercede to stop the use of the technique if it is being used improperly or if it appears that it may cause injury to the detainee. We also do not believe that the use of this technique would involve a threat of infliction of severe physical pain or suffering or other predicate act for purposes of severe mental pain or suffering under the statute. Rather, this technique is designed to shock the detainee and disrupt his expectations that he will not be treated forcefully and to wear down his resistance to interrogation. Based on these understandings, we conclude that the authorized use of this technique by adequately trained interrogators could not reasonably be considered specifically intended to cause severe physical or mental pain or suffering in violation of sections 2340-2340A.[38]

5. *Facial hold.* Like the attention grasp, this technique involves no physical pain or suffering and does not involve any predicate act for purposes of severe mental pain or suffering. Accordingly, we conclude that its authorized use by adequately trained interrogators could not

---

[38] In *Interrogation Memorandum*, we did not describe the walling technique as involving the number of repetitions that we understand may be applied. Our advice with respect to walling in the present memorandum is specifically based on the understanding that the repetitive use of walling is intended only to increase the drama and shock of the technique, to wear down the detainee's resistance, and to disrupt expectations that he will not be treated with force, and that such use is not intended to, and does not in fact, cause severe physical pain to the detainee. Moreover, our advice specifically assumes that the use of walling will be stopped if there is any indication that the use of the technique is or may be causing severe physical pain to a detainee.

reasonably be considered specifically intended to cause severe physical or mental pain or suffering.

6. *Facial slap or insult slap.* Although this technique involves a degree of physical pain, the pain associated with a slap to the face, as you have described it to us, could not be expected to constitute severe physical pain. We understand that the purpose of this technique is to cause shock, surprise, or humiliation, not to inflict physical pain that is severe or lasting; we assume it will be used accordingly. Similarly, the physical distress that may be caused by an abrupt slap to the face, even if repeated several times, would not constitute an extended state or condition of physical suffering and also would not likely involve the level of intensity required for severe physical suffering under the statute. Finally, a facial slap would not involve a predicate act for purposes of severe mental pain or suffering. Therefore, the authorized use of this technique by adequately trained interrogators could not reasonably be considered specifically intended to cause severe physical or mental pain or suffering in violation of sections 2340-2340A.[39]

7. *Abdominal slap.* Although the abdominal slap technique might involve some minor physical pain, it cannot, as you have described it to us, be said to involve even moderate, let alone *severe*, physical pain or suffering. Again, because the technique cannot be expected to cause severe physical pain or suffering, we conclude that its authorized use by an adequately trained interrogator could not reasonably be considered specifically intended to do so. Nor could it be considered specifically intended to cause severe mental pain or suffering within the meaning of sections 2340-2340A, as none of the statutory predicate acts would be present.

8. *Cramped confinement.* This technique does not involve any significant physical pain or suffering. It also does not involve a predicate act for purposes of severe mental pain or suffering. Specifically, we do not believe that placing a detainee in a dark, cramped space for the limited period of time involved here could reasonably be considered a procedure calculated to disrupt profoundly the senses so as to cause prolonged mental harm. Accordingly, we conclude that its authorized use by adequately trained interrogators could not reasonably be considered specifically intended to cause severe physical or mental pain or suffering in violation of sections 2340-2340A.

9. *Wall standing.* The wall standing technique, as you have described it, would not involve severe physical pain within the meaning of the statute. It also cannot be expected to cause severe physical suffering. Even if the physical discomfort of muscle fatigue associated with wall standing might be substantial, we understand that the duration of the technique is self-limited by the individual detainee's ability to sustain the position; thus, the short duration of the discomfort means that this technique would not be expected to cause, and could not reasonably be considered specifically intended to cause, severe physical suffering. Our advice also assumes that the detainee's position is not designed to produce severe pain that might result from contortions or twisting of the body, but only temporary muscle fatigue. Nor does wall standing

---

[39] Our advice about both the facial slap and the abdominal slap assumes that the interrogators will apply those techniques as designed and will not strike the detainee with excessive force or repetition in a manner that might result in severe physical pain.

involve any predicate act for purposes of severe mental pain or suffering. Accordingly, we conclude that the authorized use of this technique by adequately trained interrogators could not reasonably be considered specifically intended to cause severe physical or mental pain or suffering in violation of the statute.

10. *Stress positions*. For the same reasons that the use of wall standing would not violate the statute, we conclude that the authorized use of stress positions such as those described in *Interrogation Memorandum*, if employed by adequately trained interrogators, could not reasonably be considered specifically intended to cause severe physical or mental pain or suffering in violation of sections 2340-2340A. As with wall standing, we understand that the duration of the technique is self-limited by the individual detainee's ability to sustain the position; thus, the short duration of the discomfort means that this technique would not be expected to cause, and could not reasonably be considered specifically intended to cause, severe physical suffering. Our advice also assumes that stress positions are not designed to produce severe pain that might result from contortions or twisting of the body, but only temporary muscle fatigue.[40]

11. *Water dousing*. As you have described it to us, water dousing involves dousing the detainee with water from a container or a hose without a nozzle, and is intended to wear him down both physically and psychologically. You have informed us that the water might be as cold as 41°F, though you have further advised us that the water generally is not refrigerated and therefore is unlikely to be less than 50°F. (Nevertheless, for purposes of our analysis, we will assume that water as cold as 41°F might be used.) OMS has advised that, based on the extensive experience in SERE training, the medical literature, and the experience with detainees to date, water dousing as authorized is not designed or expected to cause significant physical pain, and certainly not severe physical pain. Although we understand that prolonged *immersion* in very cold water may be physically painful, as noted above, this interrogation technique does not involve immersion and a substantial margin of safety is built into the time limitation on the use of the CIA's water dousing technique—use of the technique with water of a given temperature must be limited to no more than two-thirds of the time in which hypothermia could be expected to occur from *total immersion* in water of the same temperature.[41] While being cold can involve physical discomfort, OMS also advises that in their professional judgment any resulting discomfort is not expected to be intense, and the duration is limited by specific times tied to

---

[40] A stress position that involves such contortion or twisting, as well as one held for so long that it could not be viewed only as producing temporary muscle fatigue, might raise more substantial questions under the statute. *Cf. Army Field Manual 34-52: Intelligence Interrogation* at 1-8 (1992) (indicating that "[f]orcing an individual to stand, sit, or kneel in abnormal positions for prolonged periods of time" may constitute "torture" within the meaning of the Third Geneva Convention's requirement that "[n]o physical or mental torture, nor any other form of coercion, may be inflicted on prisoners of war," but not addressing 18 U.S.C. §§ 2340-2340A); United Nations General Assembly, *Report of the Special Rapporteur on Torture and Other Cruel, Inhuman or Degrading Treatment or Punishment*, U.N. Doc. A/59/150 at 6 (Sept. 1, 2004) (suggesting that "holding detainees in painful and/or stressful positions" might in certain circumstances be characterized as torture).

[41] Moreover, even in the extremely unlikely event that hypothermia set in, under the circumstances in which this technique is used—including close medical supervision and, if necessary, medical attention—we understand that the detainee would be expected to recover fully and rapidly.

water temperature. Any discomfort caused by this technique, therefore, would not qualify as "severe physical suffering" within the meaning of sections 2340-2340A. Consequently, given that there is no expectation that the technique will cause severe physical pain or suffering when properly used, we conclude that the authorized use of this technique by an adequately trained interrogator could not reasonably be considered specifically intended to cause these results.

With respect to mental pain or suffering, as you have described the procedure, we do not believe that any of the four statutory predicate acts necessary for a possible finding of severe mental pain or suffering under the statute would be present. Nothing, for example, leads us to believe that the detainee would understand the procedure to constitute a threat of imminent death, especially given that care is taken to ensure that no water will get into the detainee's mouth or nose. Nor would a detainee reasonably understand the prospect of being doused with cold water as the threatened infliction of severe pain. Furthermore, even were we to conclude that there could be a qualifying predicate act, nothing suggests that the detainee would be expected to suffer any prolonged mental harm as a result of the procedure. OMS advises that there has been no evidence of such harm in the SERE training, which utilizes a much more extreme technique involving total immersion. The presence of psychologists who monitor the detainee's mental condition makes such harm even more unlikely. Consequently, we conclude that the authorized use of the technique by adequately trained interrogators could not reasonably be considered specifically intended to cause severe mental pain or suffering within the meaning of the statute.

The flicking technique, which is subject to the same temperature limitations as water dousing but would involve substantially less water, *a fortiori* would not violate the statute.

12. *Sleep deprivation*. In the *Interrogation Memorandum*, we concluded that sleep deprivation did not violate sections 2340-2340A. *See id.* at 10, 14-15. This question warrants further analysis for two reasons. First, we did not consider the potential for physical pain or suffering resulting from the shackling used to keep detainees awake or any impact from the diapering of the detainee. Second, we did not address the possibility of severe physical suffering that does not involve severe physical pain.

Under the limitations adopted by the CIA, sleep deprivation may not exceed 180 hours, which we understand is approximately two-thirds of the maximum recorded time that humans have gone without sleep for purposes of medical study, as discussed below.[42] Furthermore, any detainee who has undergone 180 hours of sleep deprivation must then be allowed to sleep without interruption for at least eight straight hours. Although we understand that the CIA's guidelines would allow another session of sleep deprivation to begin after the detainee has gotten

---

[42] The *IG Report* described the maximum allowable period of sleep deprivation at that time as 264 hours or 11 days. *See IG Report* at 15. You have informed us that you have since established a limit of 180 hours, that in fact no detainee has been subjected to more than 180 hours of sleep deprivation, and that sleep deprivation will rarely exceed 120 hours. To date, only three detainees have been subjected to sleep deprivation for more than 96 hours.

at least eight hours of uninterrupted sleep following 180 hours of sleep deprivation, we will evaluate only one application of up to 180 hours of sleep deprivation.[43]

We understand from OMS, and from our review of the literature on the physiology of sleep, that even very extended sleep deprivation does not cause physical pain, let alone severe physical pain.[44] "The longest studies of sleep deprivation in humans ... [involved] volunteers [who] were deprived of sleep for 8 to 11 days. ... Surprisingly, little seemed to go wrong with the subjects physically. The main effects lay with sleepiness and impaired brain functioning, but even these were no great cause for concern." James Horne, *Why We Sleep: The Functions of Sleep in Humans and Other Mammals* 23-24 (1988) ("*Why We Sleep*") (footnote omitted). We note that there are important differences between sleep deprivation as an interrogation technique used by the CIA and the controlled experiments documented in the literature. The subjects of the experiments were free to move about and engage in normal activities and often led a "tranquil existence" with "plenty of time for relaxation," *see id.* at 24, whereas a detainee in CIA custody would be shackled and prevented from moving freely. Moreover, the subjects in the experiments often increased their food consumption during periods of extended sleep loss, *see id.* at 38, whereas the detainee undergoing interrogation may be placed on a reduced-calorie diet, as discussed above. Nevertheless, we understand that experts who have studied sleep deprivation have concluded that "[t]he most plausible reason for the uneventful physical findings with these human beings is that ... sleep loss is not particularly harmful." *Id.* at 24. We understand that this conclusion does not depend on the extent of physical movement or exercise by the subject or whether the subject increases his food consumption. OMS medical staff members have also informed us, based on their experience with detainees who have undergone extended sleep deprivation and their review of the relevant medical literature, that extended sleep deprivation does not cause physical pain. Although edema, or swelling, of the lower legs may sometimes develop as a result of the long periods of standing associated with sleep deprivation, we understand from OMS that such edema is not painful and will quickly dissipate once the subject is removed from the standing position. We also understand that if any case of significant edema develops, the team will intercede to ensure that the detainee is moved from the standing position and that he receives any medical attention necessary to relieve the swelling and allow the edema to dissipate. For these reasons, we conclude that the authorized use of extended sleep

---

[43] As noted above, we are not concluding that additional use of sleep deprivation, subject to close and careful medical supervision, would violate the statute, but at the present time we express no opinion on whether additional sleep deprivation would be consistent with sections 2340-2340A.

[44] Although sleep deprivation is not itself physically painful, we understand that some studies have noted that extended total sleep deprivation may have the effect of reducing tolerance to some forms of pain in some subjects. *See, e.g.*, B. Kundermann, et al., *Sleep Deprivation Affects Thermal Pain Thresholds but not Somatosensory Thresholds in Healthy Volunteers*, 66 Psychosomatic Med. 932 (2004) (finding a significant decrease in heat pain thresholds and some decrease in cold pain thresholds after one night without sleep); S. Hakki Onen, et al., *The Effects of Total Sleep Deprivation, Selective Sleep Interruption and Sleep Recovery on Pain Tolerance Thresholds in Healthy Subjects*, 10 J. Sleep Research 35, 41 (2001) (finding a statistically significant drop of 8-9% in tolerance thresholds for mechanical or pressure pain after 40 hours); *id.* at 35-36 (discussing other studies). We will discuss the potential interactions between sleep deprivation and other interrogation techniques in the separate memorandum, to which we referred in footnote 6, addressing whether the combined use of certain techniques is consistent with the legal requirements of sections 2340-2340A.

deprivation by adequately trained interrogators would not be expected to cause and could not reasonably be considered specifically intended to cause severe physical pain.

In addition, OMS personnel have informed us that the shackling of detainees is not designed to and does not result in significant physical pain. A detainee subject to sleep deprivation would not be allowed to hang by his wrists, and we understand that no detainee subjected to sleep deprivation to date has been allowed to hang by his wrists or has otherwise suffered injury.[45] If necessary, we understand that medical personnel will intercede to prevent any such injury and would require either that interrogators use a different method to keep the detainee awake (such as through the use of sitting or horizontal positions), or that the use of the technique be stopped altogether. When the sitting position is used, the detainee is seated on a small stool to which he is shackled; the stool supports his weight but is too small to let the detainee balance himself and fall asleep. We also specifically understand that the use of shackling with horizontal sleep deprivation, which has only been used rarely, is done in such a way as to ensure that there is no additional stress on the detainee's arm or leg joints that might force the limbs beyond natural extension or create tension on any joint. Thus, shackling cannot be expected to result in severe physical pain, and we conclude that its authorized use by adequately trained interrogators could not reasonably be considered specifically intended to do so. Finally, we believe that the use of a diaper cannot be expected to—and could not reasonably be considered intended to—result in any physical pain, let alone severe physical pain.

Although it is a more substantial question, particularly given the imprecision in the statutory standard and the lack of guidance from the courts, we also conclude that extended sleep deprivation, subject to the limitations and conditions described herein, would not be expected to cause "severe physical suffering." We understand that some individuals who undergo extended sleep deprivation would likely at some point experience physical discomfort and distress. We assume that some individuals would eventually feel weak physically and may experience other unpleasant physical sensations from prolonged fatigue, including such symptoms as impairment to coordinated body movement, difficulty with speech, nausea, and blurred vision. *See Why We Sleep* at 30. In addition, we understand that extended sleep deprivation will often cause a small drop in body temperature, *see id.* at 31, and we assume that such a drop in body temperature may also be associated with unpleasant physical sensations. We also assume that any physical discomfort that might be associated with sleep deprivation would likely increase, at least to a point, the longer the subject goes without sleep. Thus, on these assumptions, it may be the case that at some point, for some individuals, the degree of physical distress experienced in sleep deprivation might be substantial.[46]

On the other hand, we understand from OMS, and from the literature we have reviewed on the physiology of sleep, that many individuals may tolerate extended sleep deprivation well

---

[45] This includes a total of more than 25 detainees subjected to at least some period of sleep deprivation. *See* January 4 ▓▓▓ *Fax* at 1-3.

[46] The possibility noted above that sleep deprivation might heighten susceptibility to pain, *see supra* note 44, magnifies this concern.

and with little apparent distress, and that this has been the CIA's experience."⁴⁷ Furthermore, the principal physical problem associated with standing is edema, and in any instance of significant edema, the interrogation team will remove the detainee from the standing position and will seek medical assistance. The shackling is used only as a passive means of keeping the detainee awake and, in both the tightness of the shackles and the positioning of the hands, is not intended to cause pain. A detainee, for example, will not be allowed to hang by his wrists. Shackling in the sitting position involves a stool that is adequate to support the detainee's weight. In the rare instances when horizontal sleep deprivation may be used, a thick towel or blanket is placed under the detainee to protect against reduction of body temperature from contact with the floor, and the manacles and shackles are anchored so as not to cause pain or create tension on any joint. If the detainee is nude and is using an adult diaper, the diaper is checked regularly to prevent skin irritation. The conditions of sleep deprivation are thus aimed at preventing severe physical suffering. Because sleep deprivation does not involve physical pain and would not be expected to cause extreme physical distress to the detainee, the extended duration of sleep deprivation, within the 180-hour limit imposed by the CIA, is not a sufficient factor alone to constitute severe physical suffering within the meaning of sections 2340-2340A. We therefore believe that the use of this technique, under the specified limits and conditions, is not "extreme and outrageous" and does not reach the high bar set by Congress for a violation of sections 2340-2340A. *See Price v. Socialist People's Libyan Arab Jamahiriya*, 294 F.3d at 92 (to be torture under the TVPA, conduct must be "extreme and outrageous"); *cf. Mehinovic v. Vuckovic*, 198 F. Supp. 2d at 1332-40, 1345-46 (standard met under the TVPA by a course of conduct that included severe beatings to the genitals, head, and other parts of the body with metal pipes and various other items; removal of teeth with pliers; kicking in the face and ribs; breaking of bones and ribs and dislocation of fingers; cutting a figure into the victim's forehead; hanging the victim and beating him; extreme limitations of food and water; and subjection to games of "Russian roulette").

Nevertheless, because extended sleep deprivation could in some cases result in substantial physical distress, the safeguards adopted by the CIA, including ongoing medical monitoring and intervention by the team if needed, are important to ensure that the CIA's use of extended sleep deprivation will not run afoul of the statute. Different individual detainees may react physically to sleep deprivation in different ways. We assume, therefore, that the team will separately monitor each individual detainee who is undergoing sleep deprivation, and that the application of this technique will be sensitive to the individualized physical condition and reactions of each detainee. Moreover, we emphasize our understanding that OMS will intervene to alter or stop the course of sleep deprivation for a detainee if OMS concludes in its medical judgment that the detainee is or may be experiencing extreme physical distress."⁴⁸ The team, we

---

⁴⁷ Indeed, although it may seem surprising to those not familiar with the extensive medical literature relating to sleep deprivation, based on that literature and its experience with the technique, in its guidelines, OMS lists sleep deprivation as less intense than water dousing, stress positions, walling, cramped confinement, and the waterboard. *See OMS Guidelines* at 8.

⁴⁸ For example, any physical pain or suffering associated with standing or with shackles might become more intense with an extended use of the technique on a particular detainee whose condition and strength do not permit him to tolerate it, and we understand that personnel monitoring the detainee will take this possibility into account and, if necessary, will ensure that the detainee is placed into a sitting or horizontal position or will direct that the sleep deprivation be discontinued altogether. *See OMS Guidelines* at 14-16.

understand, will intervene not only if the sleep deprivation itself may be having such effects, but also if the shackling or other conditions attendant to the technique appear to be causing severe physical suffering. With these precautions in place, and based on the assumption that they will be followed, we conclude that the authorized use of extended sleep deprivation by adequately trained interrogators would not be expected to and could not reasonably be considered specifically intended to cause severe physical suffering in violation of 18 U.S.C. §§ 2340-2340A.

Finally, we also conclude that extended sleep deprivation cannot be expected to cause "severe mental pain or suffering" as defined in sections 2340-2340A, and that its authorized use by adequately trained interrogators could not reasonably be considered specifically intended to do so. First, we do not believe that use of the sleep deprivation technique, subject to the conditions in place, would involve one of the predicate acts necessary for "severe mental pain or suffering" under the statute. There would be no infliction or threatened infliction of severe physical pain or suffering, within the meaning of the statute, and there would be no threat of imminent death. It may be questioned whether sleep deprivation could be characterized as a "procedure[] calculated to disrupt profoundly the senses or the personality" within the meaning of section 2340(2)(B), since we understand from OMS and from the scientific literature that extended sleep deprivation might induce hallucinations in some cases. Physicians from OMS have informed us, however, that they are of the view that, in general, no "profound" disruption would result from the length of sleep deprivation contemplated by the CIA, and again the scientific literature we have reviewed appears to support this conclusion. Moreover, we understand that any team member would direct that the technique be immediately discontinued if there were any sign that the detainee is experiencing hallucinations. Thus, it appears that the authorized use of sleep deprivation by the CIA would not be expected to result in a profound disruption of the senses, and if it did, it would be discontinued. Even assuming, however, that the extended use of sleep deprivation may result in hallucinations that could fairly be characterized as a "profound" disruption of the subject's senses, we do not believe it tenable to conclude that in such circumstances the use of sleep deprivation could be said to be "calculated" to cause such profound disruption to the senses, as required by the statute. The term "calculated" denotes something that is planned or thought out beforehand: "Calculate," as used in the statute, is defined to mean "to plan the nature of beforehand: think out"; "to design, prepare, or adapt by forethought or careful plan: fit or prepare by appropriate means." *Webster's Third New International Dictionary* at 315 (defining "calculate"—"used chiefly [as it is in section 2340(2)(B)] as [a] past part[iciple] with complementary infinitive <*calculated* to succeed>"). Here, it is evident that the potential for any hallucinations on the part of a detainee undergoing sleep deprivation is not something that would be a "calculated" result of the use of this technique, particularly given that the team would intervene immediately to stop the technique if there were signs the subject was experiencing hallucinations.

Second, even if we were to assume, out of an abundance of caution, that extended sleep deprivation could be said to be a "procedure[] calculated to disrupt profoundly the senses or the personality" of the subject within the meaning of section 2340(2)(B), we do not believe that this technique would be expected to—or that its authorized use by adequately trained interrogators could reasonably be considered specifically intended to—cause "*prolonged* mental harm" as required by the statute, because, as we understand it, any hallucinatory effects of sleep deprivation would dissipate rapidly. OMS has informed us, based on the scientific literature and

TOP SECRET/████████/NOFORN

on its own experience with detainees who have been sleep deprived, that any such hallucinatory effects would not be prolonged. We understand from OMS that *Why We Sleep* provides an accurate summary of the scientific literature on this point. As discussed there, the longest documented period of time for which any human has gone without sleep is 264 hours. *See id.* at 29-34. The longest study with more than one subject involved 205 hours of sleep deprivation. *See id.* at 37-42. We understand that these and other studies constituting a significant body of scientific literature indicate that sleep deprivation temporarily affects the functioning of the brain but does not otherwise have significant physiological effects. *See id.* at 100. Sleep deprivation's effects on the brain are generally not severe but can include impaired cognitive performance and visual hallucinations; however, these effects dissipate rapidly, often with as little as one night's sleep. *See id.* at 31-32, 34-37, 40, 47-53. Thus, we conclude, any temporary hallucinations that might result from extended sleep deprivation could not reasonably be considered "prolonged mental harm" for purposes of sections 2340-2340A.[49]

In light of these observations, although in its extended uses it may present a substantial question under sections 2340-2340A, we conclude that the authorized use of sleep deprivation by adequately trained interrogators, subject to the limitations and monitoring in place, could not reasonably be considered specifically intended to cause severe mental pain or suffering. Finally, the use of a diaper for sanitary purposes on an individual subjected to sleep deprivation, while potentially humiliating, could not be considered specifically intended to inflict severe mental pain or suffering within the meaning of the statute, because there would be no statutory predicate act and no reason to expect "prolonged mental harm" to result.[50]

---

[49] Without determining the minimum time for mental harm to be considered "prolonged," we do not believe that "prolonged mental harm" would occur during the sleep deprivation itself. As noted, OMS would order that the technique be discontinued if hallucinations occurred. Moreover, even if OMS personnel were not aware of any such hallucinations, whatever time would remain between the onset of such hallucinations, which presumably would be well into the period of sleep deprivation, and the 180-hour maximum for sleep deprivation would not constitute "prolonged" mental harm within the meaning of the statute. Nevertheless, we note that this aspect of the technique calls for great care in monitoring by OMS personnel, including psychologists, especially as the length of the period of sleep deprivation increases.

[50] We note that the court of appeals in *Hilao v. Estate of Marcos*, 103 F.3d 789 (9th Cir. 1996), stated that a variety of techniques taken together, one of which was sleep deprivation, amounted to torture. The court, however, did not specifically discuss sleep deprivation apart from the other conduct at issue, and it did not conclude that sleep deprivation alone amounted to torture. In *Ireland v. United Kingdom*, the European Court of Human Rights concluded by a vote of 13-4 that sleep deprivation, even in conjunction with a number of other techniques, did not amount to torture under the European Charter. The duration of the sleep deprivation at issue was not clear, *see* separate opinion of Judge Fitzmaurice at ¶ 19, but may have been 96-120 hours, *see* majority opinion at ¶ 104. Finally, we note that the Committee Against Torture of the Office of the High Commissioner for Human Rights, in *Concluding Observations of the Committee Against Torture: Israel*, U.N. Doc. A/52/44, at ¶ 257 (May 9, 1997), concluded that a variety of practices taken together, including "sleep deprivation for prolonged periods," "constitute torture as defined in article 1 of the [CAT]." *See also* United Nations General Assembly, *Report of the Committee Against Torture*, U.N. Doc. A/52/44 at ¶ 56 (Sept. 10, 1997) ("sleep deprivation practised on suspects . . . may in some cases constitute torture"). The Committee provided no details on the length of the sleep deprivation or how it was implemented and no analysis to support its conclusion. These precedents provide little or no helpful guidance in our review of the CIA's use of sleep deprivation under sections 2340-2340A. While we do not rely on this fact in interpreting sections 2340-2340A, we note that we are aware of no decision of any foreign court or international tribunal finding that the techniques analyzed here, if subject to the limitations and conditions set out, would amount to torture.

TOP SECRET//NOFORN

TOP SECRET / ████████ / NOFORN

13. *Waterboard.* We previously concluded that the use of the waterboard did not constitute torture under sections 2340-2340A. *See Interrogation Memorandum* at 11, 15. We must reexamine the issue, however, because the technique, as it would be used, could involve more applications in longer sessions (and possibly using different methods) than we earlier considered.[51]

We understand that in the escalating regimen of interrogation techniques, the waterboard is considered to be the most serious, requires a separate approval that may be sought only after other techniques have not worked (or are considered unlikely to work in the time available), and in fact has been—and is expected to be—used on very few detainees. We accept the assessment of OMS that the waterboard "is by far the most traumatic of the enhanced interrogation techniques." *OMS Guidelines* at 15. This technique could subject a detainee to a high degree of distress. A detainee to whom the technique is applied will experience the physiological sensation of drowning, which likely will lead to panic. We understand that even a detainee who knows he is not going to drown is likely to have this response. Indeed, we are informed that even individuals very familiar with the technique experience this sensation when subjected to the waterboard.

Nevertheless, although this technique presents the most substantial question under the statute, we conclude for the reasons discussed below that the authorized use of the waterboard by adequately trained interrogators, subject to the limitations and conditions adopted by the CIA and in the absence of any medical contraindications, would not violate sections 2340-2340A. (We understand that a medical contraindication may have precluded the use of this particular technique on ████████ In reaching this conclusion, we do not in any way minimize the

---

[51] The *IG Report* noted that in some cases the waterboard was used with far greater frequency than initially indicated, *see IG Report* at 5, 44, 46, 103-04, and also that it was used in a different manner. *See id.* at 37 ("[T]he waterboard technique ... was different from the technique described in the DoJ opinion and used in the SERE training. The difference was in the manner in which the detainee's breathing was obstructed. At the SERE school and in the DoJ opinion, the subject's airflow is disrupted by the firm application of a damp cloth over the air passages; the interrogator applies a small amount of water to the cloth in a controlled manner. By contrast, the Agency interrogator ... applied large volumes of water to a cloth that covered the detainee's mouth and nose. One of the psychologists/interrogators acknowledged that the Agency's use of the technique is different from that used in SERE training because it is 'for real' and is more poignant and convincing."); *see also id.* at 14 n.14. The Inspector General further reported that "OMS contends that the expertise of the SERE psychologist/interrogators on the waterboard was probably misrepresented at the time, as the SERE waterboard experience is so different from the subsequent Agency usage as to make it almost irrelevant. Consequently, according to OMS, there was no *a priori* reason to believe that applying the waterboard with the frequency and intensity with which it was used by the psychologist/interrogators was either efficacious or medically safe." *Id.* at 21 n.26. We have carefully considered the *IG Report* and discussed it with OMS personnel. As noted, OMS input has resulted in a number of changes in the application of the waterboard, including limits on the frequency and cumulative use of the technique. Moreover, OMS personnel are carefully instructed in monitoring this technique and are personally present whenever it is used. *See OMS Guidelines* at 17-20. Indeed, although physician assistants can be present when other enhanced techniques are applied, "use of the waterboard requires the presence of a physician." *Id.* at 9 n.2.

TOP SECRET ████████ NOFORN

experience. The panic associated with the feeling of drowning could undoubtedly be significant. There may be few more frightening experiences than feeling that one is unable to breathe.[52]

However frightening the experience may be, OMS personnel have informed us that the waterboard technique is not physically painful. This conclusion, as we understand the facts, accords with the experience in SERE training, where the waterboard has been administered to several thousand members of the United States Armed Forces.[53] To be sure, in SERE training, the technique is confined to at most two applications (and usually only one) of no more than 40 seconds each. Here, there may be two sessions, of up to two hours each, during a 24-hour period, and each session may include multiple applications, of which six may last 10 seconds or longer (but none more than 40 seconds), for a total time of application of as much as 12 minutes in a 24-hour period. Furthermore, the waterboard may be used on up to five days during the 30-day period for which it is approved. *See August 19* ▓▓▓ *Letter* at 1-2. As you have informed us, the CIA has previously used the waterboard repeatedly on two detainees, and, as far as can be determined, these detainees did not experience physical pain or, in the professional judgment of doctors, is there any medical reason to believe they would have done so. Therefore, we conclude that the authorized use of the waterboard by adequately trained interrogators could not reasonably be considered specifically intended to cause "severe physical pain."

We also conclude that the use of the waterboard, under the strict limits and conditions imposed, would not be expected to cause "severe physical suffering" under the statute. As noted above, the difficulty of specifying a category of physical suffering apart from both physical pain and mental pain or suffering, along with the requirement that any such suffering be "severe," calls for an interpretation under which "severe physical suffering" is reserved for physical distress that is severe considering both its intensity and duration. To the extent that in some applications the use of the waterboard could cause choking or similar physical—as opposed to mental—sensations, those physical sensations might well have an intensity approaching the degree contemplated by the statute. However, we understand that any such physical—as opposed to mental—sensations caused by the use of the waterboard end when the application

---

[52] As noted above, in most uses of the technique, the individual is in fact able to breathe, though his breathing is restricted. Because in some uses breathing would not be possible, for purposes of our analysis we assume that the detainee is unable to breathe during applications of water.

[53] We understand that the waterboard is currently used only in Navy SERE training. As noted in the *IG Report*, "[a]ccording to individuals with authoritative knowledge of the SERE program, ... [e]xcept for Navy SERE training, use of the waterboard was discontinued because of its dramatic effect on the students who were subjects." *IG Report* at 14 n.14. We understand that use of the waterboard was discontinued by the other services not because of any concerns about possible physical or mental harm, but because students were not successful at resisting the technique and, as such, it was not considered to be a useful training technique. We note that OMS has concluded that "[w]hile SERE trainers believe that trainees are unable to maintain psychological resistance to the waterboard, our experience was otherwise. Some subjects unquestionably can withstand a large number of applications, with no immediately discernible cumulative impact beyond their strong aversion to the experience." *OMS Guidelines* at 17. We are aware that at a recent Senate Judiciary Committee hearing, Douglas Johnson, Executive Director of the Center for Victims of Torture, testified that some U.S. military personnel who have undergone waterboard training have apparently stated "that it's taken them 15 years of therapy to get over it." You have informed us that, in 2002, the CIA made inquiries to Department of Defense personnel involved in SERE training and that the Department of Defense was not aware of any information that would substantiate such statements, nor is the CIA aware of any such information.

ends. Given the time limits imposed, and the fact that any physical distress (as opposed to possible mental suffering, which is discussed below) would occur only during the actual application of water, the physical distress caused by the waterboard would not be expected to have the duration required to amount to severe physical suffering.[54] Applications are strictly limited to at most 40 seconds, and a total of at most 12 minutes in any 24-hour period, and use of the technique is limited to at most five days during the 30-day period we consider. Consequently, under these conditions, use of the waterboard cannot be expected to cause "severe physical suffering" within the meaning of the statute, and we conclude that its authorized use by adequately trained interrogators could not reasonably be considered specifically intended to cause "severe physical suffering."[55] Again, however, we caution that great care should be used in adhering to the limitations imposed and in monitoring any detainee subjected to it to prevent the detainee from experiencing severe physical suffering.

The most substantial question raised by the waterboard relates to the statutory definition of "severe mental pain or suffering." The sensation of drowning that we understand accompanies the use of the waterboard arguably could qualify as a "threat of imminent death" within the meaning of section 2340(2)(C) and thus might constitute a predicate act for "severe mental pain or suffering" under the statute.[56] Although the waterboard is used with safeguards that make actual harm quite unlikely, the detainee may not know about these safeguards, and even if he does learn of them, the technique is still likely to create panic in the form of an acute instinctual fear arising from the physiological sensation of drowning.

Nevertheless, the statutory definition of "severe mental pain or suffering" also requires that the predicate act produce "prolonged mental harm." 18 U.S.C. § 2340(2). As we understand from OMS personnel familiar with the history of the waterboard technique, as used both in SERE training (though in a substantially different manner) and in the previous CIA interrogations, there is no medical basis to believe that the technique would produce any mental effect beyond the distress that directly accompanies its use and the prospect that it will be used again. We understand from the CIA that to date none of the thousands of persons who have undergone the more limited use of the technique in SERE training has suffered prolonged mental harm as a result. The CIA's use of the technique could far exceed the one or two applications to which SERE training is limited, and the participant in SERE training presumably understands that the technique is part of a training program that is not intended to hurt him and will end at some foreseeable time. But the physicians and psychologists at the CIA familiar with the facts

---

[54] We emphasize that physical suffering differs from physical pain in this respect. Physical pain may be "severe" even if lasting only seconds; whereas, by contrast, physical distress may amount to "severe physical suffering" only if it is severe both in intensity and duration.

[55] As with sleep deprivation, the particular condition of the individual detainee must be monitored so that, with extended or repeated use of the technique, the detainee's experience does not depart from these expectations.

[56] It is unclear whether a detainee being subjected to the waterboard in fact experiences it as a "threat of imminent death." We understand that the CIA may inform a detainee on whom this technique is used that he would not be allowed to drown. Moreover, after multiple applications of the waterboard, it may become apparent to the detainee that, however frightening the experience may be, it will not result in death. Nevertheless, for purposes of our analysis, we will assume that the physiological sensation of drowning associated with the use of the waterboard may constitute a "threat of imminent death" within the meaning of sections 2340-2340A.

have informed us that in the case of the two detainees who have been subjected to more extensive use of the waterboard technique, no evidence of prolonged mental harm has appeared in the period since the use of the waterboard on those detainees, a period which now spans at least 25 months for each of these detainees. Moreover, in their professional judgment based on this experience and the admittedly different SERE experience, OMS officials inform us that they would not expect the waterboard to cause such harm. Nor do we believe that the distress accompanying use of the technique on five days in a 30-day period, in itself, could be the "prolonged mental harm" to which the statute refers. The technique may be designed to create fear at the time it is used on the detainee, so that the detainee will cooperate to avoid future sessions. Furthermore, we acknowledge that the term "prolonged" is imprecise. Nonetheless, without in any way minimizing the distress caused by this technique, we believe that the panic brought on by the waterboard during the very limited time it is actually administered, combined with any residual fear that may be experienced over a somewhat longer period, could not be said to amount to the "prolonged mental harm" that the statute covers.[57] For these reasons, we conclude that the authorized use of the waterboard by adequately trained interrogators could not reasonably be considered specifically intended to cause "prolonged mental harm." Again, however, we caution that the use of this technique calls for the most careful adherence to the limitations and safeguards imposed, including constant monitoring by both medical and psychological personnel of any detainee who is subjected to the waterboard.

---

[57] In *Hilao v. Estate of Marcos*, the Ninth Circuit stated that a course of conduct involving a number of techniques, one of which has similarities to the waterboard, constituted torture. The court described the course of conduct as follows:

> He was then interrogated by members of the military, who blindfolded and severely beat him while he was handcuffed and fettered; they also threatened him with death. When this round of interrogation ended, he was denied sleep and repeatedly threatened with death. In the next round of interrogation, all of his limbs were shackled to a cot and a towel was placed over his nose and mouth; his interrogators then poured water down his nostrils so that he felt as though he were drowning. This lasted for approximately six hours, during which time interrogators threatened [him] with electric shock and death. At the end of this water torture, [he] was left shackled to the cot for the following three days, during which time he was repeatedly interrogated. He was then imprisoned for seven months in a suffocatingly hot and unlit cell, measuring 2.5 meters square; during this time he was shackled to his cot, at first by all his limbs and later by one hand and one foot, for all but the briefest periods (in which he was allowed to eat or use the toilet). The handcuffs were often so tight that the slightest movement ... made them cut into his flesh. During this period, he felt 'extreme pain, almost undescribable, the boredom' and 'the feeling that tons of lead ... were falling on [his] brain. [He] was never told how long the treatment inflicted upon him would last. After his seven months shackled to his cot, [he] spent more than eight years in detention, approximately five of them in solitary confinement and the rest in near-solitary confinement.

103 F.3d at 790-91. The court then concluded, "it seems clear that all of the abuses to which [a plaintiff] testified—including the eight years during which he was held in solitary or near-solitary confinement—constituted a single course of conduct of torture." *Id.* at 795. In addition to the obvious differences between the technique in *Hilao* and the CIA's use of the waterboard subject to the careful limits described above (among other things, in *Hilao* the session lasted six hours and followed explicit threats of death and severe physical beatings), the court reached no conclusion that the technique by itself constituted torture. However, the fact that a federal appellate court would even colloquially describe a technique that may share some of the characteristics of the waterboard as "water torture" counsels continued care and careful monitoring in the use of this technique.

TOP SECRET/_____/NOFORN

Even if the occurrence of one of the predicate acts could, depending on the circumstances of a particular case, give rise to an inference of intent to cause "prolonged mental harm," no such circumstances exist here. On the contrary, experience with the use of the waterboard indicates that prolonged mental harm would not be expected to occur, and CIA's use of the technique is subject to a variety of safeguards, discussed above, designed to ensure that prolonged mental harm does not result. Therefore, the circumstances here would negate any potential inference of specific intent to cause such harm.

Assuming adherence to the strict limitations discussed herein, including the careful medical monitoring and available intervention by the team as necessary, we conclude that although the question is substantial and difficult, the authorized use of the waterboard by adequately trained interrogators and other team members could not reasonably be considered specifically intended to cause severe physical or mental pain or suffering and thus would not violate sections 2340-2340A.[58]

* * *

In sum, based on the information you have provided and the limitations, procedures, and safeguards that would be in place, we conclude that—although extended sleep deprivation and use of the waterboard present more substantial questions in certain respects under the statute and the use of the waterboard raises the most substantial issue—none of these specific techniques, considered individually, would violate the prohibition in sections 2340-2340A. The universal rejection of torture and the President's unequivocal directive that the United States not engage in torture warrant great care in analyzing whether particular interrogation techniques are consistent with the requirements of sections 2340-2340A, and we have attempted to employ such care throughout our analysis. We emphasize that these are issues about which reasonable persons may disagree. Our task has been made more difficult by the imprecision of the statute and the relative absence of judicial guidance, but we have applied our best reading of the law to the specific facts that you have provided. As is apparent, our conclusion is based on the assumption that close observation, including medical and psychological monitoring of the detainees, will continue during the period when these techniques are used; that the personnel present are authorized to, and will, stop the use of a technique at any time if they believe it is being used improperly or threatens a detainee's safety or that a detainee may be at risk of suffering severe physical or mental pain or suffering; that the medical and psychological personnel are continually assessing the available literature and ongoing experience with detainees, and that, as they have done to date, they will make adjustments to techniques to ensure that they do not cause severe physical or mental pain or suffering to the detainees; and that all interrogators and other team members understand the proper use of the techniques, that the techniques are not designed

---

[58] As noted, medical personnel are instructed to exercise special care in monitoring and reporting on use of the waterboard. *See OMS Guidelines* at 20 ("NOTE: In order to best inform future medical judgments and recommendations, it is important that every application of the waterboard be thoroughly documented: how long each application (and the entire procedure) lasted, how much water was used in the process (realizing that much splashes off), how exactly the water was applied, if a seal was achieved, if the naso- or oropharynx was filled, what sort of volume was expelled, how long was the break between applications, and how the subject looked between each treatment.") (emphasis omitted).

TOP SECRET/_____/NOFORN

TOP SECRET / NOFORN

or intended to cause severe physical or mental pain or suffering, and that they must cooperate with OMS personnel in the exercise of their important duties.

Please let us know if we may be of further assistance.

Steven G. Bradbury
Steven G. Bradbury
Principal Deputy Assistant Attorney General

MEMO THREE

DATED MAY 10, 2005, FROM STEVEN BRADBURY, ACTING ASSISTANT ATTORNEY GENERAL, OLC, TO JOHN A. RIZZO, GENERAL COUNSEL CIA

U.S. Department of Justice

Office of Legal Counsel

Office of the Principal Deputy Assistant Attorney General   Washington, D.C. 20530

May 10, 2005

MEMORANDUM FOR JOHN A. RIZZO
SENIOR DEPUTY GENERAL COUNSEL, CENTRAL INTELLIGENCE AGENCY

Re: Application of 18 U.S.C. §§ 2340-2340A to the Combined Use of Certain Techniques in the Interrogation of High Value al Qaeda Detainees

In our Memorandum for John A. Rizzo, Senior Deputy General Counsel, Central Intelligence Agency, from Steven G. Bradbury, Principal Deputy Assistant Attorney General, Office of Legal Counsel, *Re: Application of 18 U.S.C. §§ 2340-2340A to Certain Techniques That May Be Used in the Interrogation of a High Value al Qaeda Detainee* (May 10, 2005) ("*Techniques*"), we addressed the application of the anti-torture statute, 18 U.S.C. §§ 2340-2340A, to certain interrogation techniques that the CIA might use in the questioning of a specific al Qaeda operative. There, we considered each technique individually. We now consider the application of the statute to the use of these same techniques in combination. Subject to the conditions and limitations set out here and in *Techniques*, we conclude that the authorized combined use of these specific techniques by adequately trained interrogators would not violate sections 2340-2340A.

Techniques, which set out our general interpretation of the statutory elements, guides us here.[1] While referring to the analysis provided in that opinion, we do not repeat it, but instead

---

[1] As noted in *Techniques*, the Criminal Division of the Department of Justice is satisfied that our general interpretation of the legal standards under sections 2340-2340A, found in *Techniques*, is consistent with its concurrence in our Memorandum for James B. Comey, Deputy Attorney General, from Daniel Levin, Acting Assistant Attorney General, Office of Legal Counsel, *Re: Legal Standards Applicable Under 18 U.S.C. §§ 2340-2340A* (Dec. 30, 2004). In the present memorandum, we address only the application of 18 U.S.C. §§ 2340-2340A to combinations of interrogation techniques. Nothing in this memorandum or in our prior advice to the CIA should be read to suggest that the use of these techniques would conform to the requirements of the Uniform Code of Military Justice that governs members of the Armed Forces or to United States obligations under the Geneva Conventions in circumstances where those Conventions would apply. We do not address the possible application of article 16 of the United Nations Convention Against Torture and Other Cruel, Inhuman or Degrading Treatment or Punishment, Dec. 10, 1984, S. Treaty Doc. 100-20, 1465 U.N.T.S. 85 (entered into force for U.S. Nov. 20,

presume a familiarity with it. Furthermore, in referring to the individual interrogation techniques whose combined use is our present subject, we mean those techniques as we described them in *Techniques*, including all of the limitations, presumptions, and safeguards described there.

One overarching point from *Techniques* bears repeating: Torture is abhorrent and universally repudiated, *see Techniques* at 1, and the President has stated that the United States will not tolerate it. *Id.* at 1-2 & n.2 (citing Statement on United Nations International Day in Support of Victims of Torture, 40 Weekly Comp. Pres. Doc. 1167-68 (July 5, 2004)). In *Techniques*, we accordingly exercised great care in applying sections 2340-2340A to the individual techniques at issue; we apply the same degree of care in considering the combined use of these techniques.

I.

Under 18 U.S.C. § 2340A, it is a crime to commit, attempt to commit, or conspire to commit torture outside the United States. "Torture" is defined as "an act committed by a person acting under color of law specifically intended to inflict severe physical or mental pain or suffering (other than pain or suffering incidental to lawful sanctions) upon another person within his custody or physical control." 18 U.S.C. § 2340(1). "Severe mental pain or suffering" is defined as "the prolonged mental harm caused by or resulting from" any of four predicate acts. *Id.* § 2340(2). These acts are (1) "the intentional infliction or threatened infliction of severe physical pain or suffering"; (2) "the administration or application, or threatened administration or application, of mind-altering substances or other procedures calculated to disrupt profoundly the senses or the personality"; (3) "the threat of imminent death"; and (4) "the threat that another person will imminently be subjected to death, severe physical pain or suffering, or the administration or application of mind-altering substances or other procedures calculated to disrupt profoundly the senses or personality."

In *Techniques*, we concluded that the individual authorized use of several specific interrogation techniques, subject to a variety of limitations and safeguards, would not violate the statute when employed in the interrogation of a specific member of al Qaeda, though we concluded that at least in certain respects two of the techniques presented substantial questions under sections 2340-2340A. The techniques that we analyzed were dietary manipulation, nudity, the attention grasp, walling, the facial hold, the facial slap or insult slap, the abdominal slap, cramped confinement, wall standing, stress positions, water dousing, extended sleep deprivation, and the "waterboard." *Techniques* at 7-15.

1994), nor do we address any question relating to conditions of confinement or detention, as distinct from the interrogation of detainees. We stress that our advice on the application of sections 2340-2340A does not represent the policy views of the Department of Justice concerning interrogation practices. Finally, we note that section 6057(a) of H.R. 1268 (109th Cong. 1st Sess.), if it becomes law, would forbid expending or obligating funds made available by that bill "to subject any person in the custody or under the physical control of the United States to torture," but because the bill would define "torture" to have "the meaning given that term in section 2340(1) of title 18, United States Code," § 6057(b)(1), the provision (to the extent it might apply here at all) would merely reaffirm the preexisting prohibitions on torture in sections 2340-2340A.

techniques analyzed only the use of these techniques individually. As we have previously advised, however, "courts tend to take a totality-of-the-circumstances approach and consider an entire course of conduct to determine whether torture has occurred." Memorandum for John Rizzo, Acting General Counsel, Central Intelligence Agency, from Jay S. Bybee, Assistant Attorney General, Office of Legal Counsel, Re: Interrogation of al Qaeda Operative at 9 (Aug. 1, 2002) ("*Interrogation Memorandum*") (TS). A complete analysis under sections 2340-2340A thus entails an examination of the combined effects of any techniques that might be used.

In conducting this analysis, there are two additional areas of general concern. First, it is possible that the application of certain techniques might render the detainee unusually susceptible to physical or mental pain or suffering. If that were the case, use of a second technique that would not ordinarily be expected to—and could not reasonably be considered specifically intended to—cause severe physical or mental pain or suffering by itself might in fact cause severe physical or mental pain or suffering because of the enhanced susceptibility created by the first technique. Depending on the circumstances, and the knowledge and mental state of the interrogator, one might conclude that severe pain or suffering was specifically intended by the application of the second technique to a detainee who was particularly vulnerable because of the application of the first technique. Because the use of these techniques in combination is intended to, and in fact can be expected to, physically wear down a detainee, because it is difficult to assess as to a particular individual whether the application of multiple techniques renders that individual more susceptible to physical pain or suffering, and because sleep deprivation, in particular, has a number of documented physiological effects that, in some circumstances, could be problematic it is important that all participating CIA personnel, particularly interrogators and personnel of the CIA Office of Medical Services ("OMS"), be aware of the potential for enhanced susceptibility to pain and suffering from each interrogation technique. We also assume that there will be active and ongoing monitoring by medical and psychological personnel of each detainee who is undergoing a regimen of interrogation, and active intervention by a member of the team or medical staff as necessary, so as to avoid the possibility of severe physical or mental pain or suffering within the meaning of 18 U.S.C. §§ 2340-2340A as a result of such combined effects.

Second, it is possible that certain techniques that do not themselves cause severe physical or mental pain or suffering might do so in combination, particularly when used over the 30-day interrogation period with which we deal here. Again, depending on the circumstances, and the mental state of the interrogator, their use might be considered to be specifically intended to cause such severe pain or suffering. This concern calls for an inquiry into the totality of the circumstances, looking at which techniques are combined and how they are combined.

Your office has outlined the manner in which many of the individual techniques we previously considered could be combined in *Background Paper on CIA's Combined Use of Interrogation Techniques* (undated, but transmitted Dec. 30, 2004) ("*Background Paper*"). The *Background Paper*, which provides the principal basis for our analysis, first divides the process of interrogation into three phases: "Initial Conditions," "Transition to Interrogation," and "Interrogation." *Id.* at 1. After describing these three phases, *see id.* at 1-9, the *Background Paper* "provides a look at a prototypical interrogation with an emphasis on the application of

TOP SECRET/ NOFORN

interrogation techniques, in combination and separately," *id.* at 9-18. The *Background Paper* does not include any discussion of the waterboard; however, you have separately provided to us a description of how the waterboard may be used in combination with other techniques, particularly dietary manipulation and sleep deprivation. *See* Fax for Steven G. Bradbury, Principal Deputy Assistant Attorney General, Office of Legal Counsel, from ▓▓▓▓▓▓ Assistant General Counsel, CIA, at 3-4 (Apr. 22, 2005) ("*April 22* ▓▓▓ *Fax*").

Phases of the Interrogation Process

The first phase of the interrogation process, "Initial Conditions," does not involve interrogation techniques, and you have not asked us to consider any legal question regarding the CIA's practices during this phase. The "Initial Conditions" nonetheless set the stage for use of the interrogation techniques, which come later.[2]

According to the *Background Paper*, before being flown to the site of interrogation, a detainee is given a medical examination. He then is "securely shackled and is deprived of sight and sound through the use of blindfolds, earmuffs, and hoods" during the flight. *Id.* at 2. An on-board medical officer monitors his condition. Security personnel also monitor the detainee for signs of distress. Upon arrival at the site, the detainee "finds himself in complete control of Americans" and is subjected to "precise, quiet, and almost clinical" procedures designed to underscore "the enormity and suddenness of the change in environment, the uncertainty about what will happen next, and the potential dread [a detainee] may have of US custody." *Id.* His head and face are shaved; his physical condition is documented through photographs taken while he is nude; and he is given medical and psychological interviews to assess his condition and to make sure there are no contraindications to the use of any particular interrogation techniques. *See Id.* at 2-3.

The detainee then enters the next phase, the "Transition to Interrogation." The interrogators conduct an initial interview, "in a relatively benign environment," to ascertain whether the detainee is willing to cooperate. The detainee is "normally clothed but seated and shackled for security purposes." *Id.* at 3. The interrogators take "an open, non-threatening approach," but the detainee "would have to provide information on actionable threats and location information on High-Value Targets at large—not lower-level information—for interrogators to continue with [this] neutral approach." *Id.* If the detainee does not meet this "very high" standard, the interrogators submit a detailed interrogation plan to CIA headquarters

---

[2] Although the *OMS Guidelines on Medical and Psychological Support to Detainee Rendition, Interrogation and Detention* (Dec. 2004) ("*OMS Guidelines*") refer to the administration of sedatives during transport if necessary to protect the detainee or the rendition team, *id.* at 4-5, the *OMS Guidelines* do not provide for the use of sedatives for interrogation. The *Background Paper* does not mention the administration of any drugs during the detainee's transportation to the site of the interrogation or at any other time, and we do not address any such administration. OMS, we understand, is unaware of any use of sedation during the transport of a detainee in the last two years and states that the interrogation program does not use sedation or medication for the purpose of interrogation. We caution that any use of sedatives should be carefully evaluated, including under 18 U.S.C. § 2340(2)(B). For purposes of our analysis, we assume that no drugs are administered during the relevant period or that there are no ongoing effects from any administration of any drugs; if that assumption does not hold, our analysis and conclusions could change.

TOP SECRET/ NOFORN

TOP SECRET/~~█~~/NOFORN

for approval. If the medical and psychological assessments find no contraindications to the proposed plan, and if senior CIA officers at headquarters approve some or all of the plan through a cable transmitted to the site of the interrogation, the interrogation moves to the next phase. *Id.*[3]

Three interrogation techniques are typically used to bring the detainee to "a baseline, dependent state," "demonstrat[ing] to the [detainee] that he has no control over basic human needs" and helping to make him "perceive and value his personal welfare, comfort, and immediate needs more than the information he is protecting." *Id.* at 4. The three techniques used to establish this "baseline" are nudity, sleep deprivation (with shackling and, at least at times, with use of a diaper), and dietary manipulation. These techniques, which *Techniques* described in some detail, "require little to no physical interaction between the detainee and interrogator." *Background Paper* at 5.

Other techniques, which "require physical interaction between the interrogator and detainee," are characterized as "corrective" and "are used principally to correct, startle, or ... achieve another enabling objective with the detainee." *Id.* These techniques "are not used simultaneously but are often used interchangeably during an individual interrogation session." *Id.* The insult slap is used "periodically throughout the interrogation process when the interrogator needs to immediately correct the detainee or provide a consequence to a detainee's response or non-response." *Id.* at 5-6. The insult slap "can be used in combination with water dousing or kneeling stress positions"—techniques that are not characterized as "corrective." *Id.* at 6. Another corrective technique, the abdominal slap, "is similar to the insult slap in application and desired result" and "provides the variation necessary to keep a high level of unpredictability in the interrogation process." *Id.* The abdominal slap may be simultaneously combined with water dousing, stress positions, and wall standing. A third corrective technique, the facial hold, "is used sparingly throughout interrogation." *Id.* It is not painful, but "demonstrates the interrogator's control over the [detainee]." *Id.* It too may be simultaneously combined with water dousing, stress positions, and wall standing. *Id.* Finally, the attention grasp "may be used several times in the same interrogation" and may be simultaneously combined with water dousing or kneeling stress positions. *Id.*

Some techniques are characterized as "coercive." These techniques "place the detainee in more physical and psychological stress." *Id.* at 7. Coercive techniques "are typically not used

---

[3] The CIA maintains certain "detention conditions" at all of its detention facilities. (These conditions "are not interrogation techniques," *Id.* at 4, and you have not asked us to assess their lawfulness under the statute.) The detainee is "exposed to white noise/loud sounds (not to exceed 79 decibels) and constant light during portions of the interrogation process." *Id.* These conditions enhance security. The noise prevents the detainee from overhearing conversations of staff members, precludes him from picking up "auditory clues" about his surroundings, and disrupts any efforts to communicate with other detainees. *Id.* The light provides better conditions for security and for monitoring by the medical and psychological staff and the interrogators. Although we do not address the lawfulness of using white noise (not to exceed 79 decibels) and constant light, we note that according to materials you have furnished to us, (1) the Occupational Safety and Health Administration has determined that there is no risk of permanent hearing loss from continuous, 24-hour per day exposure to noise of up to 82 decibels, and (2) detainees typically adapt fairly quickly to the constant light and it does not interfere unduly with their ability to sleep. *See* Fax for Dan Levin, Acting Assistant Attorney General, Office of Legal Counsel, from ~~█~~ Assistant General Counsel, Central Intelligence Agency at 3 (Jan. 4, 2005) ("~~█~~ Fax").

in combination, although some combined use is possible." *Id.* Walling "is one of the most effective interrogation techniques because it wears down the [detainee] physically, heightens uncertainty in the detainee about what the interrogator may do to him, and creates a sense of dread when the [detainee] knows he is about to be walled again." *Id.*[4] A detainee "may be walled one time (one impact with the wall) to make a point or twenty to thirty times consecutively when the interrogator requires a more significant response to a question," and "will be walled multiple times" during a session designed to be intense. *Id.* Walling cannot practically be used at the same time as other interrogation techniques.

Water temperature and other considerations of safety established by OMS limit the use of another coercive technique, water dousing. *See id.* at 7-8. The technique "may be used frequently within those guidelines." *Id.* at 8. As suggested above, interrogators may combine water dousing with other techniques, such as stress positions, wall standing, the insult slap, or the abdominal slap. *See id.* at 8.

The use of stress positions is "usually self-limiting in that temporary muscle fatigue usually leads to the [detainee's] being unable to maintain the stress position after a period of time." *Id.* Depending on the particular position, stress positions may be combined with water dousing, the insult slap, the facial hold, and the attention grasp. *See id.* Another coercive technique, wall standing, is "usually self-limiting" in the same way as stress positions. *Id.* It may be combined with water dousing and the abdominal slap. *See id.* OMS guidelines limit the technique of cramped confinement to no more than eight hours at a time and 18 hours a day, and confinement in the "small box" is limited to two hours. *Id.* Cramped confinement cannot be used in simultaneous combination with corrective or other coercive techniques.

We understand that the CIA's use of all these interrogation techniques is subject to ongoing monitoring by interrogation team members who will direct that techniques be discontinued if there is a deviation from prescribed procedures and by medical and psychological personnel from OMS who will direct that any or all techniques be discontinued if in their professional judgment the detainee may otherwise suffer severe physical or mental pain or suffering. *See Techniques* at 6-7.

A Prototypical Interrogation

In a "prototypical interrogation," the detainee begins his first interrogation session stripped of his clothes, shackled, and hooded, with the walling collar over his head and around

---

[4] Although walling "wears down the [detainee] physically," *Background Paper* at 7, and undoubtedly may startle him, we understand that it is not significantly painful. The detainee hits "a flexible false wall," designed to create a loud sound when the individual hits it" and thus to cause "shock and surprise." *Interrogation Memorandum* at 2. But the detainee's "head and neck are supported with a rolled hood or towel that provides a c-collar effect to help prevent whiplash"; it is the detainee's shoulder blades that hit the wall; and the detainee is allowed to rebound from the flexible wall in order to reduce the chances of any injury. *See id.* You have informed us that a detainee is expected to feel "dread" at the prospect of walling because of the shock and surprise caused by the technique and because of the sense of powerlessness that comes from being roughly handled by the interrogators, not because the technique causes significant pain.

his neck. *Background Paper* at 9-10. The interrogators remove the hood and explain that the detainee can improve his situation by cooperating and may say that the interrogators "will do what it takes to get important information." *Id.*[5] As soon as the detainee does anything inconsistent with the interrogators' instructions, the interrogators use an insult slap or abdominal slap. They employ walling if it becomes clear that the detainee is not cooperating in the interrogation. This sequence "may continue for several more iterations as the interrogators continue to measure the [detainee's] resistance posture and apply a negative consequence to [his] resistance efforts." *Id.* The interrogators and security officers then put the detainee into position for standing sleep deprivation, begin dietary manipulation through a liquid diet, and keep the detainee nude (except for a diaper). *See id.* at 10-11. The first interrogation session, which could have lasted from 30 minutes to several hours, would then be at an end. *See id.* at 11.

If the interrogation team determines there is a need to continue, and if the medical and psychological personnel advise that there are no contraindications, a second session may begin. *See id.* at 12. The interval between sessions could be as short as an hour or as long as 24 hours. *See id.* at 11. At the start of the second session, the detainee is released from the position for standing sleep deprivation, is hooded, and is positioned against the walling wall, with the walling collar over his head and around his neck. *See id.* Even before removing the hood, the interrogators use the attention grasp to startle the detainee. The interrogators take off the hood and begin questioning. If the detainee does not give appropriate answers to the first questions, the interrogators use an insult slap or abdominal slap. *See id.* They employ walling if they determine that the detainee "is intent on maintaining his resistance posture." *Id.* at 13. This sequence "may continue for multiple iterations as the interrogators continue to measure the [detainee's] resistance posture." *Id.* The interrogators then increase the pressure on the detainee by using a hose to douse the detainee with water for several minutes. They stop and start the dousing as they continue the interrogation. *See id.* They then end the session by placing the detainee into the same circumstances as at the end of the first session: the detainee is in the standing position for sleep deprivation, is nude (except for a diaper), and is subjected to dietary manipulation. Once again, the session could have lasted from 30 minutes to several hours. *See id.*

Again, if the interrogation team determines there is a need to continue, and if the medical and psychological personnel find no contraindications, a third session may follow. The session begins with the detainee positioned as at the beginning of the second. *See id.* at 14. If the detainee continues to resist, the interrogators continue to use walling and water dousing. The corrective techniques—the insult slap, the abdominal slap, the facial hold, the attention grasp—"may be used several times during this session based on the responses and actions of the [detainee]." *Id.* The interrogators integrate stress positions and wall standing into the session. Furthermore, "[i]ntense questioning and walling would be repeated multiple times." *Id.* Interrogators "use one technique to support another." *Id.* For example, they threaten the use of walling unless the detainee holds a stress position, thus inducing the detainee to remain in the position longer than he otherwise would. At the end of the session, the interrogators and security

---

[5] We address the effects of this statement below at pp. 18-19.

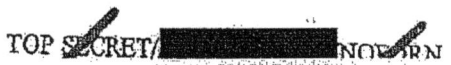

personnel place the detainee into the same circumstances as at the end of the first two sessions, with the detainee subject to sleep deprivation, nudity, and dietary manipulation. *Id.*

In later sessions, the interrogators use those techniques that are proving most effective and drop the others. Sleep deprivation "may continue to the 70 to 120 hour range, or possibly beyond for the hardest resisters, but in no case exceed the 180-hour time limit." *Id.* at 15.[6] If the medical or psychological personnel find contraindications, sleep deprivation will end earlier. *See id.* at 15-16. While continuing the use of sleep deprivation, nudity, and dietary manipulation, the interrogators may add cramped confinement. As the detainee begins to cooperate, the interrogators "begin gradually to decrease the use of interrogation techniques." *Id.* at 16. They may permit the detainee to sit, supply clothes, and provide more appetizing food. *See id.*

The entire process in this "prototypical interrogation" may last 30 days. If additional time is required and a new approval is obtained from headquarters, interrogation may go longer than 30 days. Nevertheless, "[o]n average, the actual use of interrogation techniques covers a period of three to seven days, but can vary upwards to fifteen days based on the resilience of the [detainee]." *Id.* As in *Techniques*, our advice here is limited to an interrogation process lasting no more than 30 days. *See Techniques* at 5.

Use of the Waterboard in Combination with Other Techniques

We understand that for a small number of detainees in very limited circumstances, the CIA may wish to use the waterboard technique. You have previously explained that the waterboard technique would be used only if: (1) the CIA has credible intelligence that a terrorist attack is imminent; (2) there are "substantial and credible indicators the subject has actionable intelligence that can prevent, disrupt or delay this attack"; and (3) other interrogation methods have failed or are unlikely to yield actionable intelligence in time to prevent the attack. *See* Attachment to Letter from John A. Rizzo, Acting General Counsel, CIA, to Daniel Levin, Acting Assistant Attorney General, Office of Legal Counsel (Aug. 2, 2004). You have also informed us that the waterboard may be approved for use with a given detainee only during, at most, one single 30-day period, and that during that period, the waterboard technique may be used on no more than five days. We further understand that in any 24-hour period, interrogators may use no more than two "sessions" of the waterboard on a subject—with a "session" defined to mean the time that the detainee is strapped to the waterboard—and that no session may last more than two hours. Moreover, during any session, the number of individual applications of water lasting 10 seconds or longer may not exceed six. The maximum length of any application of water is 40 seconds (you have informed us that this maximum has rarely been reached). Finally, the total cumulative time of all applications of whatever length in a 24-hour period may not exceed 12 minutes. *See* Letter from ▓▓▓▓▓▓▓▓▓▓▓▓▓▓▓▓ Associate General Counsel, CIA, to Dan Levin, Acting Assistant Attorney General, Office of Legal Counsel, at 1-2 (Aug. 19, 2004).

---

[6] As in *Techniques*, our advice here is restricted to one application of no more than 180 hours of sleep deprivation.

You have advised us that in those limited cases where the waterboard would be used, it would be used only in direct combination with two other techniques, dietary manipulation and sleep deprivation. *See April 22* ▓ *Fax* at 3-4. While an individual is physically on the waterboard, the CIA does not use the attention grasp, walling, the facial hold, the facial or insult slap, the abdominal slap, cramped confinement, wall standing, stress positions, or water dousing, though some or all of these techniques may be used with the individual before the CIA needs to resort to the waterboard, and we understand it is possible that one or more of these techniques might be used on the same day as a waterboard session, but separately from that session and not in conjunction with the waterboard. *See id.* at 3.

As we discussed in *Techniques*, you have informed us that an individual undergoing the waterboard is always placed on a fluid diet before he may be subjected to the waterboard in order to avoid aspiration of food matter. The individual is kept on the fluid diet throughout the period the waterboard is used. For this reason, and in this way, the waterboard is used in combination with dietary manipulation. *See April 22* ▓ *Fax* at 3.

You have also described how sleep deprivation may be used prior to and during the waterboard session. *Id.* at 4. We understand that the time limitation on use of sleep deprivation, as set forth in *Techniques*, continues to be strictly monitored and enforced when sleep deprivation is used in combination with the waterboard (as it is when used in combination with other techniques). *See April 22* ▓ *Fax* at 4. You have also informed us that there is no evidence in literature or experience that sleep deprivation exacerbates any harmful effects of the waterboard, though it does reduce the detainee's will to resist and thereby contributes to the effectiveness of the waterboard as an interrogation technique. *Id.* As in *Techniques*, we understand that in the event the detainee were perceived to be unable to withstand the effects of the waterboard for any reason, any member of the interrogation team has the obligation to intervene and, if necessary, to halt the use of the waterboard. *See April 22* ▓ *Fax* at 4.

II.

The issue of the combined effects of interrogation techniques raises complex and difficult questions and comes to us in a less precisely defined form than the questions treated in our earlier opinions about individual techniques. In evaluating individual techniques, we turned to a body of experience developed in the use of analogous techniques in military training by the United States, to medical literature, and to the judgment of medical personnel. Because there is less certainty and definition about the use of techniques in combination, it is necessary to draw more inferences in assessing what may be expected. You have informed us that, although "the exemplar [that is, the prototypical interrogation] is a fair representation of how these techniques are actually employed," "there is no template or script that states with certainty when and how these techniques will be used in combination during interrogation." *Background Paper* at 17. Whether any other combination of techniques would, in the relevant senses, be like the ones presented—whether the combination would be no more likely to cause severe physical or mental pain or suffering within the meaning of sections 2340-2340A—would be a question that cannot be assessed in the context of the present legal opinion. For that reason, our advice does not extend to combinations of techniques unlike the ones discussed here. For the same reason, it is especially important that the CIA use great care in applying these various techniques in

TOP SECRET/~~████~~/NOFORN

combination in a real-world scenario, and that the members of the interrogation team, and the attendant medical staff, remain watchful for indications that the use of techniques in combination may be having unintended effects, so that the interrogation regimen may be altered or halted, if necessary, to ensure that it will not result in severe physical or mental pain or suffering to any detainee in violation of 18 U.S.C. §§ 2340-2340A.

Finally, in both of our previous opinions about specific techniques, we evaluated the use of those techniques on particular identified individuals. Here, we are asked to address the combinations without reference to any particular detainee. As is relevant here, we know only that an enhanced interrogation technique, such as most of the techniques at issue in *Techniques*, may be used on a detainee only if medical and psychological personnel have determined that he is not likely, as a result, to experience severe physical or mental pain or suffering. *Techniques* at 5. Once again, whether other detainees would, in the relevant ways, be like the ones previously at issue would be a factual question we cannot now decide. Our advice, therefore, does not extend to the use of techniques on detainees unlike those we have previously considered. Moreover, in this regard, it is also especially important, as we pointed out in *Techniques* with respect to certain techniques, *see, e.g., id.* at 37 (discussing sleep deprivation), that the CIA will carefully assess the condition of each individual detainee and that the CIA's use of these techniques in combination will be sensitive to the individualized physical condition and reactions of each detainee, so that the regimen of interrogation would be altered or halted, if necessary, in the event of unanticipated effects on a particular detainee.

Subject to these cautions and to the conditions, limitations, and safeguards set out below and in *Techniques*, we nonetheless can reach some conclusions about the combined use of these techniques. Although this is a difficult question that will depend on the particular detainee, we do not believe that the use of the techniques in combination as you have described them would be expected to inflict "severe physical or mental pain or suffering" within the meaning of the statute. 18 U.S.C. § 2340(1). Although the combination of interrogation techniques will wear a detainee down physically, we understand that the principal effect, as well as the primary goal, of interrogation using these techniques is psychological—"to create a state of learned helplessness and dependence conducive to the collection of intelligence in a predictable, reliable, and sustainable manner," *Background Paper* at 1—and numerous precautions are designed to avoid inflicting "severe physical or mental pain or suffering."

For present purposes, we may divide "severe physical or mental pain or suffering" into three categories: "severe physical . . . pain," "severe physical . . . suffering," and "severe . . . mental pain or suffering" (the last being a defined term under the statute). *See Techniques* at 22-26; Memorandum for James B. Comey, Deputy Attorney General, from Daniel Levin, Acting Assistant Attorney General, Office of Legal Counsel, *Re: Legal Standards Applicable Under 18 U.S.C. §§ 2340-2340A* (Dec. 30, 2004).

As explained below, any physical pain resulting from the use of these techniques, even in combination, cannot reasonably be expected to meet the level of "severe physical pain" contemplated by the statute. We conclude, therefore, that the authorized use in combination of these techniques by adequately trained interrogators, as described in the *Background Paper* and the *April 22* ~~████~~ *Fax*, could not reasonably be considered specifically intended to do so.

TOP SECRET/~~████~~/NOFORN

TOP SECRET/NOFORN

Moreover, although it presents a closer question under sections 2340-2340A, we conclude that the combined use of these techniques also cannot reasonably be expected to—and their combined use in the authorized manner by adequately trained interrogators could not reasonably be considered specifically intended to—cause severe physical suffering. Although two techniques, extended sleep deprivation and the waterboard, may involve a more substantial risk of physical distress, nothing in the other specific techniques discussed in the *Background Paper* and the *April 22 ▓▓ Fax*, or, as we understand it, in the CIA's experience to date with the interrogations of more than two dozen detainees (three of whose interrogations involved the use of the waterboard), would lead to the expectation that any physical discomfort from the combination of sleep deprivation or the waterboard and other techniques would involve the degree of intensity and duration of physical distress sufficient to constitute severe physical suffering under the statute. Therefore, the use of the technique could not reasonably be viewed as specifically intended to cause severe physical suffering. We stress again, however, that these questions concerning whether the combined effects of different techniques may rise to the level of physical suffering within the meaning of sections 2340-2340A are difficult ones, and they reinforce the need for close and ongoing monitoring by medical and psychological personnel and by all members of the interrogation team and active intervention if necessary.

Analyzing the combined techniques in terms of severe mental pain or suffering raises two questions under the statute. The first is whether the risk of hallucinations from sleep deprivation may become exacerbated when combined with other techniques, such that a detainee might be expected to experience "prolonged mental harm" from the combination of techniques. Second, the description in the *Background Paper* that detainees may be specifically told that interrogators will "do what it takes" to elicit information, *id.* at 10, raises the question whether this statement might qualify as a threat of infliction of severe physical pain or suffering or another of the predicate acts required for "severe mental pain or suffering" under the statute. After discussing both of those possibilities below, however, we conclude that the authorized use by adequately trained interrogators of the techniques in combination, as you have described them, would not reasonably be expected to cause prolonged mental harm and could not reasonably be considered specifically intended to cause severe mental pain or suffering. We stress that these possible questions about the combined use of the techniques under the statutory category of severe mental pain or suffering are difficult ones and they serve to reinforce the need for close and ongoing monitoring and active intervention if necessary.

Severe Physical Pain

Our two previous opinions have not identified any techniques that would inflict pain that approaches the "sever[ity]" required to violate the statute. A number of the techniques—dietary manipulation, nudity, sleep deprivation, the facial hold, and the attention grasp—are not expected to cause physical pain at all. *See Techniques* at 30-36. Others might cause some pain, but the level of pain would not approach that which would be considered "severe." These techniques are the abdominal slap, water dousing, various stress positions, wall standing, cramped confinement, walling, and the facial slap. *See Id.* We also understand that the waterboard is not physically painful. *Id.* at 41. In part because none of these techniques would individually cause pain that even approaches the "severe" level required to violate the statute, the combined use of the techniques under the conditions outlined here would not be expected to—

TOP SECRET/▓▓ NOFORN

TOP SECRET/ ████████ NOFORN

and we conclude that their authorized use by adequately trained interrogators could not reasonably be considered specifically intended to—reach that level.'

We recognize the theoretical possibility that the use of one or more techniques would make a detainee more susceptible to severe pain or that the techniques, in combination, would operate differently from the way they would individually and thus cause severe pain. But as we understand the experience involving the combination of various techniques, the OMS medical and psychological personnel have not observed any such increase in susceptibility. Other than the waterboard, the specific techniques under consideration in this memorandum—including sleep deprivation—have been applied to more than 25 detainees. See ████ Fax at 1-3. No apparent increase in susceptibility to severe pain has been observed either when techniques are used sequentially or when they are used simultaneously—for example, when an insult slap is simultaneously combined with water dousing or a kneeling stress position, or when wall standing is simultaneously combined with an abdominal slap and water dousing. Nor does experience show that, even apart from changes in susceptibility to pain, combinations of these techniques cause the techniques to operate differently so as to cause severe pain. OMS doctors and psychologists, moreover, confirm that they expect that the techniques, when combined as described in the *Background Paper* and in the *April 22* ████ *Fax*, would not operate in a different manner from the way they do individually, so as to cause severe pain.

We understand that experience supports these conclusions even though the *Background Paper* does give examples where the distress caused by one technique would be increased by use of another. The "conditioning techniques"—nudity, sleep deprivation, and dietary manipulation—appear designed to wear down the detainee, physically and psychologically, and to allow other techniques to be more effective, *see Background Paper* at 5, 12; *April 22* ████ *Fax* at 4; and "these [conditioning] techniques are used in combination in almost all cases," *Background Paper* at 17. And, in another example, the threat of walling is used to cause a detainee to hold a stress position longer than he otherwise would. *See id.* at 14. The issue raised by the statute, however, is whether the techniques would be specifically intended to cause the detainee to experience "severe . . . pain." 18 U.S.C. § 2340(1). In the case of the conditioning

---

¹ We are not suggesting that combinations or repetitions of acts that do not individually cause severe physical pain could not result in severe physical pain. Other than the repeated use of the "walling" technique, however, nothing in the *Background Paper* suggests the kind of repetition that might raise an issue about severe physical pain; and, in the case of walling, we understand that this technique involves a false, flexible wall and is not significantly painful, even with repetition. Our advice with respect to walling in the present memorandum is based on the understanding that the repetitive use of walling is intended only to increase the shock and drama of the technique, to wear down the detainee's resistance, and to disrupt expectations that he will not be treated with force, and that such use is not intended to, and does not in fact, cause severe physical pain to the detainee. Along these lines, we understand that the repeated use of the insult slap and the abdominal slap gradually reduces their effectiveness and that their use is therefore limited to times when the detainee's overt disrespect for the question or questioner requires immediate correction, when the detainee displays obvious efforts to misdirect or ignore the question or questioner, or when the detainee attempts to provide an obvious lie in response to a specific question. Our advice assumes that the interrogators will apply those techniques as designed and will not strike the detainee with excessive force or repetition in a manner that might result in severe physical pain. As to all techniques, our advice assumes that the use of the technique will be stopped if there is any indication that it is or may be causing severe physical pain to the detainee.

TOP SECRET/ ████████ NOFORN

techniques, the principal effect, as you have described it, is on the detainee's will to resist other techniques, rather than on the pain that the other techniques cause. *See Background Paper* at 5, 12; *April 22 [redacted] Fax* at 4. Moreover, the stress positions and wall standing, while inducing muscle fatigue, do not cause "severe physical . . . pain," and there is no reason to believe that a position, held somewhat longer than otherwise, would create such pain. *See Techniques* at 33-34.[8]

In any particular case, a combination of techniques might have unexpected results, just as an individual technique could produce surprising effects. But the *Background Paper* and the *April 22 [redacted] Fax*, as well as *Techniques*, describe a system of medical and psychological monitoring of the detainee that would very likely identify any such unexpected results as they begin to occur and would require an interrogation to be modified or stopped if a detainee is in danger of severe physical pain. Medical and psychological personnel assess the detainee before any interrogation starts. *See, e.g., Techniques* at 5. Physical and psychological evaluations are completed daily during any period in which the interrogators use enhanced techniques, including those at issue in *Techniques* (leaving aside dietary manipulation and sleep deprivation of less than 48 hours). *See id.* at 5-7. Medical and psychological personnel are on scene throughout the interrogation, and are physically present or are otherwise observing during many of the techniques. *See id.* at 6-7. These safeguards, which were critically important to our conclusions about individual techniques, are even more significant when techniques are combined.

In one specific context, monitoring the effects on detainees appears particularly important. The *Background Paper* and the *April 22 [redacted] Fax* illustrate that sleep deprivation is a central part of the "prototypical interrogation." We noted in *Techniques* that extended sleep deprivation may cause a small decline in body temperature and increased food consumption. *See Techniques* at 33-34. Water dousing and dietary manipulation and perhaps even nudity may thus raise dangers of enhanced susceptibility to hypothermia or other medical conditions for a detainee undergoing sleep deprivation. As in *Techniques*, we assume that medical personnel will be aware of these possible interactions and will monitor detainees closely for any signs that such interactions are developing. *See id.* at 33-35. This monitoring, along with quick intervention if any signs of problematic symptoms develop, can be expected to prevent a detainee from experiencing severe physical pain.

We also understand that some studies suggest that extended sleep deprivation may be associated with a reduced tolerance for some forms of pain.[9] Several of the techniques used by

---

[8] Our advice about wall standing and stress positions assumes that the positions used in each technique are not designed to produce severe pain that might result from contortions or twisting of the body, but only temporary muscle fatigue.

[9] For example, one study found a statistically significant drop of 8-9% in subjects' tolerance thresholds for mechanical or pressure pain after 40 hours of total sleep deprivation. *See* S. Hakki Onen, et al., *The Effects of Total Sleep Deprivation, Selective Sleep Interruption and Sleep Recovery on Pain Tolerance Thresholds in Healthy Subjects*, 10 J. Sleep Research 35, 41 (2001); *see also id.* at 35-36 (discussing other studies). Another study of extended total sleep deprivation found a significant decrease in the threshold for heat pain and some decrease in the cold pain threshold. *See* B. Kundermann, et al., *Sleep Deprivation Affects Thermal Pain Thresholds but not Somatosensory Thresholds in Healthy Volunteers*, 66 Psychosomatic Med. 932 (2004).

the CIA may involve a degree of physical pain, as we have previously noted, including facial and abdominal slaps, walling, stress positions, and water dousing. Nevertheless, none of these techniques would cause anything approaching severe physical pain. Because sleep deprivation appears to cause at most only relatively moderate decreases in pain tolerance, the use of these techniques in combination with extended sleep deprivation would not be expected to cause severe physical pain.

Therefore, the combined use of techniques, as set out in the *Background Paper* and the April 22 ▇▇▇ *Fax*, would not reasonably be expected by the interrogators to result in severe physical pain. We conclude that the authorized use of these techniques in combination by adequately trained interrogators, as you have described it, could not reasonably be considered specifically intended to cause such pain for purposes of sections 2340-2340A. The close monitoring of each detainee for any signs that he is at risk of experiencing severe physical pain reinforces the conclusion that the combined use of interrogation techniques is not intended to inflict such pain. OMS has directed that "[m]edical officers must remain cognizant at all times of their obligation to prevent 'severe physical or mental pain or suffering.'" *OMS Guidelines* at 10. The obligation of interrogation team members and medical staff to intercede if their observations indicate a detainee is at risk of experiencing severe physical pain, and the expectation that all interrogators understand the important role played by OMS and will cooperate with them in the exercise of this duty, are here, as in *Techniques*, essential to our advice. *See Techniques* at 14.

Severe Physical Suffering

We noted in *Techniques* that, although the statute covers a category of "severe physical ... suffering" distinct from "severe physical pain," this category encompasses only "physical distress that is 'severe' considering its intensity and duration or persistence, rather than merely mild or transitory." *Id.* at 23 (internal quotation marks omitted). Severe physical suffering for purposes of sections 2340-2340A, we have concluded, means a state or condition of physical distress, misery, affliction, or torment, usually involving physical pain, that is both extreme in intensity and significantly protracted in duration or persistent over time. *Id.* Severe physical suffering is distinguished from suffering that is purely mental or psychological in nature, since mental suffering is encompassed by the separately defined statutory category of "severe mental pain or suffering," discussed below. To amount to torture, conduct must be "sufficiently extreme and outrageous to warrant the universal condemnation that the term 'torture' both connotes and invokes." *See Price v. Socialist People's Libyan Arab Jamahiriya*, 294 F.3d 82, 92 (D.C. Cir. 2002) (interpreting the TVPA); *cf. Mehinovic v. Vuckovic*, 198 F. Supp. 2d 1322, 1332-40, 1345-46 (N.D. Ga. 2002) (standard met under the TVPA by a course of conduct that included severe beatings to the genitals, head, and other parts of the body with metal pipes and various other items; removal of teeth with pliers; kicking in the face and ribs; breaking of bones and ribs and dislocation of fingers; cutting a figure into the victim's forehead; hanging the victim and beating him; extreme limitations of food and water; and subjection to games of "Russian roulette").

In *Techniques*, we recognized that, depending on the physical condition and reactions of a given individual, extended sleep deprivation might cause physical distress in some cases. *Id.* at 34. Accordingly, we advised that the strict limitations and safeguards adopted by the CIA are

MEMO THREE: BRADBURY TO RIZO, MAY 10, 2005

TOP SECRET/ NOFORN

important to ensure that the use of extended sleep deprivation would not cause severe physical suffering. *Id.* at 34-35. We pointed to the close medical monitoring by OMS of each detainee subjected to sleep deprivation, as well as to the power of any member of the interrogation team or detention facility staff to intervene and, in particular, to intervention by OMS if OMS concludes in its medical judgment that the detainee may be experiencing extreme physical distress. With those safeguards in place, and based on the assumption that they would be strictly followed, we concluded that the authorized use of sleep deprivation by adequately trained interrogators could not reasonably be considered specifically intended to cause such severe physical suffering. *Id.* at 34. We pointed out that "[d]ifferent individual detainees may react physically to sleep deprivation in different ways," *id.*, and we assumed that the interrogation team and medical staff "will separately monitor each individual detainee who is undergoing sleep deprivation, and that the application of this technique will be sensitive to the individualized physical condition and reactions of each detainee." *Id.*

Although it is difficult to calculate the additional effect of combining other techniques with sleep deprivation, we do not believe that the addition of the other techniques as described in the *Background Paper* would result in "severe physical ... suffering." The other techniques do not themselves inflict severe physical pain. They are not of the intensity and duration that are necessary for "severe physical suffering"; instead, they only increase, over a short time, the discomfort that a detainee subjected to sleep deprivation experiences. They do not extend the time at which sleep deprivation would end, and although it is possible that the other techniques increase the physical discomfort associated with sleep deprivation itself, we cannot say that the effect would be so significant as to cause "physical distress that is 'severe' considering its intensity and duration or persistence." *Techniques* at 23 (internal quotation marks omitted). We emphasize that the question of "severe physical suffering" in the context of a combination of techniques is a substantial and difficult one, particularly in light of the imprecision in the statutory standard and the relative lack of guidance in the case law. Nevertheless, we believe that the combination of techniques in question here would not be "extreme and outrageous" and thus would not reach the high bar established by Congress in sections 2340-2340A, which is reserved for actions that "warrant the universal condemnation that the term 'torture' both connotes and invokes." *See Price v. Socialist People's Libyan Arab Jamahiriya*, 294 F.3d at 92 (interpreting the TVPA)

As we explained in *Techniques*, experience with extended sleep deprivation shows that "'[s]urprisingly, little seemed to go wrong with the subjects physically. The main effects lay with sleepiness and impaired brain functioning, but even these were no great cause for concern.'" *Id.* at 36 (quoting James Horne, *Why We Sleep: The Functions of Sleep in Humans and Other Mammals* 23-24 (1988)). The aspects of sleep deprivation that might result in substantial physical discomfort, therefore, are limited in scope; and although the degree of distress associated with sleepiness, as noted above, may differ from person to person, the CIA has found that many of the at least 25 detainees subjected to sleep deprivation have tolerated it well. The general conditions in which sleep deprivation takes place would not change this conclusion. Shackling is employed as a passive means of keeping a detainee awake and is used in a way designed to prevent causing significant pain. A detainee is not allowed to hang by his wrists. When the detainee is shackled in a sitting position, he is on a stool adequate to bear his weight; and if a horizontal position is used, there is no additional stress on the detainee's arm or leg

TOP SECRET/

joints that might force his limbs beyond their natural extension or create tension on any joint. Furthermore, team members, as well as medical staff, watch for the development of edema and will act to relieve that condition, should significant edema develop. If a detainee subject to sleep deprivation is using an adult diaper, the diaper is checked regularly and changed as needed to prevent skin irritation.

Nevertheless, we recognize, as noted above, the possibility that sleep deprivation might lower a detainee's tolerance for pain. *See supra* p.13 & n.9. This possibility suggests that use of extended sleep deprivation in combination with other techniques might be more likely than the separate use of the techniques to place the detainee in a state of severe physical distress and, therefore, that the detainee might be more likely to experience severe physical suffering. However, you have informed us that the interrogation techniques at issue would not be used during a course of extended sleep deprivation with such frequency and intensity as to induce in the detainee a persistent condition of extreme physical distress such as may constitute "severe physical suffering" within the meaning of sections 2340-2340A. We understand that the combined use of these techniques with extended sleep deprivation is not designed or expected to cause that result. Even assuming there could be such an effect, members of the interrogation team and medical staff from OMS monitor detainees and would intercede if there were indications that the combined use of the techniques may be having that result, and the use of the techniques would be reduced in frequency or intensity or halted altogether, as necessary. In this regard, we assume that if a detainee started to show an atypical, adverse reaction during sleep deprivation, the system for monitoring would identify this development.

These considerations underscore that the combination of other techniques with sleep deprivation magnifies the importance of adhering strictly to the limits and safeguards applicable to sleep deprivation as an individual technique, as well as the understanding that team personnel, as well as OMS medical personnel, would intervene to alter or stop the use of an interrogation technique if they conclude that a detainee is or may be experiencing extreme physical distress.

The waterboard may be used simultaneously with two other techniques: it may be used during a course of sleep deprivation, and as explained above, a detainee subjected to the waterboard must be under dietary manipulation, because a fluid diet reduces the risks of the technique. Furthermore, although the insult slap, abdominal slap, attention grasp, facial hold, walling, water dousing, stress positions, and cramped confinement cannot be employed during the actual session when the waterboard is being employed, they may be used at a point in time close to the waterboard, including on the same day. *See* April 22 ▮▮ Fax at 3.

In *Techniques*, we explained why neither sleep deprivation nor the waterboard would impose distress of such intensity and duration as to amount to "severe physical suffering," and, depending on the circumstances and the individual detainee, we do not believe the combination of the techniques, even if close in time with other techniques, would change that conclusion. The physical distress of the waterboard, as explained in *Techniques*, lasts only during the relatively short periods during a session when the technique is actually being used. Sleep deprivation would not extend that period. Moreover, we understand that there is nothing in the literature or experience to suggest that sleep deprivation would exacerbate any harmful effects of the waterboard. *See supra* p. 9. Similarly, the use of the waterboard would not extend the time of sleep deprivation or increase its distress, except during the relatively brief times that the technique is actually being used. And the use of other techniques that do not involve the intensity and duration required for "severe physical suffering" would not lengthen the time during which the waterboard would be used or increase, in any apparent way, the intensity of the distress it would cause. Nevertheless, because both the waterboard and sleep deprivation raise substantial questions, the combination of the techniques only heightens the difficulty of the issues. Furthermore, particularly because the waterboard is so different from other techniques in its effects, its use in combination with other techniques is particularly difficult to judge in the abstract and calls for the utmost vigilance and care.

Based on these assumptions, and those described at length in *Techniques*, we conclude that the combination of techniques, as described in the *Background Paper* and the *April 22 Fax*, would not be expected by the interrogators to cause "severe physical . . . suffering," and that the authorized use of these techniques in combination by adequately trained interrogators could not reasonably be considered specifically intended to cause severe physical suffering within the meaning of sections 2340-2340A.

Severe Mental Pain or Suffering

As we explained in *Techniques*, the statutory definition of "severe mental pain or suffering" requires that one of four specified predicate acts cause "prolonged mental harm." 18 U.S.C. § 2340(2); *see Techniques* at 24-25. In *Techniques*, we concluded that only two of the techniques at issue here—sleep deprivation and the waterboard—could even arguably involve a predicate act. The statute provides that "the administration or application . . . of . . . procedures calculated to disrupt profoundly the senses or the personality" can be a predicate act. 18 U.S.C. § 2340(2)(B). Although sleep deprivation may cause hallucinations, OMS, supported by the scientific literature of which we are aware, would not expect a profound disruption of the senses and would order sleep deprivation discontinued if hallucinations occurred. We nonetheless assumed in *Techniques* that any hallucinations resulting from sleep deprivation would amount to a profound disruption of the senses. Even on this assumption, we concluded that sleep deprivation should not be deemed "calculated" to have that effect. *Techniques* at 35-36. Furthermore, even if sleep deprivation could be said to be "calculated" to disrupt the senses profoundly and thus to qualify as a predicate act, we expressed the understanding in *Techniques* that, as demonstrated by the scientific literature about which we knew and by relevant experience in CIA interrogations, the effects of sleep deprivation, including the effects of any associated hallucinations, would rapidly dissipate. Based on that understanding, sleep deprivation therefore would not cause "prolonged mental harm" and would not meet the statutory definition for "severe mental pain or suffering." *Id.* at 36.

We noted in *Techniques* that the use of the waterboard might involve a predicate act. A detainee subjected to the waterboard experiences a sensation of drowning, which arguably qualifies as a "threat of imminent death." 18 U.S.C. § 2340(2)(C). We noted, however, that there is no medical basis for believing that the technique would produce any prolonged mental harm. As explained in *Techniques*, there is no evidence for such prolonged mental harm in the CIA's experience with the technique, and we understand that it has been used thousands of times (albeit in a somewhat different way) during the military training of United States personnel, without producing any evidence of such harm.

There is no evidence that combining other techniques with sleep deprivation or the waterboard would change these conclusions. We understand that none of the detainees subjected to sleep deprivation has exhibited any lasting mental harm, and that, in all but one case, these detainees have been subjected to at least some other interrogation technique besides the sleep deprivation itself. Nor does this experience give any reason to believe that, should sleep deprivation cause hallucinations, the use of these other techniques in combination with sleep deprivation would change the expected result that, once a person subjected to sleep deprivation is allowed to sleep, the effects of the sleep deprivation, and of any associated hallucinations, would rapidly dissipate.

Once again, our advice assumes continuous, diligent monitoring of the detainee during sleep deprivation and prompt intervention at the first signs of hallucinatory experiences. The absence of any atypical, adverse reaction during sleep deprivation would buttress the inference that, like others deprived of sleep for long periods, the detainee would fit within the norm established by experience with sleep deprivation, both the general experience reflected in the medical literature and the CIA's specific experience with other detainees. We understand that, based on these experiences, the detainee would be expected to return quickly to his normal mental state once he has been allowed to sleep and would suffer no "prolonged mental harm."

Similarly, the CIA's experience has produced no evidence that combining the waterboard and other techniques causes prolonged mental harm, and the same is true of the military training in which the technique was used. We assume, again, continuous and diligent monitoring during the use of the technique, with a view toward quickly identifying any atypical, adverse reactions and intervening as necessary.

The *Background Paper* raises one other issue about "severe mental pain or suffering." According to the *Background Paper*, the interrogators may tell detainees that they "will do what it takes to get important information." *Background Paper* at 10. (We understand that interrogators may instead use other statements that might be taken to have a similar import.) Conceivably, a detainee might understand such a statement as a threat that, if necessary, the interrogators will imminently subject him to "severe physical pain or suffering" or to "the administration or application of mind-altering substances or other procedures calculated to disrupt profoundly the senses or the personality," or he perhaps even could interpret the statement as a threat of imminent death (although, as the detainee himself would probably realize, killing a detainee would end the flow of information). 18 U.S.C. § 2340(2)(A)-(C).

We doubt that this statement is sufficiently specific to qualify as a predicate act under section 2340(2). Nevertheless, we do not have sufficient information to judge whether, in context, detainees understand the statement in any of these ways. If they do, this statement at the beginning of the interrogation arguably requires considering whether it alters the detainee's perception of the interrogation techniques and whether, in light of this perception, prolonged mental harm would be expected to result from the combination throughout the interrogation process of all of the techniques used. We do not have any body of experience, beyond the CIA's

TOP SECRET/   /NOFORN

own experience with detainees, on which to base an answer to this question. SERE training, for example, or other experience with sleep deprivation, does not involve its use with the standing position used here, extended nudity, extended dietary manipulation, and the other techniques which are intended "to create a state of learned helplessness," *Background Paper* at 1, and SERE training does not involve repeated applications of the waterboard. A statement that the interrogators "will do what it takes to get important information" moves the interrogations at issue here even further from this body of experience.

Although it may raise a question, we do not believe that, under the careful limitations and monitoring in place, the combined use outlined in the *Background Paper*, together with a statement of this kind, would violate the statute. We are informed that, in the opinion of OMS, none of the detainees who have heard such a statement in their interrogations has experienced "prolonged mental harm," such as post-traumatic stress disorder, *see Techniques* at 26 n.31, as a result of it or the various techniques utilized on them. This body of experience supports the conclusion that the use of the statement does not alter the effects that would be expected to follow from the combined use of the techniques. Nevertheless, in light of these uncertainties, you may wish to evaluate whether such a statement is a necessary part of the interrogation regimen or whether a different statement might be adequate to convey to the detainee the seriousness of his situation.

* * *

In view of the experience from past interrogations, the judgment of medical and psychological personnel, and the interrogation team's diligent monitoring of the effects of combining interrogation techniques, interrogators would not reasonably expect that the combined use of the interrogation methods under consideration, subject to the conditions and safeguards set forth here and in *Techniques*, would result in severe physical or mental pain or suffering within the meaning of sections 2340-2340A. Accordingly, we conclude that the authorized use, as described in the *Background Paper* and the *April 22   Fax*, of these techniques in combination by adequately trained interrogators could not reasonably be considered specifically intended to cause severe physical or mental pain or suffering, and thus would not violate sections 2340-2340A. We nonetheless underscore that when these techniques are combined in a real-world scenario, the members of the interrogation team and the attendant medical staff must be vigilant in watching for unintended effects, so that the individual characteristics of each detainee are constantly taken into account and the interrogation may be modified or halted, if necessary, to avoid causing severe physical or mental pain or suffering to any detainee. Furthermore, as noted above, our advice does not extend to combinations of techniques unlike the ones discussed here, and whether any other combination of techniques would be more likely to cause severe physical or mental pain or suffering within the meaning of sections 2340-2340A would be a question that we cannot assess here. Similarly, our advice does not extend to the use of techniques on detainees unlike those we have previously considered; and whether other detainees would, in the relevant ways, be like the ones at issue in our previous advice would be a factual question we cannot now decide. Finally, we emphasize that these are issues about which reasonable persons may disagree. Our task has been made more difficult by the imprecision of the statute and the relative absence of judicial guidance, but we have applied our best reading of the law to the specific facts that you have provided.

TOP SECRET/   /NOFORN

TOP SECRET/ ▮▮▮▮ /NOFORN

Please let us know if we may be of further assistance.

Steven G. Bradbury
Steven G. Bradbury
Principal Deputy Assistant Attorney General

TOP SECRET/ ▮▮▮▮ /NOFORN

MEMO FOUR

DATED MAY 30, 2005, FROM STEVEN BRADBURY, ACTING ASSISTANT ATTORNEY GENERAL, OLC, TO JOHN A. RIZZO, GENERAL COUNSEL CIA

~~TOP SECRET/~~ ███████ ~~NOFORN~~   0000011

U.S. Department of Justice

Office of Legal Counsel

Office of the Principal Deputy Assistant Attorney General   Washington, D.C. 20530

May 30, 2005

MEMORANDUM FOR JOHN A. RIZZO
SENIOR DEPUTY GENERAL COUNSEL, CENTRAL INTELLIGENCE AGENCY

Re: *Application of United States Obligations Under Article 16 of the Convention Against Torture to Certain Techniques that May Be Used in the Interrogation of High Value al Qaeda Detainees*

You have asked us to address whether certain "enhanced interrogation techniques" employed by the Central Intelligence Agency ("CIA") in the interrogation of high value al Qaeda detainees are consistent with United States obligations under Article 16 of the United Nations Convention Against Torture and Other Cruel, Inhuman or Degrading Treatment or Punishment, Dec. 10, 1984, S. Treaty Doc. No. 100-20, 1465 U.N.T.S. 85 (entered into force for U.S. Nov. 20, 1994) ("CAT"). We conclude that use of these techniques, subject to the CIA's careful screening criteria and limitations and its medical safeguards, is consistent with United States obligations under Article 16.[1]

By its terms, Article 16 is limited to conduct within "territory under [United States] jurisdiction." We conclude that territory under United States jurisdiction includes, at most, areas

---

[1] Our analysis and conclusions are limited to the specific legal issues we address in this memorandum. We note that we have previously concluded that use of these techniques, subject to the limits and safeguards required by the interrogation program, does not violate the federal prohibition on torture, codified at 18 U.S.C. §§ 2340-2340A. *See* Memorandum for John A. Rizzo, Senior Deputy General Counsel, Central Intelligence Agency, from Steven G. Bradbury, Principal Deputy Assistant Attorney General, Office of Legal Counsel, *Re: Application of 18 U.S.C. §§ 2340-2340A to Certain Techniques that May Be Used in the Interrogation of a High Value al Qaeda Detainee* (May 10, 2005); *see also* Memorandum for John A. Rizzo, Senior Deputy General Counsel, Central Intelligence Agency, from Steven G. Bradbury, Principal Deputy Assistant Attorney General, Office of Legal Counsel, *Re: Application of 18 U.S.C. §§ 2340-2340A to the Combined Use of Certain Techniques in the Interrogation of High Value al Qaeda Detainees* (May 10, 2005) (concluding that the anticipated combined use of these techniques would not violate the federal prohibition on torture). The legal advice provided in this memorandum does not represent the policy views of the Department of Justice concerning the use of any interrogation methods.

TOP SECRET/ NOFORN

over which the United States exercises at least de facto authority as the government. Based on CIA assurances, we understand that the interrogations do not take place in any such areas. We therefore conclude that Article 16 is inapplicable to the CIA's interrogation practices and that those practices thus cannot violate Article 16. Further, the United States undertook its obligations under Article 16 subject to a Senate reservation, which, as relevant here, explicitly limits those obligations to "the cruel, unusual and inhumane treatment ... prohibited by the Fifth Amendment ... to the Constitution of the United States."[2] There is a strong argument that through this reservation the Senate intended to limit the scope of United States obligations under Article 16 to those imposed by the relevant provisions of the Constitution. As construed by the courts, the Fifth Amendment does not apply to aliens outside the United States. The CIA has assured us that the interrogation techniques are not used within the United States or against United States persons, including both United States citizens and lawful permanent residents. Because the geographic limitation on the face of Article 16 renders it inapplicable to the CIA interrogation program in any event, we need not decide in this memorandum the precise effect, if any, of the Senate reservation on the geographic reach of United States obligations under Article 16. For these reasons, we conclude in Part II that the interrogation techniques where and as used by the CIA are not subject to, and therefore do not violate, Article 16.

Notwithstanding these conclusions, you have also asked whether the interrogation techniques at issue would violate the substantive standards applicable to the United States under Article 16 if, contrary to our conclusion in Part II, those standards did extend to the CIA interrogation program. As detailed below in Part III, the relevant constraint here, assuming Article 16 did apply, would be the Fifth Amendment's prohibition of executive conduct that "shocks the conscience." The Supreme Court has emphasized that whether conduct "shocks the conscience" is a highly context-specific and fact-dependent question. The Court, however, has not set forth with precision a specific test for ascertaining whether conduct can be said to "shock the conscience" and has disclaimed the ability to do so. Moreover, there are few Supreme Court cases addressing whether conduct "shocks the conscience," and the few cases there are have all arisen in very different contexts from that which we consider here.

For these reasons, we cannot set forth or apply a precise test for ascertaining whether conduct can be said to "shock the conscience." Nevertheless, the Court's "shocks the conscience" cases do provide some signposts that can guide our inquiry. In particular, on balance the cases are best read to require a determination whether the conduct is "'arbitrary in the constitutional sense,'" *County of Sacramento v. Lewis*, 523 U.S. 833, 846 (1998) (citation

---

[2] The reservation provides in full:

That the United States considers itself bound by the obligation under Article 16 to prevent "cruel, inhuman or degrading treatment or punishment," only insofar as the term "cruel, inhuman or degrading treatment or punishment" means the cruel, unusual and inhumane treatment or punishment prohibited by the Fifth, Eighth, and/or Fourteenth Amendments to the Constitution of the United States.

136 Cong. Rec. 36198 (1990). As we explain below, the Eighth and Fourteenth Amendments are not applicable in this context.

TOP SECRET/ NOFORN

2

omitted); that is, whether it involves the "exercise of power without any reasonable justification in the service of a legitimate governmental objective," *id.* "[C]onduct intended to injure in some way unjustifiable by any government interest is the sort of official action most likely to rise to the conscience-shocking level." *Id.* at 849. Far from being constitutionally arbitrary, the interrogation techniques at issue here are employed by the CIA only as reasonably deemed necessary to protect against grave threats to United States interests, a determination that is made at CIA Headquarters, with input from the on-scene interrogation team, pursuant to careful screening procedures that ensure that the techniques will be used as little as possible on as few detainees as possible. Moreover, the techniques have been carefully designed to minimize the risk of suffering or injury and to avoid inflicting any serious or lasting physical or psychological harm. Medical screening, monitoring, and ongoing evaluations further lower such risk. Significantly, you have informed us that the CIA believes that this program is largely responsible for preventing a subsequent attack within the United States. Because the CIA interrogation program is carefully limited to further a vital government interest and designed to avoid unnecessary or serious harm, we conclude that it cannot be said to be constitutionally arbitrary.

The Supreme Court's decisions also suggest that it is appropriate to consider whether, in light of "traditional executive behavior, of contemporary practice, and the standards of blame generally applied to them," use of the techniques in the CIA interrogation program "is so egregious, so outrageous, that it may fairly be said to shock the contemporary conscience." *Id.* at 847 n.8. We have not found evidence of traditional executive behavior or contemporary practice either condemning or condoning an interrogation program carefully limited to further a vital government interest and designed to avoid unnecessary or serious harm. We recognize, however, that use of coercive interrogation techniques in other contexts—in different settings, for other purposes, or absent the CIA's safeguards—might be thought to "shock the conscience." *Cf., e.g., Rochin v. California*, 342 U.S. 165, 172 (1952) (finding that pumping the stomach of a criminal defendant to obtain evidence "shocks the conscience"); *U.S. Army Field Manual 34-52: Intelligence Interrogation* (1992) ("*Field Manual 34-52*") (detailing guidelines for interrogations in the context of traditional warfare); Department of State, Country Reports on Human Rights Practices (describing human-rights abuses condemned by the United States). We believe, however, that each of these other contexts, which we describe more fully below, differs critically from the CIA interrogation program in ways that would be unreasonable to ignore in examining whether the conduct involved in the CIA program "shock[s] the contemporary conscience." Ordinary criminal investigations within the United States, for example, involve fundamentally different government interests and implicate specific constitutional guarantees, such as the privilege against self-incrimination, that are not at issue here. Furthermore, the CIA interrogation techniques have all been adapted from military Survival, Evasion, Resistance, Escape ("SERE") training. Although there are obvious differences between training exercises and actual interrogations, the fact that the United States uses similar techniques on its own troops ~~for training purposes strongly suggests that these techniques are not categorically beyond the~~ pale.

Given that the CIA interrogation program is carefully limited to further the Government's paramount interest in protecting the Nation while avoiding unnecessary or serious harm, we conclude that the interrogation program cannot "be said to shock the contemporary conscience" when considered in light of "traditional executive behavior" and "contemporary practice." *Lewis*, 523 U.S. at 847 n.8.

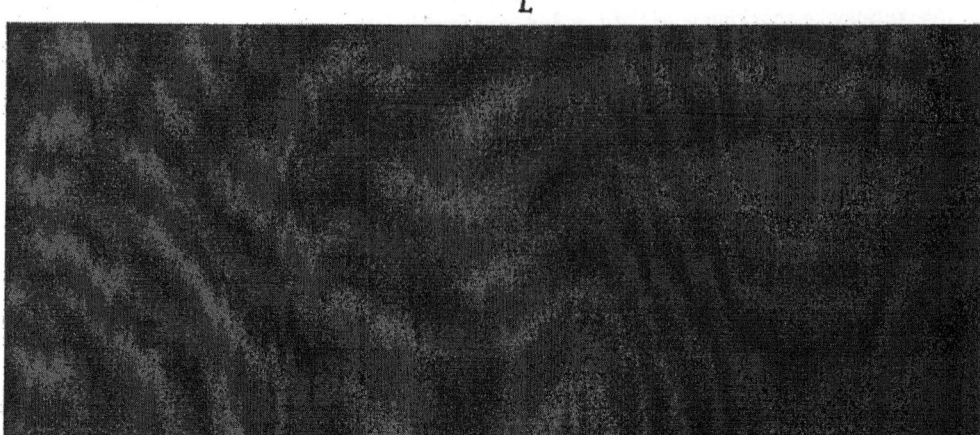

Elsewhere, we have described the CIA interrogation program in great detail. *See* Memorandum for John A. Rizzo, Senior Deputy General Counsel, Central Intelligence Agency, from Steven G. Bradbury, Principal Deputy Assistant Attorney General, Office of Legal Counsel, *Re: Application of 18 U.S.C. §§ 2340-2340A to Certain Techniques that May Be Used in the Interrogation of a High Value al Qaeda Detainee* at 4-15, 28-45 (May 10, 2005) ("*Techniques*"); Memorandum for John A. Rizzo, Senior Deputy General Counsel, Central Intelligence Agency, from Steven G. Bradbury, Principal Deputy Assistant Attorney General, Office of Legal Counsel, *Re: Application of 18 U.S.C. §§ 2340-2340A to the Combined Use of Certain Techniques in the Interrogation of High Value al Qaeda Detainees* at 3-9 (May 10, 2005) ("*Combined Use*"). The descriptions of the techniques, including all limitations and safeguards applicable to their use, set forth in *Techniques* and *Combined Use* are incorporated by reference herein, and we assume familiarity with those descriptions. Here, we highlight those aspects of the program that are most important to the question under consideration. Where appropriate, throughout this opinion we also provide more detailed background information regarding specific high value detainees who are representative of the individuals on whom the techniques might be used.[3]

A.

Under the CIA's guidelines, several conditions must be satisfied before the CIA considers employing enhanced techniques in the interrogation of any detainee. The CIA must,

---

[3] The CIA has reviewed and confirmed the accuracy of our description of the interrogation program, including its purposes, methods, limitations, and results.

MEMO FOUR: BRADBURY TO RIZO, MAY 30, 2005

TOP SECRET//  //NOFORN

based on available intelligence, conclude that the detainee is an important and dangerous member of an al Qaeda-affiliated group. The CIA must then determine, at the Headquarters level and on a case-by-case basis with input from the on-scene interrogation team, that enhanced interrogation methods are needed in a particular interrogation. Finally, the enhanced techniques, which have been designed and implemented to minimize the potential for serious or unnecessary harm to the detainees, may be used only if there are no medical or psychological contraindications.

I.

▓▓▓▓▓▓▓▓▓▓▓▓▓▓▓▓▓▓▓ the CIA uses enhanced interrogation techniques only if the CIA's Counterterrorist Center ("CTC") determines an individual to be a "High Value Detainee," which the CIA defines as:

> a detainee who, until time of capture, we have reason to believe: (1) is a senior member of al-Qai'da or an al-Qai'da associated terrorist group (Jemaah Islamiyyah, Egyptian Islamic Jihad, al-Zarqawi Group, etc.); (2) has knowledge of imminent terrorist threats against the USA, its military forces, its citizens and organizations, or its allies; or that has/had direct involvement in planning and preparing terrorist actions against the USA or its allies, or assisting the al-Qai'da leadership in planning and preparing such terrorist actions; and (3) if released, constitutes a clear and continuing threat to the USA or its allies.

Fax for Daniel Levin, Acting Assistant Attorney General, Office of Legal Counsel, from ▓▓▓▓▓▓ Assistant General Counsel, Central Intelligence Agency at 4 (Jan. 4, 2005) ("January 4 ▓▓▓ Fax"). The CIA, therefore, must have reason to believe that the detainee is a senior member (rather than a mere "foot soldier") of al Qaeda or an associated terrorist organization, who likely has actionable intelligence concerning terrorist threats, and who poses a significant threat to United States interests.

The "waterboard," which is the most intense of the CIA interrogation techniques, is subject to additional limits. It may be used on a High Value Detainee only if the CIA has "credible intelligence that a terrorist attack is imminent"; "substantial and credible indicators that the subject has actionable intelligence that can prevent, disrupt or delay this attack"; and "[o]ther interrogation methods have failed to elicit the information [or] CIA has clear indications that other . . . methods are unlikely to elicit this information *within the perceived time limit for preventing the attack*." Letter from John A. Rizzo, Acting General Counsel, Central Intelligence Agency, to Daniel Levin, Acting Assistant Attorney General, Office of Legal Counsel at 5 (Aug. 2, 2004) ("*August 2 Rizzo Letter*") (attachment).

To date, the CIA has taken custody of 94 detainees ▓▓▓▓▓▓▓▓▓▓▓▓▓ and has employed enhanced techniques to varying degrees in the interrogations of 28 of these detainees. We understand that two individuals, ▓▓

TOP SECRET// ▓▓▓▓▓▓▓▓ //NOFORN

TOP SECRET/ ███████ //NOFORN

███████ are representative of the high value detainees on whom enhanced techniques have been, or might be, used. On ███████ the CIA took custody of ███████ whom the CIA believed had actionable intelligence concerning the pre-election threat to the United States. *See* Letter from ███████, Associate General Counsel, Central Intelligence Agency, to Daniel Levin, Acting Assistant Attorney General, Office of Legal Counsel at 2 (Aug. 25, 2004) ("*August 25* ███████ *Letter*"). ███████ extensive connections to various al Qaeda leaders, members of the Taliban, and the al-Zarqawi network, and intelligence indicated ███████ arranged a ... meeting between ███████ and ███████ at which elements of the pre-election threat were discussed." *Id.* at 2-3; *see also* Undated CIA Memo.

Intelligence indicated that prior to his capture, ███████ "perform[ed] critical facilitation and finance activities for al-Qa'ida," including "transporting people, funds, and documents." Fax for Jack L. Goldsmith, III, Assistant Attorney General, Office of Legal Counsel, from ███████ Assistant General Counsel, Central Intelligence Agency (March 12, 2004). The CIA also suspected ███████ played an active part in planning attacks against United States forces ███████ had extensive contacts with key members of al Qaeda, including, prior to their captures, Khalid Shaykh Muhammad ("KSM") and Abu Zubaydah. *See id.* ███████ was captured while on a mission from ███████ to establish contact" with al-Zarqawi. *See* CIA Directorate of Intelligence, *US Efforts Grinding Down al-Qa'ida* 2 (Feb. 21, 2004).

Consistent with its heightened standard for use of the waterboard, the CIA has used this technique in the interrogations of only three detainees to date (KSM, Zubaydah, and 'Abd Al-Rahim Al-Nashiri) and has not used it since the March 2003 interrogation of KSM. *See* Letter from Scott W. Muller, General Counsel, Central Intelligence Agency, to Jack L. Goldsmith III, Assistant Attorney General, Office of Legal Counsel at 1 (June 14, 2004).

We understand that Abu Zubaydah and KSM are representative of the types of detainees on whom the waterboard has been, or might be, used. Prior to his capture, Zubaydah was "one of Usama Bin Laden's key lieutenants." CIA, *Zayn al-Abidin Muhammad Husayn ABU ZUBAYDAH* at 1 (Jan. 7, 2002) ("*Zubaydah Biography*"). Indeed, Zubaydah was al Qaeda's third or fourth highest ranking member and had been involved "in every major terrorist operation carried out by al Qaeda." Memorandum for John Rizzo, Acting General Counsel, Central Intelligence Agency, from Jay S. Bybee, Assistant Attorney General, Office of Legal Counsel, *Re: Interrogation of al Qaeda Operative* at 7 (Aug. 1, 2002) ("*Interrogation Memorandum*"); Zubaydah Biography (noting Zubaydah's involvement in the September 11 attacks). Upon his capture on March 27, 2002, Zubaydah became the most senior member of al Qaeda in United States custody. *See IG Report* at 12.

KSM, "a mastermind" of the September 11, 2001, attacks, was regarded as "one of al-Qa'ida's most dangerous and resourceful operatives." CIA, *Khalid Shaykh Muhammad* ███████ (Nov. 1, 2002) ("*CIA KSM Biography*"). ███████ Prior to his capture, the CIA considered KSM to be one of al Qaeda's "most important operational leaders ... based on his

TOP SECRET/ ███████ //NOFORN

6

close relationship with Usama Bin Laden and his reputation among the al-Qa'ida rank and file." *Id.* After the September 11 attacks, KSM assumed "the role of operations chief for al-Qa'ida around the world." CIA Directorate of Intelligence, *Khalid Shaykh Muhammad: Preeminent Source on Al-Qa'ida* 7 (July 13, 2004) ("*Preeminent Source*"). KSM also planned additional attacks within the United States both before and after September 11. *See id.* at 7-8; *see also The 9/11 Commission Report: Final Report of the National Commission on Terrorist Attacks Upon the United States* 150 (official gov't ed. 2004) ("*9/11 Commission Report*").[4]

2.

Even with regard to detainees who satisfy these threshold requirements, enhanced techniques are considered only if the on-scene interrogation team determines that the detainee is withholding or manipulating information. In order to make this assessment, interrogators conduct an initial interview "in a relatively benign environment." Fax for Daniel Levin, Acting Assistant Attorney General, Office of Legal Counsel, from ▌▌▌▌▌ Associate General Counsel, Central Intelligence Agency, *Re: Background Paper on CIA's Combined Use of Interrogation Techniques* at 3 (Dec. 30, 2004) ("*Background Paper*"). At this stage, the detainee is "normally clothed but seated and shackled for security purposes," and the interrogators take "an open, non-threatening approach." *Id.* In order to be judged participatory, however, a high value detainee "would have to willingly provide information on actionable threats and location information on High-Value Targets at large—not lower level information." *Id.* If the detainee fails to meet this "very high" standard, the interrogation team develops an interrogation plan, which generally calls for the use of enhanced techniques only as necessary and in escalating fashion. *See id.* at 3-4; *Techniques* at 5.

Any interrogation plan that involves the use of enhanced techniques must be reviewed and approved by "the Director, DCI Counterterrorist Center, with the concurrence of the Chief, CTC Legal Group." George J. Tenet, Director of Central Intelligence, *Guidelines on Interrogations Conducted Pursuant to the* ▌▌▌▌▌ at 3 (Jan. 28, 2003) ("*Interrogation Guidelines*").[5] Each approval lasts for a period of at most 30 days, *see id.* at 1-2, although enhanced interrogation techniques are generally not used for more than seven days, *see Background Paper* at 17.

For example, after medical and psychological examinations found no contraindications, ▌▌▌▌▌'s interrogation team sought and obtained approval to use the following techniques: attention grasp, walling, facial hold, facial slap, wall standing, stress positions, and sleep deprivation. *See August 25* ▌▌▌▌ *Letter* at 2. The interrogation team "carefully analyzed Gul's responsiveness to different areas of inquiry" during this time and noted that his resistance increased as questioning moved to his "knowledge of operational terrorist activities." *Id.* at 3.

---

[4] Al-Nashiri, the only other detainee to be subjected to the waterboard, planned the bombing of the U.S.S. Cole and was subsequently "recognized as the chief of al Qaeda operations in and around the Arabian Peninsula." *9/11 Commission Report* at 153.

[5] You have informed us that the current practice is for the Director of the Central Intelligence Agency to make this determination personally.

TOP SECRET/███████████ NOFORN

███████ feigned memory problems (which CIA psychologists ruled out through intelligence and memory tests) in order to avoid answering questions. *Id.*

At that point, the interrogation team believed ███████ "maintains a tough, Mujahidin fighter mentality and has conditioned himself for a physical interrogation." *Id.* The team therefore concluded that "more subtle interrogation measures designed more to weaken ███ physical ability and mental desire to resist interrogation over the long run are likely to be more effective." *Id.* For these reasons, the team sought authorization to use dietary manipulation, nudity, water dousing, and abdominal slap. *Id.* at 4-5. In the team's view, adding these techniques would be especially helpful ███████ because he appeared to have a particular weakness for food and also seemed especially modest. *See id.* at 4.

The CIA used the waterboard extensively in the interrogations of KSM and Zubaydah, but did so only after it became clear that standard interrogation techniques were not working. Interrogators used enhanced techniques in the interrogation of al-Nashiri with notable results as early as the first day. *See IG Report* at 35-36. Twelve days into the interrogation, the CIA subjected al-Nashiri to one session of the waterboard during which water was applied two times. *See id.* at 36.

3.

Medical and psychological professionals from the CIA's Office of Medical Services ("OMS") carefully evaluate detainees before any enhanced technique is authorized in order to ensure that the detainee "is not likely to suffer any severe physical or mental pain or suffering as a result of interrogation." *Techniques* at 4; *see OMS Guidelines on Medical and Psychological Support to Detainee Rendition, Interrogation and Detention* at 9 (Dec. 2004) ("*OMS Guidelines*"). In addition, OMS officials continuously monitor the detainee's condition throughout any interrogation using enhanced techniques, and the interrogation team will stop the use of particular techniques or the interrogation altogether if the detainee's medical or psychological condition indicates that the detainee might suffer significant physical or mental harm. *See Techniques* at 5-6. OMS has, in fact, prohibited the use of certain techniques in the interrogations of certain detainees. *See id.* at 5. Thus, no technique is used in the interrogation of any detainee—no matter how valuable the information the CIA believes the detainee has—if the medical and psychological evaluations or ongoing monitoring suggest that the detainee is likely to suffer serious harm. Careful records are kept of each interrogation, which ensures accountability and allows for ongoing evaluation of the efficacy of each technique and its potential for any unintended or inappropriate results. *See id.*

B.

Your office has informed us that the CIA believes that "the intelligence acquired from these interrogations has been a key reason why al-Qa'ida has failed to launch a spectacular attack in the West since 11 September 2001." Memorandum for Steven G. Bradbury, Principal Deputy Assistant Attorney General, Office of Legal Counsel, from ███████ ███████ DCI Counterterrorist Center, *Re: Effectiveness of the CIA Counterintelligence Interrogation Techniques* at 2 (Mar. 2, 2005) ("*Effectiveness Memo*"). In particular, the CIA

TOP SECRET/███████████ NOFORN

believes that it would have been unable to obtain critical information from numerous detainees, including KSM and Abu Zubaydah, without these enhanced techniques. Both KSM and Zubaydah had "expressed their belief that the general US population was 'weak,' lacked resilience, and would be unable to 'do what was necessary' to prevent the terrorists from succeeding in their goals." *Id.* at 1. Indeed, before the CIA used enhanced techniques in its interrogation of KSM, KSM resisted giving any answers to questions about future attacks, simply noting, "Soon, you will know." *Id.* We understand that the use of enhanced techniques in the interrogations of KSM, Zubaydah, and others, by contrast, has yielded critical information. *See IG Report* at 86, 90-91 (describing increase in intelligence reports attributable to use of enhanced techniques). As Zubaydah himself explained with respect to enhanced techniques, "brothers who are captured and interrogated are permitted by Allah to provide information when they believe they have 'reached the limit of their ability to withhold it' in the face of psychological and physical hardships." *Effectiveness Memo* at 2. And, indeed, we understand that since the use of enhanced techniques, "KSM and Abu Zubaydah have been pivotal sources because of their ability and willingness to provide their analysis and speculation about the capabilities, methodologies, and mindsets of terrorists." *Preeminent Source* at 4.

Nevertheless, current CIA threat reporting indicates that, despite substantial setbacks over the last year, al Qaeda continues to pose a grave threat to the United States and its interests. *See* CIA  You have informed us that the CIA believes that enhanced interrogation techniques remain essential to obtaining vital intelligence necessary to detect and disrupt such emerging threats.

In understanding the effectiveness of the interrogation program, it is important to keep two related points in mind. First, the total value of the program cannot be appreciated solely by focusing on individual pieces of information. According to the CIA Inspector General:

> CTC frequently uses the information from one detainee, as well as other sources, to vet the information of another detainee. Although lower-level detainees provide less information than the high value detainees, information from these detainees has, on many occasions, supplied the information needed to probe the high value detainees further. . . . [T]he triangulation of intelligence provides a fuller knowledge of Al-Qa'ida activities than would be possible from a single detainee.

IG Report at 86. As illustrated below, we understand that even interrogations of comparatively lower-tier high value detainees supply information that the CIA uses to validate and assess information elicited in other interrogations and through other methods. Intelligence acquired from the interrogation program also enhances other intelligence methods and has helped to build the CIA's overall understanding of al Qaeda and its affiliates. Second, it is difficult to quantify with confidence and precision the effectiveness of the program. As the *IG Report* notes, it is difficult to determine conclusively whether interrogations have provided information critical to interdicting specific imminent attacks. *See id.* at 88. And, because the CIA has used enhanced techniques sparingly, "there is limited data on which to assess their individual effectiveness." *Id.* at 89. As discussed below, however, we understand that interrogations have led to specific, actionable intelligence as well as a general increase in the amount of intelligence regarding al Qaeda and its affiliates. *See id.* at 85-91.

With these caveats, we turn to specific examples that you have provided to us. You have informed us that the interrogation of KSM—once enhanced techniques were employed—led to the discovery of a KSM plot, the "Second Wave," "to use East Asian operatives to crash a hijacked airliner into" a building in Los Angeles. *Effectiveness Memo* at 3. You have informed us that information obtained from KSM also led to the capture of Riduan bin Isomuddin, better known as Hambali, and the discovery of the Guraba Cell, a 17-member Jemaah Islamiyah cell tasked with executing the "Second Wave." *See id.* at 3-4; CIA Directorate of Intelligence, *Al-Qa'ida's Ties to Other Key Terror Groups: Terrorists Links in a Chain* 2 (Aug. 28, 2003). More specifically, we understand that KSM admitted that he had tasked Majid Khan with delivering a large sum of money to an al Qaeda associate. *See* Fax from ███████ ███████ DCI Counterterrorist Center, *Briefing Notes on the Value of Detainee Reporting* at 1 (Apr. 15, 2005) ("*Briefing Notes*"). Khan subsequently identified the associate (Zubair), who was then captured. Zubair, in turn, provided information that led to the arrest of Hambali. *See id.* The information acquired from these captures allowed CIA interrogators to pose more specific questions to KSM, which led the CIA to Hambali's brother, al-Hadi. Using information obtained from multiple sources, al-Hadi was captured, and he subsequently identified the Guraba cell. *See id.* at 1-2. With the aid of this additional information, interrogations of Hambali confirmed much of what was learned from KSM.[6]

Interrogations of Zubaydah—again, once enhanced techniques were employed—furnished detailed information regarding al Qaeda's "organizational structure, key operatives, and modus operandi" and identified KSM as the mastermind of the September 11 attacks. *See Briefing Notes* at 4. You have informed us that Zubaydah also "provided significant information on two operatives, [including] Jose Padilla[,] who planned to build and detonate a 'dirty bomb' in the Washington DC area." *Effectiveness Memo* at 4. Zubaydah and KSM have also supplied important information about al-Zarqawi and his network. *See* Fax for Jack L. Goldsmith III, Assistant Attorney General, Office of Legal Counsel, from ███████ ███████ Office of General Counsel, CIA, ███████████████████████████████

---

[6] We discuss only a small fraction of the important intelligence CIA interrogators have obtained from KSM.

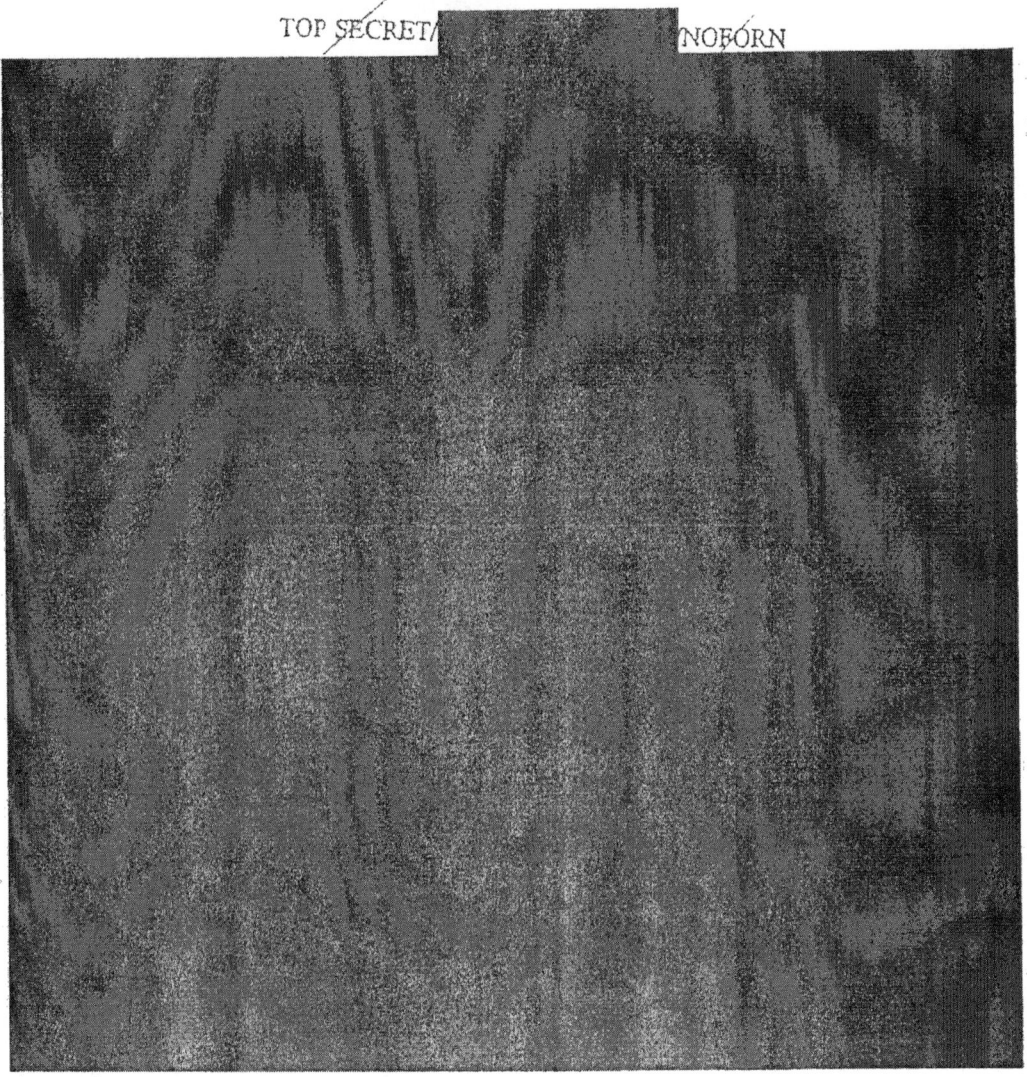

More generally, the CIA has informed us that, since March 2002, the intelligence derived from CIA detainees has resulted in more than 6,000 intelligence reports and, in 2004, accounted for approximately half of CTC's reporting on al Qaeda. *See Briefing Notes* at 1; *see also IG Report* at 86 (noting that from September 11, 2001, through April 2003, the CIA "produced over 3,000 intelligence reports from" a few high value detainees). You have informed us that the substantial majority of this intelligence has come from detainees subjected to enhanced interrogation techniques. In addition, the CIA advises us that the program has been virtually indispensable to the task of deriving actionable intelligence from other forms of collection.

---

[7] As with KSM, we discuss only a portion of the intelligence obtained through interrogations of Zubaydah.

C.

There are three categories of enhanced interrogation techniques: conditioning techniques, corrective techniques, and coercive techniques. *See Background Paper* at 4. As noted above, each of the specific enhanced techniques has been adapted from SERE training, where similar techniques have been used, in some form, for years on United States military personnel. *See Techniques* at 6; *IG Report* at 13-14.

1. Conditioning techniques

Conditioning techniques are used to put the detainee in a "baseline" state, and to "demonstrate to the [detainee] that he has no control over basic human needs." *Background Paper* at 4. This "creates . . . a mindset in which [the detainee] learns to perceive and value his personal welfare, comfort, and immediate needs more than the information he is protecting." *Id.* Conditioning techniques are not designed to bring about immediate results. Rather, these techniques are useful in view of their "cumulative effect . . . , used over time and in combination with other interrogation techniques and intelligence exploitation methods." *Id.* at 5. The specific conditioning techniques are nudity, dietary manipulation, and sleep deprivation.

Nudity is used to induce psychological discomfort and because it allows interrogators to reward detainees instantly with clothing for cooperation. *See Techniques* at 7. Although this technique might cause embarrassment, it does not involve any sexual abuse or threats of sexual abuse. *See id.* at 7-8. Because ambient air temperatures are kept above 68°F, the technique is at most mildly physically uncomfortable and poses no threat to the detainee's health. *Id.* at 7.

Dietary manipulation involves substituting a bland, commercial liquid meal for a detainee's normal diet. We understand that its use can increase the effectiveness of other techniques, such as sleep deprivation. As a guideline, the CIA uses a formula for caloric intake that depends on a detainee's body weight and expected level of activity and that ensures that caloric intake will always be set at or above 1,000 kcal/day. *See id.* at 7 & n.10.[8] By comparison, commercial weight-loss programs used within the United States not uncommonly limit intake to 1000 kcal/day regardless of body weight. Detainees are monitored at all times to ensure that they do not lose more than 10% of their starting body weight. *See id.* at 7. The CIA also sets a minimum fluid intake, but a detainee undergoing dietary manipulation may drink as much water as he pleases. *See id.*

Sleep deprivation involves subjecting a detainee to an extended period of sleeplessness. Interrogators employ sleep deprivation in order to weaken a detainee's resistance. Although up to 180 hours may be authorized, the CIA has in fact subjected only three detainees to more than

---

[8] As we explained in *Techniques*: "The CIA generally follows as a guideline a calorie requirement of 900 kcal/day + 10 kcal/kg/day. This quantity is multiplied by 1.2 for a sedentary activity level or 1.4 for a moderate activity level. Regardless of this formula, the recommended minimum calorie intake is 1500 kcal/day, and in no event is the detainee allowed to receive less than 1000 kcal/day." *Id.* at 7 (footnote omitted). The guideline caloric intake for a detainee who weighs 150 pounds (approximately 68 kilograms) would therefore be nearly 1,900 kcal/day for sedentary activity and would be more than 2,200 kcal/day for moderate activity.

TOP SECRET/NOFORN

96 hours of sleep deprivation. Generally, a detainee undergoing this technique is shackled in a standing position with his hands in front of his body, which prevents him from falling asleep but also allows him to move around within a two- to three-foot diameter. The detainee's hands are generally positioned below his chin, although they may be raised above the head for a period not to exceed two hours. *See id.* at 11-13 (explaining the procedures at length). As we have previously noted, sleep deprivation itself generally has few negative effects (beyond temporary cognitive impairment and transient hallucinations), though some detainees might experience transient "unpleasant physical sensations from prolonged fatigue, including such symptoms as impairment to coordinated body movement, difficulty with speech, nausea, and blurred vision." *Id.* at 37; *see also id.* 37-38. Subjects deprived of sleep in scientific studies for longer than the 180-hour limit imposed by the CIA generally return to normal neurological functioning with as little as one night of normal sleep. *See id.* at 40. In light of the ongoing and careful medical monitoring undertaken by OMS and the authority and obligation of all members of the interrogation team, and of OMS personnel and other facility staff, to stop the procedure if necessary, this technique is not be expected to result in any detainee experiencing extreme physical distress. *See id.* at 38-39.[9]

With respect to the shackling, the procedures in place (which include constant monitoring by detention personnel, via closed-circuit television, and intervention if necessary) minimize the risk that a detainee will hang by his wrists or otherwise suffer injury from the shackling. *See id.* at 11. Indeed, these procedures appear to have been effective, as no detainee has suffered any lasting harm from the shackling. *See id.*

Because releasing a detainee from the shackles would present a security problem and would interfere with the effectiveness of the technique, a detainee undergoing sleep deprivation frequently wears an adult diaper. *See* Letter from ▓▓▓▓▓▓▓▓▓▓ Associate General Counsel, Central Intelligence Agency, to Dan Levin, Acting Assistant Attorney General, Office of Legal Counsel at 4 (Oct. 12, 2004) ("*October 12* ▓▓▓▓ *Letter*"). Diapers are checked and changed as needed so that no detainee would be allowed to remain in a soiled diaper, and the detainee's skin condition is monitored. *See Techniques* at 12. You have informed us that diapers are used solely for sanitary and health reasons and not in order to humiliate the detainee.

2. *Corrective techniques*

Corrective techniques entail some degree of physical interaction with the detainee and are used "to correct, startle, or to achieve another enabling objective with the detainee." *Background Paper* at 5. These techniques "condition a detainee to pay attention to the interrogator's questions and . . . dislodge expectations that the detainee will not be touched." *Techniques* at 9.

---

[9] In addition, as we observed in *Techniques*, certain studies indicate that sleep deprivation might lower pain thresholds in some detainees. *See Techniques* at 36 n.44. The ongoing medical monitoring is therefore especially important when interrogators employ this technique in conjunction with other techniques. *See Combined Use* at 13-14 & n.9, 16. In this regard, we note once again that the CIA has "informed us that the interrogation techniques at issue would not be used during a course of extended sleep deprivation with such frequency and intensity as to induce in the detainee a persistent condition of extreme physical distress such as may constitute 'severe physical suffering.'" *Id.* at 16.

TOP SECRET/NOFORN

This category comprises the following techniques: insult (facial) slap, abdominal slap, facial hold, and attention grasp. *See Background Paper* at 5; *see also Techniques* at 8-9 (describing these techniques).[10] In the facial hold technique, for example, the interrogator uses his hands to immobilize the detainee's head. The interrogator's fingers are kept closely together and away from the detainee's eyes. *See* Pre-Academic Laboratory (PREAL) Operating Instructions at 19 ("*PREAL Manual*"). The technique instills fear and apprehension with minimal physical force. Indeed, each of these techniques entails only mild uses of force and does not cause any significant pain or any lasting harm. *See Background Paper* at 5-7.

3. Coercive techniques

Coercive techniques "place the detainee in more physical and psychological stress" than the other techniques and are generally "considered to be more effective tools in persuading a resistant [detainee] to participate with CIA interrogators." *Background Paper* at 7. These techniques are typically not used simultaneously. The *Background Paper* lists walling, water dousing, stress positions, wall standing, and cramped confinement in this category. We will also treat the waterboard as a coercive technique.

Walling is performed by placing the detainee against what seems to be a normal wall but is in fact a flexible false wall. *See Techniques* at 8. The interrogator pulls the detainee towards him and then quickly slams the detainee against the false wall. The false wall is designed, and a c-collar or similar device is used, to help avoid whiplash or similar injury. *See id*. The technique is designed to create a loud sound and to shock the detainee without causing significant pain. The CIA regards walling as "one of the most effective interrogation techniques because it wears down the [detainee] physically, heightens uncertainty in the detainee about what the interrogator may do to him, and creates a sense of dread when the [detainee] knows he is about to be walled again." *Background Paper* at 7. A detainee "may be walled one time (one impact with the wall) to make a point or twenty to thirty times consecutively when the interrogator requires a more significant response to a question," and "will be walled multiple times" during a session designed to be intense. *Id*. At no time, however, is the technique employed in such a way that could cause severe physical pain. *See Techniques* at 32 n.38.[11]

In the water dousing technique, potable cold water is poured on the detainee either from a container or a hose without a nozzle. Ambient air temperatures are kept above 64°F. The

---

[10] As noted in our previous opinions, the slap techniques are not used in a way that could cause severe pain. *See, e.g., Techniques* at 8-9, 33 & n.39; *Combined Use* at 11.

[11] Although walling "wears down the [detainee] physically," *Background Paper* at 7, and undoubtedly may startle him, we understand that it is not significantly painful. The detainee hits a flexible false wall designed to create a loud sound when the individual hits it and thus to cause shock and surprise. *See Combined Use* at 6 n.4. But the detainee's head and neck are supported with a rolled hood or towel that provides a C-collar effect to help prevent whiplash; it is the detainee's shoulder blades that hit the wall; and the detainee is allowed to rebound from the flexible wall in order to reduce the chances of any injury. *See id.* You have informed us that a detainee is expected to feel "dread" at the prospect of walling because of the shock and surprise caused by the technique and because of the sense of powerlessness that comes from being roughly handled by the interrogators, not because the technique causes significant pain. *See id.*

maximum permissible duration of water exposure depends on the water temperature, which may be no lower than 41°F and is usually no lower than 50°F. *See id.* at 10. Maximum exposure durations have been "set at two-thirds the time at which, based on extensive medical literature and experience, hypothermia could be expected to develop in healthy individuals who are submerged in water of the same temperature" in order to provide adequate safety margins against hypothermia. *Id.* This technique can easily be used in combination with other techniques and "is intended to weaken the detainee's resistance and persuade him to cooperate with interrogators." *Id.* at 9.

Stress positions and wall standing are used to induce muscle fatigue and the attendant discomfort. *See Techniques* at 9 (describing techniques); *see also PREAL Manual* at 20 (explaining that stress positions are used "to create a distracting pressure" and "to humiliate or insult"). The use of these techniques is "usually self-limiting in that temporary muscle fatigue usually leads to the [detainee's] being unable to maintain the stress position after a period of time." *Background Paper* at 8. We understand that these techniques are used only to induce temporary muscle fatigue; neither of these techniques is designed or expected to cause severe physical pain. *See Techniques* at 33-34.

Cramped confinement involves placing the detainee in an uncomfortably small container. Such confinement may last up to eight hours in a relatively large container or up to two hours in a smaller container. *See Background Paper* at 8; *Techniques* at 9. The technique "accelerate[s] the physical and psychological stresses of captivity." *PREAL Manual* at 22. In OMS's view, however, cramped confinement "ha[s] not proved particularly effective" because it provides "a safehaven offering respite from interrogation." *OMS Guidelines* at 16.

The waterboard is generally considered to be "the most traumatic of the enhanced interrogation techniques," *id.* at 17, a conclusion with which we have readily agreed, *see Techniques* at 41. In this technique, the detainee is placed face-up on a gurney with his head inclined downward. A cloth is placed over his face on which cold water is then poured for periods of at most 40 seconds. This creates a barrier through which it is either difficult or impossible to breathe. The technique thereby "induce[s] a sensation of drowning." *Id.* at 13. The waterboard may be authorized for, at most, one 30-day period, during which the technique can actually be applied on no more than five days. *See id.* at 14 (describing, in detail, these and additional limitations); *see also* Letter from ▮▮▮▮▮▮▮, Associate General Counsel, Central Intelligence Agency, to Dan Levin, Acting Assistant Attorney General, Office of Legal Counsel at 1 (Aug. 19, 2004) ("*August 19 ▮▮▮▮ Letter*"). Further, there can be no more than two sessions in any 24-hour period. Each session—the time during which the detainee is strapped to the waterboard—lasts no more than two hours. There may be at most six applications of water lasting 10 seconds or longer during any session, and water may be applied for a total of no more than 12 minutes during any 24-hour period. *See Techniques* at 14.

As we have explained, "these limitations have been established with extensive input from OMS, based on experience to date with this technique and OMS's professional judgment that the health risks associated with use of the waterboard on a healthy individual subject to these limitations would be 'medically acceptable.'" *Id.* at 14 (citing *OMS Guidelines* at 18-19). In addition, although the waterboard induces fear and panic, it is not painful. *See id.* at 13.

TOP SECRET//NOFORN

II.

We conclude, first, that the CIA interrogation program does not implicate United States obligations under Article 16 of the CAT because Article 16 has limited geographic scope. By its terms, Article 16 places no obligations on a State Party outside "territory under its jurisdiction." The ordinary meaning of the phrase, the use of the phrase elsewhere in the CAT, and the negotiating history of the CAT demonstrate that the phrase "territory under its jurisdiction" is best understood as including, at most, areas where a State exercises territory-based jurisdiction; that is, areas over which the State exercises at least de facto authority as the government. As we explain below, based on CIA assurances, we understand that the interrogations conducted by the CIA do not take place in any "territory under [United States] jurisdiction" within the meaning of Article 16. We therefore conclude that the CIA interrogation program does not violate the obligations set forth in Article 16.

Apart from the terms of Article 16 as stated in the CAT, the United States undertook its obligations under the CAT subject to a Senate reservation that provides: "[T]he United States considers itself bound by the obligation under Article 16 . . . only insofar as the term 'cruel, inhuman or degrading treatment or punishment' means the cruel, unusual and inhumane treatment or punishment prohibited by the Fifth, Eighth, and/or Fourteenth Amendments to the Constitution of the United States." There is a strong argument that in requiring this reservation, the Senate intended to limit United States obligations under Article 16 to the existing obligations already imposed by these Amendments. These Amendments have been construed by the courts not to extend protections to aliens outside the United States. The CIA has also assured us that the interrogation techniques are not used within the United States or against United States persons, including both U.S. citizens and lawful permanent resident aliens.

A.

"[W]e begin with the text of the treaty and the context in which the written words are used." *Eastern Airlines, Inc. v. Floyd*, 499 U.S. 530, 534 (1991) (quotation marks omitted). *See also* Vienna Convention on the Law of Treaties, May 23, 1969, art. 31(1), 1155 U.N.T.S. 331, 340 (1980) ("A treaty shall be interpreted in good faith in accordance with the ordinary meaning to be given to the terms of the treaty in their context and in light of its object and purpose.").[12] Article 16 states that "[e]ach State Party shall undertake to prevent *in any territory under its jurisdiction* other acts of cruel, inhuman or degrading treatment or punishment which do not amount to torture." CAT Art. 16(1) (emphasis added).[13] This territorial limitation is confirmed

---

[12] The United States is not a party to the Vienna Convention and is therefore not bound by it. Nevertheless, Article 31(1)'s emphasis on textual analysis reflects international interpretive practice. *See, e.g.*, Rudolf Bernhardt, "Interpretation in International Law," in 2 *Encyclopedia of Public International Law* 1416, 1420 (1995) ("According to the prevailing opinion, the starting point in any treaty interpretation is the treaty text and the normal or ordinary meaning of its terms.").

[13] Article 16(1) provides in full:

Each State Party undertakes to prevent in any territory under its jurisdiction other acts of cruel, inhuman or degrading treatment or punishment which do not amount to torture as defined in

TOP SECRET//NOFORN

16

by Article 16's explication of this basic obligation: "In particular, the obligations contained in articles 10, 11, 12 and 13 shall apply with the substitution for references to torture of references to other forms of cruel, inhuman or degrading treatment or punishment." *Id.* Articles 11 through 13 impose on each State Party certain specific obligations, each of which is expressly limited to "territory under its jurisdiction." *See infra* pp. 18-19 (describing requirements). Although Article 10, which as incorporated in Article 16 requires each State Party to "ensure that education and information regarding the prohibition" against cruel, inhuman, or degrading treatment or punishment is given to specified government personnel, does not expressly limit its obligation to "territory under [each State's] jurisdiction," Article 10's reference to the "prohibition" against such treatment or punishment can only be understood to refer to the territorially limited obligation set forth in Article 16.

The obligations imposed by the CAT are thus more limited with respect to cruel, inhuman, or degrading treatment or punishment than with respect to torture. To be sure, Article 2, like Article 16, imposes an obligation on each State Party to prevent torture "in any territory under its jurisdiction." Article 4(1), however, separately requires each State Party to "ensure that *all* acts of torture are offenses under its criminal law." (Emphasis added.) The CAT imposes no analogous requirement with respect to cruel, inhuman, or degrading treatment or punishment.[14]

Because the CAT does not define the phrase "territory under its jurisdiction," we turn to the dictionary definitions of the relevant terms. *See Olympic Airways v. Husain*, 540 U.S. 644, 654-55 (2004) (drawing on dictionary definitions in interpreting a treaty); *Sale v. Haitian Centers Council, Inc.*, 509 U.S. 155, 180-81 (1993) (same). Common dictionary definitions of "jurisdiction" include "[t]he right and power to interpret and apply the law[; a]uthority or control[; and t]he territorial range of authority or control." *American Heritage Dictionary* 711 (1973); *American Heritage Dictionary* 978 (3d ed. 1992) (same definitions); *see also Black's Law Dictionary* 766 (5th ed. 1979) ("[a]reas of authority"). Common dictionary definitions of "territory" include "[a]n area of land[; or t]he land and waters under the jurisdiction of a state, nation, or sovereign." *American Heritage Dictionary* at 1329 (1973); *American Heritage Dictionary* at 1854 (3d ed. 1992) (same); *see also Black's Law Dictionary* at 1321 ("A part of a country separated from the rest, and subject to a particular jurisdiction. Geographical area under the jurisdiction of another country or sovereign power."); *Black's Law Dictionary* at 1512 (8th ed. 2004) ("[a] geographical area included within a particular government's jurisdiction; the portion of the earth's surface that is in a state's exclusive possession and control"). Taking these

---

article 1, when such acts are committed by or at the instigation of or with the consent or acquiescence of a public official or other person acting in an official capacity. In particular, the obligations contained in articles 10, 11, 12 and 13 shall apply with the substitution for references to torture of references to other forms of cruel, inhuman or degrading treatment or punishment.

[14] In addition, although Article 2(2) emphasizes that "[n]o exceptional circumstances whatsoever, whether a state of war or a threat of war, internal political instability or any other public emergency, may be invoked as a justification of torture," the CAT has no analogous provision with respect to cruel, inhuman or degrading treatment or punishment. Because we conclude that the CIA interrogation program does not implicate United States obligations under Article 16 and that the program would conform to United States obligations under Article 16 even if that provision did apply, we need not consider whether the absence of a provision analogous to Article 2(2) implies that State Parties could derogate from their obligations under Article 16 in extraordinary circumstances.

definitions together, we conclude that the most plausible meaning of the term "territory under its jurisdiction" is the land over which a State exercises authority and control as the government. *Cf. Rasul v. Bush*, 124 S. Ct. 2686, 2696 (2004) (concluding that "the territorial jurisdiction of the United States" subsumes areas over which "the United States exercises complete jurisdiction and control") (internal quotation marks omitted); *Cunard S.S. Co. v. Mellon*, 262 U.S. 100, 123 (1923) ("It now is settled in the United States and recognized elsewhere that the territory subject to its jurisdiction includes the land areas under its dominion and control[.]").

This understanding of the phrase "territory under its jurisdiction" is confirmed by the way the phrase is used in various provisions throughout the CAT. *See Air France v. Saks*, 470 U.S. 392, 398 (1985) (treaty drafters "logically would . . . use[] the same word in each article" when they intend to convey the same meaning throughout); J. Herman Burgers & Hans Danelius, *The United Nations Convention Against Torture: A Handbook on the Convention Against Torture and Other Cruel, Inhuman or Degrading Treatment or Punishment* 53 (1988) ("*CAT Handbook*") (noting that "it was agreed that the phrase 'territory under its jurisdiction' had the same meaning" in different articles of the CAT).

For example, Article 5 provides:

Each State Party shall take such measures as may be necessary to establish its jurisdiction over the offences referred to in article 4 [requiring each State Party to criminalize all acts of torture] in the following cases:

(a) When the offences are committed in any *territory under its jurisdiction* or on board a ship or aircraft registered in that State;

(b) When the alleged offender is a national of that State;

(c) When the victim is a national of that State if that State considers it appropriate.

CAT art. 5(1) (emphasis added). The CAT thereby distinguishes jurisdiction based on territory from jurisdiction based on the nationality of either the victim or the perpetrator. Paragraph (a) also distinguishes jurisdiction based on territory from jurisdiction based on registry of ships and aircraft. To read the phrase "territory under its jurisdiction" to subsume these other types of jurisdiction would eliminate these distinctions and render most of Article 5 surplusage. Each of Article 5's provisions, however, "like all the other words of the treaty, is to be given a meaning, if reasonably possible, and rules of construction may not be resorted to to render it meaningless or inoperative." *Factor v. Laubenheimer*, 290 U.S. 276, 303-04 (1933).

Articles 11 through 13, moreover, use the phrase "territory under its jurisdiction" in ways that presuppose that the relevant State exercises the traditional authorities of the government in such areas. Article 11 requires each State to "keep under systematic review . . . arrangements for the custody and treatment of persons subjected to any form of arrest, detention or imprisonment in any territory under its jurisdiction." Article 12 mandates that "[e]ach State Party shall ensure that its competent authorities proceed to a prompt and impartial investigation, wherever there is reasonable ground to believe that an act of torture has been committed in any territory under its jurisdiction." Similarly, Article 13 requires "[e]ach State Party [to] ensure that any individual who alleges he has been subjected to torture in any territory under its jurisdiction has the right to complain to, and to have his case promptly and impartially examined by, its competent authorities." These provisions assume that the relevant State exercises traditional governmental authority—including the authority to arrest, detain, imprison, and investigate crime—within any "territory under its jurisdiction."

Three other provisions underscore this point. Article 2(1) requires each State Party to "take effective legislative, administrative, judicial or other measures to prevent such acts of torture in any territory under its jurisdiction." "Territory under its jurisdiction," therefore, is most reasonably read to refer to areas over which States exercise broad governmental authority—the areas over which States could take legislative, administrative, or judicial action. Article 5(2), moreover, enjoins "[e]ach State Party . . . to establish its jurisdiction over such offences in cases where the alleged offender is present in any territory under its jurisdiction and it does not extradite him." Article 7(1) similarly requires State Parties to extradite suspects or refer them to "competent authorities for the purpose of prosecution." These provisions evidently contemplate that each State Party has authority to extradite and prosecute those suspected of torture in any "territory under its jurisdiction." That is, each State Party is expected to operate as the government in "territory under its jurisdiction."[15]

This understanding is supported by the negotiating record. *See Zicherman v. Korean Air Lines Co.*, 516 U.S. 217, 226 (1996) ("Because a treaty ratified by the United States is not only the law of this land, see U.S. Const., Art. II, § 2, but also an agreement among sovereign powers, we have traditionally considered as aids to its interpretation the negotiating and drafting history . . . ."); Vienna Convention on the Law of Treaties, art. 32 (permitting recourse to "the preparatory work of the treaty and the circumstances of its conclusion" *inter alia* "to confirm" the ordinary meaning of the text). The original Swedish proposal, which was the basis for the first draft of the CAT, contained a predecessor to Article 16 that would have required that "[e]ach State Party undertake[] to ensure that [a proscribed act] does not take place *within its jurisdiction*." Draft International Convention Against Torture and Other Cruel, Inhuman or Degrading Treatment or Punishment, submitted by Sweden on January 18, 1978, arts. 2-3, E/CN.4/1285, in *CAT Handbook* app. 6, at 203 (emphasis added); *CAT Handbook* at 47. France objected that the phrase "within its jurisdiction" was too broad. For example, it was concerned that the phrase might extend to signatories' citizens located in territory belonging to other nations. *See Report of the Pre-Sessional Working Group*, E/CN.4/L.1470 (1979), *reprinted in*

---

[15] Article 6 may suggest an interpretation of the phrase "territory under its jurisdiction" that is potentially broader than the traditional notion of "territory." Article 6(1) directs a State Party "*in whose territory* a person alleged to have committed [certain offenses] is *present*" to take the suspected offender into custody. (Emphases added.) The use of the word "territory" in Article 6 rather than the phrase "territory under its jurisdiction" suggests that the terms have distinct meanings. *See Factor*, 290 U.S. at 303-04 (stating that treaty language should not be construed to render certain phrases "meaningless or inoperative"). Article 6 may thus support the position, discussed below, that "territory under its jurisdiction" may extend beyond sovereign territory to encompass areas where a State exercises de facto authority as the government, such as occupied territory. *See infra* p. 20. Article 20, which refers to "the territory of a State Party" may support the same inference.

Report of the United Nations Commission on Human Rights, E/CN.4/1347 35, 40 (1979); *CAT Handbook* at 48. Although France suggested replacing "within its jurisdiction" with "in its territory," the phrase "any territory under its jurisdiction" was chosen instead. *See CAT Handbook* at 48.

There is some evidence that the United States understood these phrases to mean essentially the same thing. *See, e.g.,* Exec. Report 101-30, 101st Cong., 2d Sess., 23-24 (Aug. 30, 1990) (Senate Foreign Relations Committee Report) (suggesting that the phrase "in any territory under its jurisdiction" would impose obligations on a State Party with respect to conduct committed "in its territory" but not with respect to conduct "occurring abroad"); *Convention Against Torture: Hearing Before the Committee on Foreign Relations, United State. Senate*, S. Hrg. 101-718 at 7 (Jan. 30, 1990) (prepared statement of Hon. Abraham D. Sofaer, Legal Adviser, Department of State) (stating that under Article 2, State Parties would be obligated "to take administrative, judicial or other measures to prevent torture *within their territory*") (emphasis added). Other evidence, however, suggests that the phrase "territory under its jurisdiction" has a somewhat broader meaning than "in its territory." According to the record of the negotiation relating to Articles 12 and 13 of the CAT, "[i]n response to the question on the scope of the phrase 'territory under its jurisdiction' as contained in these articles, it was said that it was intended to cover, *inter alia*, territories still under colonial rule and occupied territory." U.N. Doc. E/CN.4/1367, Mar. 5, 1980, at 13. And one commentator has stated that the negotiating record suggests that the phrase "territory under its jurisdiction" "is not limited to a State's land territory, its territorial sea and the airspace over its land and sea territory, but it also applies to territories under military occupation, to colonial territories and to any other territories over which a State has factual control." *Id.* at 131. Others have suggested that the phrase would also reach conduct occurring on ships and aircraft registered in a State. *See CAT Handbook* at 48; Message from the President of the United States Transmitting the Convention Against Torture and Other Cruel, Inhuman or Degrading Treatment or Punishment, S. Treaty Doc. No. 100-20, at 5 (1988) (Secretary of State Schultz) (asserting that "territory under its jurisdiction" "refers to all places that the State Party controls as a governmental authority, including ships and aircraft registered in that State").[16]

Thus, although portions of the negotiating record of the CAT may support reading the phrase "any territory under its jurisdiction" to include not only sovereign territory but also areas subject to de facto government authority (and perhaps registered ships and aircraft), the negotiating record as a whole tends to confirm that the phrase does not extend to places where a State Party does not exercise authority as the government.

The CIA has assured us that the interrogations at issue here do not take place within the sovereign territory or special maritime and territorial jurisdiction ("SMTJ") of the United States. *See* 18 U.S.C. § 5 (defining "United States"); *id.* § 7 (defining SMTJ). As relevant here, we

---

[16] This suggestion is in tension with the text of Article 5(1)(a), which seems to distinguish "territory under [a State's] jurisdiction" from "ship[s] or aircraft registered in that State." *See Chan v. Korean Air Lines, Ltd.*, 490 U.S. 122, 134 n.5 (1989) (noting that where treaty text is not perfectly clear, the "natural meaning" of the text "could properly be contradicted only by clear drafting history"). Because the CIA has assured us that its interrogations do not take place on ships or aircraft registered in the United States, we need not resolve this issue here.

believe that the phrase "any territory under its jurisdiction" certainly reaches no further than the sovereign territory and the SMTJ of the United States.[17] Indeed, in many respects, it probably does not reach this far. Although many provisions of the SMTJ invoke territorial bases of jurisdiction, other provisions assert jurisdiction on other grounds, including, for example, sections 7(5) through 7(9), which assert jurisdiction over certain offenses committed by or against United States citizens. Accordingly, we conclude that the interrogation program does not take place within "territory under [United States] jurisdiction" and therefore does not violate Article 16—even absent the Senate's reservation limiting United States obligations under Article 16, which we discuss in the next section.

B.

As a condition to its advice and consent to the ratification of the CAT, the Senate required a reservation that provides that the United States is

> bound by the obligation under Article 16 to prevent "cruel, inhuman or degrading treatment or punishment," only insofar as the term "cruel, inhuman or degrading treatment or punishment" means the cruel, unusual and inhumane treatment or punishment prohibited by the Fifth, Eighth, and/or Fourteenth Amendments to the Constitution of the United States.

Cong. Rec. 36,198 (1990). This reservation, which the United States deposited with its instrument of ratification, is legally binding and defines the scope of United States obligations under Article 16 of the CAT. *See Relevance of Senate Ratification History to Treaty Interpretation*, 11 Op. O.L.C. 28, 33 (1987) (Reservations deposited with the instrument of ratification "are generally binding . . . both internationally and domestically . . . in . . . subsequent interpretation of the treaty.").[18]

Under the terms of the reservation, the United States is obligated to prevent "cruel, inhuman or degrading treatment" only to the extent that such treatment amounts to "the cruel, unusual and inhumane treatment or punishment prohibited by the Fifth, Eighth, and/or Fourteenth Amendments." Giving force to the terms of this reservation, treatment that is not

---

[17] As we have explained, there is an argument that "territory under [a State's] jurisdiction" might also include occupied territory. Accordingly, at least absent the Senate's reservation, Article 16's obligations might extend to occupied territory. Because the United States is not currently an occupying power within the meaning of the laws of war anywhere in the world, we need not decide whether occupied territory is "territory under [United States] jurisdiction."

[18] "The Senate's right to qualify its consent to ratification by reservations, amendments and interpretations was established through a reservation to the Jay treaty of 1794;" Quincy Wright, *The Control of American Foreign Relations* 253 (1922), and has been frequently exercised since then. The Supreme Court has indicated its acceptance of this practice. *See Haver v. Yaker*, 76 U.S. (9 Wall.) 32, 35 (1869); *United States v. Schooner Peggy*, 5 U.S. (1 Cranch) 103, 107 (1801). *See also Constitutionality of Proposed Conditions to Senate Consent to the Interim Convention on the Conservation of North Pacific Fur Seals*, 10 Op. O.L.C. 12, 16 (1986) ("[T]he Senate's practice of conditioning its consent to particular treaties is well-established.").

"prohibited by" these amendments would not violate United States obligations as limited by the reservation.

Conceivably, one might read the text of the reservation as limiting only the substantive (as opposed to the territorial) reach of United States obligations under Article 16. That would not be an unreasonable reading of the text. Under this view, the reservation replaced only the phrase "cruel, inhuman or degrading treatment or punishment" and left untouched the phrase "in any territory under its jurisdiction," which defines the geographic scope of the Article. The text of the reservation, however, is susceptible to another reasonable reading—one suggesting that the Senate intended to ensure that the United States would, with respect to Article 16, undertake no obligations not already imposed by the Constitution itself. Under this reading, the reference to the treatment or punishment prohibited by the constitutional provisions does not distinguish between the substantive scope of the constitutional prohibitions and their geographic scope. As we discuss below, this second reading is strongly supported by the Senate's ratification history of the CAT.

The Summary and Analysis of the CAT submitted by the President to the Senate in 1988 expressed concern that "Article 16 is arguably broader than existing U.S. law." *Summary and Analysis of the Convention Against Torture and Other Cruel, Inhuman or Degrading Treatment or Punishment, in* S. Treaty Doc. No. 100-20, at 15. "In view of the ambiguity of the terms," the Executive Branch suggested "that U.S. obligations under this article [Article 16] should be limited to *conduct prohibited by the U.S. Constitution.*" S. Exec. Rep. No. 101-30, at 8 (1990) (emphasis added); *see also id.* at 25-26. Accordingly, it proposed what became the Senate's reservation in order "[t]o make clear that the United States construes the phrase ["cruel, inhuman or degrading treatment or punishment"] to be coextensive with its constitutional guarantees against cruel, unusual, and inhumane treatment." *Id.* at 25-26; S. Treaty Doc. No. 100-20, at 15 (same). As State Department Legal Adviser Abraham D. Sofaer explained, "because the Constitution of the United States directly addresses this area of the law . . . [the reservation] would limit our obligations under this Convention to the proscriptions already covered in our Constitution." *Convention Against Torture: Hearing Before the Senate Comm. on Foreign Relations*, 101st Cong. 11 (1990) (prepared statement). The Senate Foreign Relations Committee expressed the same concern about the potential scope of Article 16 and recommended the same reservation to the Senate. *See* S. Exec. Rep. No. 101-30, at 8, 25-26.

Furthermore, the Senate declared that Articles 1 through 16 of the CAT are not self-executing, *see* Cong. Rec. 36,198 (1990), and the discussions surrounding this declaration in the ratification history also indicate that the United States did not intend to undertake any obligations under Article 16 that extended beyond those already imposed by the Constitution. The Administration expressed the view that "as indicated in the original Presidential transmittal, existing Federal and State law appears sufficient to implement the Convention," except that "new Federal legislation would be required *only to establish criminal jurisdiction under Article 5.*" Letter for Senator Pressler, from Janet Mullins, Assistant Secretary, Legislative Affairs, Department of State (April 4, 1990), *in* S. Exec. Rep. No. 101-30, at 41 (emphasis added). It was understood that "the majority of the obligations to be undertaken by the United States pursuant to the Convention [were] already covered by existing law" and that "additional implementing legislation [would] be needed *only with respect to article 5.*" S. Exec. Rep. No. 101-30, at 10 (emphasis added). Congress then enacted 18 U.S.C. §§ 2340-2349A, the only "necessary legislation to implement" United States obligations under the CAT, noting that the United States would "not become a party to the Convention until the necessary implementing legislation is enacted." S. Rep. No. 103-107, at 366 (1993). Reading Article 16 to extend the substantive standards of the Constitution in contexts where they did not already apply would be difficult to square with the evident understanding of the United States that existing law would satisfy its obligations under the CAT except with respect to Article 5. The ratification history thus strongly supports the view that United States obligations under Article 16 were intended to reach no further—substantively, territorially, or in any other respect—than its obligations under the Fifth, Eighth, and Fourteenth Amendments.

The Supreme Court has repeatedly suggested in various contexts that the Constitution does not apply to aliens outside the United States. *See, e.g., United States v. Belmont*, 301 U.S. 324, 332 (1937) ("[O]ur Constitution, laws, and policies have no extraterritorial operation, unless in respect of our own citizens."); *United States v. Curtiss-Wright Export Corp.*, 299 U.S. 304, 318 (1936) ("Neither the Constitution nor the laws passed in pursuance of it have any force in foreign territory unless in respect of our own citizens . . . ."); *see also United States v. Verdugo-Urquidez*, 494 U.S. 259, 271 (1990) (noting that cases relied upon by an alien asserting constitutional rights "establish only that aliens receive constitutional protections when they have come within the territory of the United States and developed substantial connections with this country"). Federal courts of appeals, in turn, have held that "[t]he Constitution does not extend its guarantees to nonresident aliens living outside the United States," *Vancouver Women's Health Collective Soc'y v. A.H. Robins Co.*, 820 F.2d 1359, 1363 (4th Cir. 1987); that "non-resident aliens . . . plainly cannot appeal to the protection of the Constitution or laws of the United States," *Pauling v. McElroy*, 278 F.2d 252, 254 n.3 (D.C. Cir. 1960) (per curiam); and that a "foreign entity without property or presence in this country has no constitutional rights, under the due process clause or otherwise," *32 County Sovereignty Comm. v. Dep't of State*, 292 F.3d 797, 799 (D.C. Cir. 2002) (quoting *People's Mojahedin Org. of Iran v. Dep't of State*, 182 F.3d 17, 22 (D.C. Cir. 1999)).[19]

As we explain below, it is the Fifth Amendment that is potentially relevant in the present context. With respect to that Amendment, the Supreme Court has "rejected the claim that aliens are entitled to Fifth Amendment rights outside the sovereign territory of the United States." *Verdugo-Urquidez*, 494 U.S. at 269. In *Verdugo-Urquidez*, 494 U.S. at 269, the Court noted its "emphatic" "rejection of extraterritorial application of the Fifth Amendment" in *Johnson v. Eisentrager*, 339 U.S. 763 (1950), which rejected "[t]he doctrine that the term 'any person' in the Fifth Amendment spreads its protection over alien enemies anywhere in the world engaged in hostilities against us," id. at 782. Accord *Zadvydas v. Davis*, 533 U.S. 678, 693 (2001) (citing *Verdugo-Urquidez* and *Eisentrager* and noting that "[i]t is well established that" Fifth Amendment protections "are unavailable to aliens outside of our geographic borders"). Federal

---

[19] The Restatement (Third) of Foreign Relations Law asserts that "[a]lthough the matter has not been authoritatively adjudicated, at least some actions by the United States in respect to foreign nationals outside the country are also subject to constitutional limitations." Id. § 722, cmt. m. This statement is contrary to the authorities cited in the text.

TOP SECRET//  //NOFORN

courts of appeals have similarly held that "non-resident aliens who have insufficient contacts with the United States are not entitled to Fifth Amendment protections." *Jifry v. F.A.A.*, 370 F.3d 1174, 1182 (D.C. Cir. 2004); *see also Harbury v. Deutch*, 233 F.3d 596, 604 (D.C. Cir. 2000) (relying on *Eisentrager* and *Verdugo-Urquidez* to conclude that an alien could not state a due process claim for torture allegedly inflicted by United States agents abroad), *rev'd on other grounds sub nom. Christopher v. Harbury*, 536 U.S. 403 (2002); *Cuban Am. Bar Ass'n, Inc. v. Christopher*, 43 F.3d 1412, 1428-29 (11th Cir. 1995) (relying on *Eisentrager* and *Verdugo-Urquidez* to conclude that aliens held at Guantanamo Bay lack Fifth Amendment rights).[20]

The reservation required by the Senate as a condition of its advice and consent to the ratification of the CAT thus tends to confirm the territorially limited reach of U.S. obligations under Article 16. Indeed, there is a strong argument that, by limiting United States obligations under Article 16 to those that certain provisions of the Constitution already impose, the Senate's reservation limits the territorial reach of Article 16 even more sharply than does the text of Article 16 standing alone. Under this view, Article 16 would impose no obligations with respect

---

[20] The Court's decision in *Rasul v. Bush*, 124 S. Ct. 2686 (2004), is not to the contrary. To be sure, the Court stated in a footnote that:

> Petitioners' allegations—that, although they have engaged neither in combat nor in acts of terrorism against the United States, they have been held in Executive detention for more than two years in territory subject to the long-term, exclusive jurisdiction and control of the United States, without access to counsel and without being charged with any wrongdoing—unquestionably describe "custody in violation of the Constitution or laws or treaties of the United States."

Id. at 2698 n.15. We believe this footnote is best understood to leave intact the Court's settled understanding of the Fifth Amendment. First, the Court limited its holding to the issue before it: whether the federal courts have *statutory jurisdiction* over habeas petitions brought by such aliens held at Guantanamo as enemy combatants. *See id.* at 2699 ("Whether and what further proceedings may become necessary . . . are matters that we need not address now. What is presently at stake is only whether the federal courts have jurisdiction to determine the legality of the Executive's potentially indefinite detention of individuals who claim to be wholly innocent of wrongdoing."). Indeed, the Court granted the petition for writ of certiorari "limited to the following Question: Whether United States courts lack jurisdiction to consider challenges to the legality of the detention of foreign nationals captured abroad in connection with hostilities and incarcerated at the Guantanamo Bay Naval Base, Cuba." *Rasul v. Bush*, 540 U.S. 1003 (2003).

Second, the footnote relies on a portion of Justice Kennedy's concurrence in *Verdugo-Urquidez* "and the cases cited therein," *Rasul*, 124 S. Ct. at 2698 n.15. In this portion of Justice Kennedy's *Verdugo-Urquidez* concurrence, Justice Kennedy discusses the *Insular Cases*. These cases stand for the proposition that although not every provision of the Constitution applies in United States territory overseas, certain core constitutional protections may apply in certain insular territories of the United States. *See also, e.g., Reid v. Covert*, 354 U.S. 1, 74-75 (1957) (Harlan, J., concurring in judgment) (discussing *Insular Cases*); *Balzac v. Porto Rico*, 258 U.S. 298 (1922). Given that the Court in *Rasul* stressed GTMO's unique status as "territory subject to the long-term, exclusive jurisdiction and control of the United States," *Rasul*, 124 S. Ct. at 2698 n.15, in the very sentence that cited Justice Kennedy's concurrence, it is conceivable that footnote 15 might reflect, at most, a willingness to consider whether GTMO is similar in significant respects to the territories at issue in the *Insular Cases*. *See also id.* at 2696 (noting that under the agreement with Cuba "the United States exercises complete jurisdiction and control over the Guantanamo Bay Naval Base") (internal quotation marks omitted); *id.* at 2700 (Kennedy, J., concurring) (asserting that "Guantanamo Bay is in every practical respect a United States territory" and explaining that "[w]hat matters is the unchallenged and indefinite control that the United States has long exercised over Guantanamo Bay").

TOP SECRET//  //NOFORN

to aliens outside the United States.[21] And because the CIA has informed us that these techniques are not authorized for use against United States persons, or within the United States, they would not, under this view, violate Article 16. Even if the reservation is read only to confirm the territorial limits explicit in Article 16, however, or even if it is read not to bear on this question at all, the program would still not violate Article 16 for the reasons discussed in Part II.A. Accordingly, we need not decide here the precise effect, if any, of the Senate reservation on the geographic scope of U.S. obligations under Article 16.[22]

III.

You have also asked us to consider whether the CIA interrogation program would violate the substantive standards applicable to the United States under Article 16 if, contrary to the conclusions reached in Part II above, those standards did extend to the CIA interrogation program. Pursuant to the Senate's reservation, the United States is bound by Article 16 to prevent "the cruel, unusual and inhumane treatment or punishment prohibited by the Fifth, Eighth, and/or Fourteenth Amendments to the Constitution of the United States." As we explain, the relevant test is whether use of the CIA's enhanced interrogation techniques constitutes government conduct that "shocks the conscience." Based on our understanding of the relevant case law and the CIA's descriptions of the interrogation program, we conclude that use of the enhanced interrogation techniques, subject to all applicable conditions, limitations, and safeguards, does not "shock the conscience." We emphasize, however, that this analysis calls for the application of a somewhat subjective test with only limited guidance from the Court. We therefore cannot predict with confidence whether a court would agree with our conclusions, though, as discussed more fully below, we believe the interpretation of Article 16's substantive standard is unlikely to be subject to judicial inquiry.

---

[21] Additional analysis may be required in the case of aliens entitled to lawful permanent resident status. Compare *Kwong Hai Chew v. Colding*, 344 U.S. 590 (1953), with *Shaughnessy v. United States ex rel. Mezei*, 345 U.S. 206 (1953). You have informed us that the CIA does not use these techniques on any United States persons, including lawful permanent residents, and we do not here address United States obligations under Article 16 with respect to such aliens.

[22] Our analysis is not affected by the recent enactment of the Emergency Supplemental Appropriations Act for Defense, the Global War on Terror, and Tsunami Relief, 2005, Pub. L. No. 109-13, 119 Stat. 231 (2005). Section 1031(a)(1) of that law provides that

> [n]one of the funds appropriated or otherwise made available by this Act shall be obligated or expended to subject any person in the custody or under the physical control of the United States to torture or cruel, inhuman, or degrading treatment or punishment that is prohibited by the Constitution, laws, or treaties of the United States.

119 Stat. at 256. Because the Senate reservation, as deposited with the United States instrument of ratification, defines United States obligations under Article 16 of the CAT, this statute does not prohibit the expenditure of funds for conduct that does not violate United States obligations under Article 16, as limited by the Senate reservation. Furthermore, this statute itself defines "cruel, inhuman, or degrading treatment or punishment" as "the cruel, unusual, and inhumane treatment or punishment prohibited by the fifth amendment, eighth amendment, or fourteenth amendment to the Constitution of the United States." *Id.* § 1031(b)(2).

TOP SECRETNOFORN

A.

Although, pursuant to the Senate's reservation, United States obligations under Article 16 extend to "the cruel, unusual and inhumane treatment or punishment prohibited by the Fifth, Eighth, and/or Fourteenth Amendments to the Constitution of the United States," only the Fifth Amendment is potentially relevant here. The Fourteenth Amendment provides, in relevant part: "No *State* shall . . . deprive any person of life, liberty, or property, without due process of law." (Emphasis added.) This Amendment does not apply to actions taken by the federal Government. *See, e.g., San Francisco Arts & Athletics, Inc. v. United States Olympic Comm.*, 483 U.S. 522, 542 n.21 (1987) (explaining that the Fourteenth Amendment "does not apply" to the federal Government); *Bolling v. Sharpe*, 347 U.S. 497, 498-99 (1954) (noting that the Fifth Amendment rather than the Fourteenth Amendment applies to actions taken by the District of Columbia). The Eighth Amendment prohibits the infliction of "cruel and unusual *punishments*." (Emphasis added.) As the Supreme Court has repeatedly held, the Eighth Amendment does not apply until there has been a formal adjudication of guilt. *E.g., Bell v. Wolfish*, 441 U.S. 520, 535 n.16 (1979); *Ingraham v. Wright*, 430 U.S. 651, 671 n.40 (1977). *See also In re Guantanamo Detainee Cases*, 355 F. Supp. 2d 443, 480 (D.D.C. 2005) (dismissing detainees' claims based on Eighth Amendment because "the Eighth Amendment applies only after an individual is convicted of a crime") (stayed pending appeal). The same conclusion concerning the limited applicability of the Eighth Amendment under Article 16 was expressly recognized by the Senate and the Executive Branch during the CAT ratification deliberations:

> The Eighth Amendment prohibition of cruel and unusual punishment is, of the three [constitutional provisions cited in the Senate reservation], the most limited in scope, as this amendment has consistently been interpreted as protecting only "those convicted of crimes." *Ingraham v. Wright*, 430 U.S. 651, 664 (1977). The Eighth Amendment does, however, afford protection against torture and ill-treatment of persons in prison and similar situations of *criminal punishment*.

Summary and Analysis of the Convention Against Torture and Other Cruel, Inhuman or Degrading Treatment or Punishment, *in* S. Treaty Doc. No. 100-20, at 9 (emphasis added). Because the high value detainees on whom the CIA might use enhanced interrogation techniques have not been convicted of any crime, the substantive requirements of the Eighth Amendment would not be relevant here, even if we assume that Article 16 has application to the CIA's interrogation program.[23]

The Fifth Amendment, however, is not subject to these same limitations. As potentially relevant here, the substantive due process component of the Fifth Amendment protects against executive action that "shocks the conscience." *Rochin v. California*, 342 U.S. 165, 172 (1952); *see also County of Sacramento v. Lewis*, 523 U.S. 833, 846 (1998) ("To this end, for half a

---

[23] To be sure, treatment amounting to punishment (let alone, cruel and unusual punishment) generally cannot be imposed on individuals who have not been convicted of crimes. But this prohibition flows from the Fifth Amendment rather than the Eighth. *See Wolfish*, 441 U.S. at 535 n.16; *United States v. Salerno*, 481 U.S. 739, 746-47 (1987). *See also infra* note 26.

TOP SECRETNOFORN

century now we have spoken of the cognizable level of executive abuse of power as that which shocks the conscience.").[24]

B.

We must therefore determine whether the CIA interrogation program involves conduct that "shocks the conscience." The Court has indicated that whether government conduct can be said to "shock the conscience" depends primarily on whether the conduct is "arbitrary in the constitutional sense," *Lewis*, 523 U.S. at 846 (internal quotation marks omitted); that is, whether it amounts to the "exercise of power without any reasonable justification in the service of a legitimate governmental objective," *id.* "[C]onduct intended to injure in some way unjustifiable by any government interest is the sort of official action most likely to rise to the conscience-shocking level," *id.* at 849, although, in some cases, deliberate indifference to the risk of inflicting such unjustifiable injury might also "shock the conscience," *id.* at 850-51. The Court has also suggested that it is appropriate to consider whether, in light of "traditional executive behavior, of contemporary practice, and of the standards of blame generally applied to them," conduct "is so egregious, so outrageous, that it may fairly be said to shock the contemporary conscience." *Id.* at 847 n.8.[25]

Several considerations complicate our analysis. First, there are relatively few cases in which the Court has analyzed whether conduct "shocks the conscience," and these cases involve contexts that differ dramatically from the CIA interrogation program. Further, the Court has emphasized that there is "no calibrated yard stick" with which to determine whether conduct "shocks the conscience." *Id.* at 847. To the contrary: "Rules of due process are not . . . subject to mechanical application in unfamiliar territory." *Id.* at 850. A claim that government conduct "shocks the conscience," therefore, requires "an exact analysis of circumstances." *Id.* The Court has explained:

---

[24] Because what is at issue under the text of the Senate reservation is the subset of "cruel, inhuman or degrading treatment" that is "the cruel, unusual and inhumane treatment . . . prohibited by the Fifth . . . Amendment[]," we do not believe that the procedural aspects of the Fifth Amendment are relevant, at least in the context of interrogation techniques unrelated to the criminal justice system. Nor, given the language of Article 16 and the reservation, do we believe that United States obligations under this Article include other aspects of the Fifth Amendment, such as the Takings Clause or the various privacy rights that the Supreme Court has found to be protected by the Due Process Clause.

[25] It appears that conscience-shocking conduct is a necessary but perhaps not sufficient condition to establishing that executive conduct violates substantive due process. *See Lewis*, 523 U.S. at 847 n.8 ("Only if the *necessary condition* of egregious behavior were satisfied would there be a *possibility* of recognizing a substantive due process right to be free of such executive action, and only then might there be a debate about the sufficiency of historical examples of enforcement of the right claimed, or its recognition in other ways.") (emphases added); *see also, e.g., Terrell v. Larson*, 396 F.3d 975, 978 n.1 (8th Cir. 2005) ("To violate substantive due process, the conduct of an executive official must be conscience shocking *and* must violate" a fundamental right.); *Slusarchuck v. Hoff*, 346 F.3d 1178, 1181 (8th Cir. 2003). It is therefore arguable that conscience-shocking behavior would not violate the Constitution if it did not violate a fundamental right or if it were narrowly tailored to serve a compelling state interest. *See, e.g., Washington v. Glucksberg*, 521 U.S. 702, 721 (1997). Because we conclude that the CIA interrogation program does not "shock the conscience," we need not address these issues here.

TOP SECRET/███████/NOFORN

> The phrase [due process of law] formulates a concept less rigid and more fluid than those envisaged in other specific and particular provisions of the Bill of Rights. Its application is less a matter of rule. Asserted denial is to be tested by an appraisal of the totality of facts in a given case. That which may, in one setting, constitute a denial of fundamental fairness, shocking to the universal sense of justice, may, in other circumstances, and in light of other considerations, fall short of such a denial.

Id. at 850 (quoting *Betts v. Brady*, 316 U.S. 455, 462 (1942)) (alteration in *Lewis*). Our task, therefore, is to apply in a novel context a highly fact-dependent test with little guidance from the Supreme Court.

I.

We first consider whether the CIA interrogation program involves conduct that is "constitutionally arbitrary." We conclude that it does not. Indeed, we find no evidence of "conduct intended to injure in some way unjustifiable by any government interest," *id.* at 849, or of deliberate indifference to the possibility of such unjustifiable injury, *see id.* at 853.

As an initial matter, the Court has made clear that whether conduct can be considered to be constitutionally arbitrary depends vitally on whether it furthers a government interest, and, if it does, the nature and importance of that interest. The test is not merely whether the conduct is "intended to injure," but rather whether it is "intended to injure *in some way unjustifiable by any government interest.*" *Id.* at 849 (emphasis added). It is the "exercise of power *without any reasonable justification in the service of a legitimate governmental objective*" that can be said to "shock the conscience." *Id.* at 846 (emphasis added). In *United States v. Salerno*, 481 U.S. 739, 748 (1987), for example, the Court explained that the Due Process Clause "lays down [no] . . . categorical imperative," and emphasized that the Court has "repeatedly held that the Government's regulatory interest in community safety can, in appropriate circumstances, outweigh an individual's liberty interest." *See also Hamdi v. Rumsfeld*, 124 S. Ct. 2633, 2646 (2004) (plurality opinion) (explaining that the individual's interests must be weighed against the government's). The government's interest is thus an important part of the context that must be carefully considered in evaluating an asserted violation of due process.[26]

---

[26] The pretrial detention context is informative. Analysis of the government's interest and purpose in imposing a condition of confinement is essential to determining whether there is a violation of due process in this context. *See Salerno*, 481 U.S. at 747-50. The government has a legitimate interest in "effectuat[ing] th[e] detention," *Wolfish*, 441 U.S. at 537, which supports government action that "may rationally be connected" to the detention, *Salerno*, 481 U.S. at 747 (internal quotation marks omitted). By contrast, inflicting cruel and unusual punishment on such detainees would violate due process because the government has no legitimate interest in inflicting punishment prior to conviction. *See Wolfish*, 441 U.S. at 535 & n.16.

In addition, *Lewis* suggests that the Court's Eighth Amendment jurisprudence sheds at least some light on the due process inquiry. *See* 523 U.S. at 852-53 (analogizing the due process inquiry to the Eighth Amendment context and noting that in both cases "liability should turn on 'whether force was applied in a good faith effort to maintain or restore discipline or maliciously and sadistically for the very purpose of causing harm'") (quoting *Whitley v. Albers*, 475 U.S. 312, 320-21 (1986)). The interrogation program we consider does not involve or allow

TOP SECRET/███████/NOFORN

TOP SECRET/ ~~███████~~ /NOFORN

Al Qaeda's demonstrated ability to launch sophisticated attacks causing mass casualties within the United States and against United States interests worldwide, as well as its continuing efforts to plan and to execute such attacks, *see supra* p. 9, indisputably pose a grave and continuing threat. "It is 'obvious and unarguable' that no governmental interest is more compelling than the security of the Nation." *Haig v. Agee*, 453 U.S. 280, 307 (1981) (citations omitted); *see also Salerno*, 481 U.S. at 748 (noting that "society's interest is at its peak" "in times of war or insurrection"). It is this paramount interest that the Government seeks to vindicate through the interrogation program. Indeed, the program, which the CIA believes "has been a key reason why al-Qa'ida has failed to launch a spectacular attack in the West since 11 September 2001," *Effectiveness Memo* at 2, directly furthers that interest, producing substantial quantities of otherwise unavailable actionable intelligence. As detailed above, ordinary interrogation techniques had little effect on either KSM or Zubaydah. Use of enhanced techniques, however, led to critical, actionable intelligence such as the discovery of the Guraba Cell, which was tasked with executing KSM's planned Second Wave attacks against Los Angeles. Interrogations of these most valuable detainees and comparatively lower-tier high value detainees ███████████████████ have also greatly increased the CIA's understanding of our enemy and its plans.

As evidenced by our discussion in Part I, the CIA goes to great lengths to ensure that the techniques are applied only as reasonably necessary to protect this paramount interest in "the security of the Nation." Various aspects of the program ensure that enhanced techniques will be used only in the interrogations of the detainees who are most likely to have critical, actionable intelligence. The CIA screening procedures, which the CIA imposes in addition to the standards applicable to activities conducted pursuant to paragraph four of the Memorandum of Notification, ensure that the techniques are not used unless the CIA reasonably believes that the detainee is a "senior member of al-Qai'da or [its affiliates]," *and* the detainee has "knowledge of imminent terrorist threats against the USA" or has been directly involved in the planning of attacks. *January 4 ███ Fax* at 5; *supra* p. 5. The fact that enhanced techniques have been used to date in the interrogations of only 28 high value detainees out of the 94 detainees in CIA custody demonstrates this selectivity.

Use of the waterboard is limited still further, requiring "credible intelligence that a terrorist attack is imminent; . . . substantial and credible indicators that the subject has actionable intelligence that can prevent, disrupt or delay this attack; and [a determination that o]ther interrogation methods have failed to elicit the information [and that] . . . other . . . methods are unlikely to elicit this information *within the perceived time limit for preventing the attack*." *August 2 Rizzo Letter* (attachment). Once again, the CIA's practice confirms the program's selectivity. CIA interrogators have used the waterboard on only three detainees to date—KSM, Zubaydah, and Al-Nashiri—and have not used it at all since March 2003.

---

the malicious or sadistic infliction of harm. Rather, as discussed in the text, interrogation techniques are used only as reasonably deemed necessary to further a government interest of the highest order, and have been carefully designed to avoid inflicting severe pain or suffering or any other lasting or significant harm and to minimize the risk of any harm that does not further this government interest. *See infra* pp. 29-31.

TOP SECRET/  /NOFORN

29

TOP SECRET/ NOFORN

Moreover, enhanced techniques are considered only when the on-scene interrogation team considers them necessary because a detainee is withholding or manipulating important, actionable intelligence or there is insufficient time to try other techniques. For example, as recounted above, the CIA used enhanced techniques in the interrogations of KSM and Zubaydah only after ordinary interrogation tactics had failed. Even then, CIA Headquarters must make the decision whether to use enhanced techniques in any interrogation. Officials at CIA Headquarters can assess the situation based on the interrogation team's reports and intelligence from a variety of other sources and are therefore well positioned to assess the importance of the information sought.

Once approved, techniques are used only in escalating fashion so that it is unlikely that a detainee would be subjected to more duress than is reasonably necessary to elicit the information sought. Thus, no technique is used on a detainee unless use of that technique at that time appears necessary to obtaining the intelligence. And use of enhanced techniques ceases "if the detainee is judged to be consistently providing accurate intelligence or if he is no longer believed to have actionable intelligence." *Techniques* at 5. Indeed, use of the techniques usually ends after just a few days when the detainee begins participating. Enhanced techniques, therefore, would not be used on a detainee not reasonably thought to possess important, actionable intelligence that could not be obtained otherwise.

Not only is the interrogation program closely tied to a government interest of the highest order, it is also designed, through its careful limitations and screening criteria, to avoid causing any severe pain or suffering or inflicting significant or lasting harm. As the *OMS Guidelines* explain, "[i]n all instances the general goal of these techniques is a psychological impact, and not some physical effect, with a specific goal of 'dislocat[ing] [the detainee's] expectations regarding the treatment he believes he will receive.'" *OMS Guidelines* at 8-9 (second alteration in original). Furthermore, techniques can be used only if there are no medical or psychological contraindications. Thus, no technique is ever used if there is reason to believe it will cause the detainee significant mental or physical harm. When enhanced techniques are used, OMS closely monitors the detainee's condition to ensure that he does not, in fact, experience severe pain or suffering or sustain any significant or lasting harm.

This facet of our analysis bears emphasis. We do not conclude that any conduct, no matter how extreme, could be justified by a sufficiently weighty government interest coupled with appropriate tailoring. Rather, our inquiry is limited to the program under consideration, in which the techniques do not amount to torture considered independently or in combination. *See Techniques* at 28-45; *Combined Use* at 9-19. Torture is categorically prohibited both by the CAT, *see* art. 2(2) ("No exceptional circumstances whatsoever ... may be invoked as a justification of torture."), and by implementing legislation, *see* 18 U.S.C. §§ 2340-2340A.

The program, moreover, is designed to minimize the risk of injury or any suffering that is unintended or does not advance the purpose of the program. For example, in dietary manipulation, the minimum caloric intake is set at or above levels used in commercial weight-loss programs, thereby avoiding the possibility of significant weight loss. In nudity and water dousing, interrogators set ambient air temperatures high enough to guard against hypothermia. The walling technique employs a false wall and a C-collar (or similar device) to help avoid

TOP SECRET/ NOFORN

30

TOP SECRET/NOFORN

2.

We next address whether, considered in light of "an understanding of traditional executive behavior, of contemporary practice, and of the standards of blame generally applied to them," use of the enhanced interrogation techniques constitutes government behavior that "is so egregious, so outrageous, that it may fairly be said to shock the contemporary conscience." *Id.* at 847 n.8. We have not found evidence of traditional executive behavior or contemporary practice either condemning or condoning an interrogation program carefully limited to further a vital government interest and designed to avoid unnecessary or serious harm.[29] However, in many contexts, there is a strong tradition against the use of coercive interrogation techniques. Accordingly, this aspect of the analysis poses a more difficult question. We examine the traditions surrounding ordinary criminal investigations within the United States, the military's tradition of not employing coercive techniques in intelligence interrogations, and the fact that the United States regularly condemns conduct undertaken by other countries that bears at least some resemblance to the techniques at issue.

These traditions provide significant evidence that the use of enhanced interrogation techniques might "shock the contemporary conscience" in at least some contexts. *Id.* As we have explained, however, the due process inquiry depends critically on setting and circumstance, *see, e.g., id.* at 847, 850, and each of these contexts differs in important ways from the one we consider here. Careful consideration of the underpinnings of the standards of conduct expected in these other contexts, moreover, demonstrates that those standards are not controlling here. Further, as explained below, the enhanced techniques are all adapted from techniques used by the United States on its own troops, albeit under significantly different conditions. At a minimum, this confirms that use of these techniques cannot be considered to be categorically impermissible; that is, in some circumstances, use of these techniques is consistent with "traditional executive behavior" and "contemporary practice." *Id.* at 847 n.8. As explained below, we believe such circumstances are present here.

Domestic Criminal Investigations. Use of interrogation practices like those we consider here in ordinary criminal investigations might well "shock the conscience." In *Rochin v.*

---

[29] CIA interrogation practice appears to have varied over time. The *IG Report* explains that the CIA "has had intermittent involvement in the interrogation of individuals whose interests are opposed to those of the United States." *IG Report* at 9. In the early 1980s, for example, the CIA initiated the Human Resource Exploitation ("HRE") training program, "designed to train foreign liaison services on interrogation techniques." *Id.* The CIA terminated the HRE program in 1986 because of allegations of human rights abuses in Latin America. *See id.* at 10.

TOP SECRET/NOFORN

California, 342 U.S. 165 (1952), the Supreme Court reversed a criminal conviction where the prosecution introduced evidence against the defendant that had been obtained by the forcible pumping of the defendant's stomach. The Court concluded that the conduct at issue "shocks the conscience" and was "too close to the rack and the screw." *Id.* at 172. Likewise, in *Williams v. United States*, 341 U.S. 97 (1951), the Court considered a conviction under a statute that criminalized depriving an individual of a constitutional right under color of law. The defendant suspected several persons of committing a particular crime. He then

> over a period of three days took four men to a paint shack ... and used brutal methods to obtain a confession from each of them. A rubber hose, a pistol, a blunt instrument, a sash cord and other implement were used in the project. ... Each was beaten, threatened, and unmercifully punished for several hours until he confessed.

Id. at 98-99. The Court characterized this as "the classic use of force to make a man testify against himself," which would render the confessions inadmissible. *Id.* at 101. The Court concluded:

> But where police take matters in their own hands, seize victims, beat and pound them until they confess, there cannot be the slightest doubt that the police have deprived the victim of a right under the Constitution. It is the right of the accused to be tried by a legally constituted court, not by a kangaroo court.

Id. at 101.

More recently, in *Chavez v. Martinez*, 538 U.S. 760 (2003), the police had questioned the plaintiff, a gunshot wound victim who was in severe pain and believed he was dying. At issue was whether a section 1983 suit could be maintained by the plaintiff against the police despite the fact that no charges had ever been brought against the plaintiff. The Court rejected the plaintiff's Fifth Amendment Self-Incrimination Clause claim, *see id.* at 773 (opinion of Thomas, J.); *id.* at 778-79 (Souter, J., concurring in judgment), but remanded for consideration of whether the questioning violated the plaintiff's substantive due process rights, *see id.* at 779-80. Some of the justices expressed the view that the Constitution categorically prohibits such coercive interrogations. *See id.* at 783, 788 (Stevens, J., concurring in part and dissenting in part) (describing the interrogation at issue as "torturous" and asserting that such interrogation "is a classic example of a violation of a constitutional right implicit in the concept of ordered liberty") (internal quotation marks omitted); *id.* at 796 (Kennedy, J., concurring in part and dissenting in part) ("The Constitution does not countenance the official imposition of severe pain or pressure for purposes of interrogation. This is true whether the protection is found in the Self-Incrimination Clause, the broader guarantees of the Due Process Clause, or both.").

The CIA program is considerably less invasive or extreme than much of the conduct at issue in these cases. In addition, the government interest at issue in each of these cases was the general interest in ordinary law enforcement (and, in *Williams*, even that was doubtful). That government interest is strikingly different from what is at stake here: the national security—in particular, the protection of the United States and its interests against attacks that may result in

California, 342 U.S. 165 (1952), the Supreme Court reversed a criminal conviction where the prosecution introduced evidence against the defendant that had been obtained by the forcible pumping of the defendant's stomach. The Court concluded that the conduct at issue "shocks the conscience" and was "too close to the rack and the screw." *Id.* at 172. Likewise, in *Williams v. United States*, 341 U.S. 97 (1951), the Court considered a conviction under a statute that criminalized depriving an individual of a constitutional right under color of law. The defendant suspected several persons of committing a particular crime. He then

> over a period of three days took four men to a paint shack . . . and used brutal methods to obtain a confession from each of them. A rubber hose, a pistol, a blunt instrument, a sash cord and other implement were used in the project. . . . Each was beaten, threatened, and unmercifully punished for several hours until he confessed.

Id. at 98-99. The Court characterized this as "the classic use of force to make a man testify against himself," which would render the confessions inadmissible. *Id.* at 101. The Court concluded:

> But where police take matters in their own hands, seize victims, beat and pound them until they confess, there cannot be the slightest doubt that the police have deprived the victim of a right under the Constitution. It is the right of the accused to be tried by a legally constituted court, not by a kangaroo court.

Id. at 101.

More recently, in *Chavez v. Martinez*, 538 U.S. 760 (2003), the police had questioned the plaintiff, a gunshot wound victim who was in severe pain and believed he was dying. At issue was whether a section 1983 suit could be maintained by the plaintiff against the police despite the fact that no charges had ever been brought against the plaintiff. The Court rejected the plaintiff's Fifth Amendment Self-Incrimination Clause claim, *see id.* at 773 (opinion of Thomas, J.); *id.* at 778-79 (Souter, J., concurring in judgment), but remanded for consideration of whether the questioning violated the plaintiff's substantive due process rights, *see id.* at 779-80. Some of the justices expressed the view that the Constitution categorically prohibits such coercive interrogations. *See id.* at 783, 788 (Stevens, J., concurring in part and dissenting in part) (describing the interrogation at issue as "torturous" and asserting that such interrogation "is a classic example of a violation of a constitutional right implicit in the concept of ordered liberty") (internal quotation marks omitted); *id.* at 796 (Kennedy, J., concurring in part and dissenting in part) ("The Constitution does not countenance the official imposition of severe pain or pressure for purposes of interrogation. This is true whether the protection is found in the Self-Incrimination Clause, the broader guarantees of the Due Process Clause, or both.").

The CIA program is considerably less invasive or extreme than much of the conduct at issue in these cases. In addition, the government interest at issue in each of these cases was the general interest in ordinary law enforcement (and, in *Williams*, even that was doubtful). That government interest is strikingly different from what is at stake here: the national security—in particular, the protection of the United States and its interests against attacks that may result in massive civilian casualties. Specific constitutional constraints, such as the Fifth Amendment's Self-Incrimination Clause, which provides that "[n]o person . . . shall be compelled *in any criminal case* to be a witness against himself," (emphasis added), apply when the government acts to further its general interest in law enforcement and reflect explicit fundamental limitation on how the government may further that interest. Indeed, most of the Court's police interrogation cases appear to be rooted in the policies behind the Self-Incrimination Clause and concern for the fairness and integrity of the trial process. In *Rochin*, for example, the Court was concerned with the use of evidence obtained by coercion to bring about a criminal conviction. *See, e.g.*, 342 U.S. at 173 ("Due process of law, as a historic and generative principle, precludes defining, and thereby confining, these standards of conduct more precisely than to say that convictions cannot be brought about by methods that offend 'a sense of justice.'") (citation omitted); *id.* (refusing to hold that "in order to convict a man the police cannot extract by force what is in his mind but can extract what is in his stomach"). *See also Jackson v. Denno*, 378 U.S. 368, 377 (1964) (characterizing the interest at stake in police interrogation cases as the "right to be free of a conviction based upon a coerced confession"); *Lyons v. Oklahoma*, 322 U.S. 596, 605 (1944) (explaining that "[a] coerced confession is offensive to basic standards of justice, not because the victim has a legal grievance against the police, but because declarations procured by torture are not premises from which a civilized forum will infer guilt"). Even *Chavez*, which might indicate the Court's receptiveness to a substantive due process claim based on coercive police interrogation practices irrespective of whether the evidence obtained was ever used against the individual interrogated, involved an interrogation implicating ordinary law enforcement interests.

Courts have long distinguished the government's interest in ordinary law enforcement from other government interests such as national security. The Foreign Intelligence Surveillance Court of Review recently explained that, with respect to the Fourth Amendment, "the [Supreme] Court distinguishe[s] general crime control programs and those that have another particular purpose, such as protection of citizens against special hazards or protection of our borders." *In re Sealed Case*, 310 F.3d 717, 745-46 (For. Intel. Surv. Ct. Rev. 2002) (discussing the Court's "special needs" cases and distinguishing "FISA's general programmatic purpose" of "protect[ing] the nation against terrorists and espionage threats directed by foreign powers" from general crime control). Under the "special needs" doctrine, the Supreme Court has approved of warantless and even suspicionless searches that serve "special needs, beyond the normal need for law enforcement." *Vernonia School Dist. 47J v. Acton*, 515 U.S. 646, 653 (1995) (quotation marks and citation omitted). Thus, although the Court has explained that it "cannot sanction [automobile] stops justified only by the" "general interest in crime control," *Indianapolis v. Edmond*, 531 U.S. 32, 44 (2000) (quotation marks and citation omitted), it suggested that it might approve of a "roadblock set up to thwart an imminent terrorist attack," *id*. See also Memorandum for James B. Comey, Deputy Attorney General, from Noel J. Francisco, Deputy Assistant Attorney General, Office of Legal Counsel, Re: *Whether OFAC May Without Obtaining a Judicial Warrant Enter the Commercial Premises of a Designated Entity To Secure Property That Has Been Blocked Pursuant to IEEPA* (April 11, 2005). Notably, in the due process context, the Court has distinguished the Government's interest in detaining illegal aliens generally from its interest in detaining suspected terrorists. *See Zadvydas*, 533 U.S. at 691. Although the Court concluded that a statute permitting the indefinite detention of aliens subject to a final order of removal but who could not be removed to other countries would raise

TOP SECRETNOFORN

We think that a policy premised on the applicability of the Geneva Conventions and not purporting to bind the CIA does not constitute controlling evidence of executive tradition and contemporary practice with respect to untraditional armed conflict where those treaties do not apply, where the enemy flagrantly violates the laws of war by secretly attacking civilians, and where the United States cannot identify the enemy or prevent its attacks absent accurate intelligence.

State Department Reports. Each year, in the State Department's Country Reports on Human Rights Practices, the United States condemns coercive interrogation techniques and other practices employed by other countries. Certain of the techniques the United States has condemned appear to bear some resemblance to some of the CIA interrogation techniques. In their discussion of Indonesia, for example, the reports list as "[p]sychological torture" conduct that involves "food and sleep deprivation," but give no specific information as to what these techniques involve. In their discussion of Egypt, the reports list as "methods of torture" "stripping and blindfolding victims; suspending victims from a ceiling or doorframe with feet just touching the floor; beating victims [with various objects]; . . . and dousing victims with cold water." *See also, e.g.*, Algeria (describing the "chiffon" method, which involves "placing a rag drenched in dirty water in someone's mouth"); Iran (counting sleep deprivation as either torture or severe prisoner abuse); Syria (discussing sleep deprivation and "having cold water thrown on" detainees as either torture or "ill-treatment"). The State Department's inclusion of nudity, water dousing, sleep deprivation, and food deprivation among the conduct it condemns is significant and provides some indication of an executive foreign relations tradition condemning the use of these techniques.[30]

To the extent they may be relevant, however, we do not believe that the reports provide evidence that the CIA interrogation program "shocks the contemporary conscience." The reports do not generally focus on or provide precise descriptions of individual interrogation techniques. Nor do the reports discuss in any detail the contexts in which the techniques are used. From what we glean from the reports, however, it appears that the condemned techniques are often part of a course of conduct that involves techniques and is undertaken in ways that bear no resemblance to the CIA interrogation program. Much of the condemned conduct goes far beyond the CIA techniques and would almost certainly constitute torture under United States law. *See, e.g.*, Egypt (discussing "suspending victims from a ceiling or doorframe with feet just touching the floor" and "beating victims [with various objects]"); Syria (discussing finger crushing and severe beatings); Pakistan (beatings, burning with cigarettes, electric shock); Uzbekistan (electric shock, rape, sexual abuse, beatings). The condemned conduct, moreover, is often undertaken for reasons totally unlike the CIA's. For example, Indonesia security forces apparently use their techniques in order to obtain confessions, to punish, and to extort money. Egypt "employ[s] torture to extract information, coerce opposition figures to cease their political activities, and to deter others from similar activities." There is no indication that techniques are

---

[30] We recognize that as a matter of diplomacy, the United States may for various reasons in various circumstances call another nation to account for practices that may in some respects resemble conduct in which the United States might in some circumstances engage, covertly or otherwise. Diplomatic relations with regard to foreign countries are not reliable evidence of United States executive practice and thus may be of only limited relevance here.

TOP SECRETNOFORN

We think that a policy premised on the applicability of the Geneva Conventions and not purporting to bind the CIA does not constitute controlling evidence of executive tradition and contemporary practice with respect to untraditional armed conflict where those treaties do not apply, where the enemy flagrantly violates the laws of war by secretly attacking civilians, and where the United States cannot identify the enemy or prevent its attacks absent accurate intelligence.

State Department Reports. Each year, in the State Department's Country Reports on Human Rights Practices, the United States condemns coercive interrogation techniques and other practices employed by other countries. Certain of the techniques the United States has condemned appear to bear some resemblance to some of the CIA interrogation techniques. In their discussion of Indonesia, for example, the reports list as "[p]sychological torture" conduct that involves "food and sleep deprivation," but give no specific information as to what these techniques involve. In their discussion of Egypt, the reports list as "methods of torture" "stripping and blindfolding victims; suspending victims from a ceiling or doorframe with feet just touching the floor; beating victims [with various objects]; . . . and dousing victims with cold water." *See also, e.g.,* Algeria (describing the "chiffon" method, which involves "placing a rag drenched in dirty water in someone's mouth"); Iran (counting sleep deprivation as either torture or severe prisoner abuse); Syria (discussing sleep deprivation and "having cold water thrown on" detainees as either torture or "ill-treatment"). The State Department's inclusion of nudity, water dousing, sleep deprivation, and food deprivation among the conduct it condemns is significant and provides some indication of an executive foreign relations tradition condemning the use of these techniques.[30]

To the extent they may be relevant, however, we do not believe that the reports provide evidence that the CIA interrogation program "shocks the contemporary conscience." The reports do not generally focus on or provide precise descriptions of individual interrogation techniques. Nor do the reports discuss in any detail the contexts in which the techniques are used. From what we glean from the reports, however, it appears that the condemned techniques are often part of a course of conduct that involves techniques and is undertaken in ways that bear no resemblance to the CIA interrogation program. Much of the condemned conduct goes far beyond the CIA techniques and would almost certainly constitute torture under United States law. *See, e.g.,* Egypt (discussing "suspending victims from a ceiling or doorframe with feet just touching the floor" and "beating victims [with various objects]"); Syria (discussing finger crushing and severe beatings); Pakistan (beatings, burning with cigarettes, electric shock); Uzbekistan (electric shock, rape, sexual abuse, beatings). The condemned conduct, moreover, is often undertaken for reasons totally unlike the CIA's. For example, Indonesia security forces apparently use their techniques in order to obtain confessions, to punish, and to extort money. Egypt "employ[s] torture to extract information, coerce opposition figures to cease their political activities, and to deter others from similar activities." There is no indication that techniques are

---

[30] We recognize that as a matter of diplomacy, the United States may for various reasons in various circumstances call another nation to account for practices that may in some respects resemble conduct in which the United States might in some circumstances engage, covertly or otherwise. Diplomatic relations with regard to foreign countries are not reliable evidence of United States executive practice and thus may be of only limited relevance here.

used only as necessary to protect against grave terrorist threats or for any similarly vital government interests (or indeed for any legitimate government interest). On the contrary, much of the alleged abuses discussed in the reports appears to involve either the indiscriminate use of force, *see, e.g.*, Kenya, or the targeting of critics of the government, *see, e.g.*, Liberia, Rwanda. And there is certainly no indication that these countries apply careful screening procedures, medical monitoring, or any of the other safeguards required by the CIA interrogation program.

A United States foreign relations tradition of condemning torture, the indiscriminate use of force, the use of force against the government's political opponents, or the use of force to obtain confessions in ordinary criminal cases says little about the propriety of the CIA's interrogation practices. The CIA's careful screening procedures are designed to ensure that enhanced techniques are used in the relatively few interrogations of terrorists who are believed to possess vital, actionable intelligence that might avert an attack against the United States or its interests. The CIA uses enhanced techniques only to the extent reasonably believed necessary to obtain the information and takes great care to avoid inflicting severe pain or suffering or any lasting or unnecessary harm. In short, the CIA program is designed to subject detainees to no more duress than is justified by the Government's interest in protecting the United States from further terrorist attacks. In these essential respects, it differs from the conduct condemned in the State Department reports.

SERE Training. There is also evidence that use of these techniques is in some circumstances consistent with executive tradition and practice. Each of the CIA's enhanced interrogation techniques has been adapted from military SERE training, where the techniques have long been used on our own troops. *See Techniques* at 6; *IG Report* at 13-14. In some instances, the CIA uses a milder form of the technique than SERE. Water dousing, as done in SERE training, involves complete immersion in water that may be below 40°F. *See Techniques* at 10. This aspect of SERE training is done outside with ambient air temperatures as low as 10°F. *See id.* In the CIA technique, by contrast, the detainee is splashed with water that is never below 41°F and is usually warmer. *See id.* Further, ambient air temperatures are never below 64°F. *See id.* Other techniques, however, are undeniably more extreme as applied in the CIA interrogation program. Most notably, the waterboard is used quite sparingly in SERE training—at most two times on a trainee for at most 40 seconds each time. *See Id.* at 13, 42. Although the CIA program authorizes waterboard use only in narrow circumstances (to date, the CIA has used the waterboard on only three detainees), where authorized, it may be used for two "sessions" per day of up to two hours. During a session, water may be applied up to six times for ten seconds or longer (but never more than 40 seconds). In a 24-hour period, a detainee may be subjected to up to twelve minutes of water application. *See id.* at 42. Additionally, the waterboard may be used on as many as five days during a 30-day approval period. *See August 19*  *Letter* at 1-2. The CIA used the waterboard "at least 83 times during August 2002" in the interrogation of Zubaydah, *IG Report* at 90, and 183 times during March 2003 in the interrogation of KSM, *see id.* at 91.

In addition, as we have explained before:

Individuals undergoing SERE training are obviously in a very different situation from detainees undergoing interrogation; SERE trainees know it is part of a training program, not a real-life interrogation regime, they presumably know it will last only a short time, and they presumably have assurances that they will not be significantly harmed by the training.

Techniques at 6. On the other hand, the interrogation program we consider here furthers the paramount interest of the United States in the security of the Nation more immediately and directly than SERE training, which seeks to reduce the possibility that United States military personnel might reveal information that could harm the national security in the event they are captured. Again, analysis of the due process question must pay careful attention to these differences. But we can draw at least one conclusion from the existence of SERE training. Use of the techniques involved in the CIA's interrogation program (or at least the similar techniques from which these have been adapted) cannot be considered to be *categorically* inconsistent with "traditional executive behavior" and "contemporary practice" regardless of context.[31] It follows that use of these techniques will not shock the conscience in at least some circumstances. We believe that such circumstances exist here, where the techniques are used against unlawful combatants who deliberately and secretly attack civilians in an untraditional armed conflict in which intelligence is difficult or impossible to collect by other means and is essential to the protection of the United States and its interests, where the techniques are used only when necessary and only in the interrogations of key terrorist leaders reasonably thought to have actionable intelligence, and where every effort is made to minimize unnecessary suffering and to avoid inflicting significant or lasting harm.

Accordingly, we conclude that, in light of "an understanding of traditional executive behavior, of contemporary practice, and of the standards of blame generally applied to them," the use of the enhanced interrogation techniques in the CIA interrogation program as we understand it, does not constitute government behavior that "is so egregious, so outrageous, that it may fairly be said to shock the contemporary conscience." *Lewis*, 523 U.S. at 847 n.8.

C.

For the reasons stated, we conclude that the CIA interrogation techniques, with their careful screening procedures and medical monitoring, do not "shock the conscience." Given the relative paucity of Supreme Court precedent applying this test at all, let alone in anything resembling this setting, as well as the context-specific, fact-dependent, and somewhat subjective nature of the inquiry, however, we cannot predict with confidence that a court would agree with our conclusion. We believe, however, that the question whether the CIA's enhanced interrogation techniques violate the substantive standard of United States obligations under Article 16 is unlikely to be subject to judicial inquiry.

As discussed above, Article 16 imposes no legal obligations on the United States that implicate the CIA interrogation program in view of the language of Article 16 itself and,

---

[31] In addition, the fact that individuals voluntarily undergo the techniques in SERE training is probative. *See Breithaupt v. Abram*, 352 U.S. 432, 436-37 (1957) (noting that people regularly voluntarily allow their blood to be drawn and concluding that involuntary blood testing does not "shock the conscience").

independently, the Senate's reservation. But even if this were less clear (indeed, even if it were false), Article 16 itself has no domestic legal effect because the Senate attached a non-self-execution declaration to its resolution of ratification. *See* Cong. Rec. 36,198 (1990) ("the United States declares that the provisions of Articles 1 through 16 of the Convention are not self-executing"). It is well settled that non-self-executing treaty provisions "can only be enforced pursuant to legislation to carry them into effect." *Whitney v. Robertson*, 124 U.S. 190, 194 (1888); *see also Foster v. Neilson*, 27 U.S. (2 Pet.) 253, 314 (1829) ("A treaty is in its nature a contract between two nations, not a legislative act. It does not generally effect, of itself, the object to be accomplished, . . . but is carried into execution by the sovereign power of the respective parties to the instrument."). One implication of the fact that Article 16 is non-self-executing is that, with respect to Article 16, "the courts have nothing to do and can give no redress." *Head Money Cases*, 112 U.S. 580, 598 (1884). As one court recently explained in the context of the CAT itself, "Treaties that are not self-executing do not create judicially-enforceable rights unless they are first given effect by implementing legislation." *Auguste v. Ridge*, 395 F.3d 123, 132 n.7 (3d Cir. 2005) (citations omitted). Because (with perhaps one narrow exception[32]) Article 16 has not been legislatively implemented, the interpretation of its substantive standard is unlikely to be subject to judicial inquiry.[33]

* * *

Based on CIA assurances, we understand that the CIA interrogation program is not conducted in the United States or "territory under [United States] jurisdiction," and that it is not authorized for use against United States persons. Accordingly, we conclude that the program does not implicate Article 16. We also conclude that the CIA interrogation program, subject to its careful screening, limits, and medical monitoring, would not violate the substantive standards

---

[32] As noted above, Section 1031 of Public Law 109-13 provides that "[n]one of the funds appropriated or otherwise made available by this Act shall be obligated or expended to subject any person in the custody or under the physical control of the United States to . . . cruel, inhuman, or degrading treatment or punishment that is prohibited by the Constitution, laws, or treaties of the United States." To the extent this appropriations rider implements Article 16, it creates a narrow domestic law obligation not to expend funds appropriated under Public Law 109-13 for conduct that violates Article 16. This appropriations rider, however, is unlikely to result in judicial interpretation of Article 16's substantive standards since it does not create a private right of action. *See, e.g., Alexander v. Sandoval*, 532 U.S. 275, 286 (2001) ("Like substantive federal law itself, private rights of action to enforce federal law must be created by Congress."); *Resident Council of Allen Parkway Vill. v. Dep't of Hous. & Urban Dev.*, 980 F.2d 1043, 1052 (5th Cir. 1993) ("courts have been reluctant to infer congressional intent to create private rights under appropriations measures") (citing *California v. Sierra Club*, 451 U.S. 287 (1981)).

It is possible that a court could address the scope of Article 16 if a prosecution were brought under the Antideficiency Act, 31 U.S.C. § 1341 (2000), for a violation of section 1031's spending restriction. Section 1341(a)(1)(A) of title 31 provides that officers or employees of the United States may not "make or authorize an expenditure or obligation exceeding an amount available in an appropriation or fund for the expenditure or obligation." "[K]nowing[] and willful[] violati[ons]" of section 1341(a) are subject to criminal penalties. *Id.* § 1350.

[33] Although the interpretation of Article 16 is unlikely to be subject to judicial inquiry, it is conceivable that a court might attempt to address substantive questions under the Fifth Amendment if, for example, the United States sought a criminal conviction of a high value detainee in an Article III court in the United States using evidence that had been obtained from the detainee through the use of enhanced interrogation techniques.

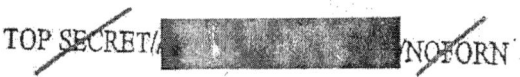

TOP SECRET/  NOFORN

applicable to the United States under Article 16 even if those standards extended to the CIA interrogation program. Given the paucity of relevant precedent and the subjective nature of the inquiry, however, we cannot predict with confidence whether a court would agree with this conclusion, though, for the reasons explained, the question is unlikely to be subject to judicial inquiry.

Please let us know if we may be of further assistance.

Steven G. Bradbury
Principal Deputy Assistant Attorney General

www.ArcManor.com

www.ingramcontent.com/pod-product-compliance
Ingram Content Group UK Ltd.
Pitfield, Milton Keynes, MK11 3LW, UK
UKHW051251180426
11947UKWH00020B/1647